HV
6598 Lawrence, Bobbi
.L38   The child snatchers
1983

DATE DUE

NOV	DEC 0 7 1992
DEC 7 1984	
APR 29 1985	JUN 2 1998
MAY 11 1985	
AUG 13 1985	
OCT 21 1985	
MAY 7 1987	
AP 25 '88	OC 13 '89
JY 11 '88	NO 3 '89
DE 9	DEC 1S
AP 21 '89	MAY 12 1990

The Child Snatchers

The Child Snatchers

Bobbi Lawrence
and
Olivia Taylor-Young

Charles River Books, Inc.
Boston

Library of Congress Cataloging in Publication Data

Lawrence, Bobbi.
　The child snatchers.

　Bibliography: p.
　1. Kidnapping, Parental — United States —
Case studies. 2. Kidnapping, Parental —
Information services — United States — Directories.
I. Taylor-Young, Olivia.　II. Title.
HV6598.L38　　　362.8′2　　　　　　82-1152
ISBN 0-89182-050-7　　　　　　　　　AACR2

Published by Charles River Books, Inc.
One Thompson Square, Charlestown, MA 02129
Copyright 1983 by Bobbi Lawrence and
Olivia Taylor-Young

The lines from "On Children" are reprinted from *The Prophet* by Kahlil Gibran, copyright 1923, with permission of the publisher, Alfred A. Knopf, Inc.

All rights reserved. No part of this work may be reproduced or transmitted in any form by any means, electronic or mechanical, including photocopying and recording or by an information storage or retrieval system, without the written permission of the publisher, except for brief passages quoted by a reviewer.

ISBN 0 89182 050 7
Library of Congress Card Number 82-1152
Printed in the United States of America

*This book is dedicated to the real
Bryan Simmons, and to those who may find
that we've also told their story.*

Your children are not your children.

They are sons and daughters of Life's longing for itself.

They come through you but not from you,
And though they are with you yet they belong not to you. . . .

> Kahlil Gibran

Preface

The events described in Part One of *The Child Snatchers* were experienced by one or both of the authors, or related to us by others. In those instances where fragments had to be pieced together based on memory, intuitive knowledge, legal documents or hearsay, we believe we have remained close to the truth as it actually happened.

Due to the sensitive nature of the story, we have changed names, some locations and for literary purposes, composited a few of the minor characters and details.

In Part Two, parental names have been omitted unless implied permission was granted through prior use in the media. We hope we have satisfied both those who desire privacy and those who wish attention drawn to their cases in the hopes of eliciting action or making a public statement.

We wish to thank the many people who gave so generously of their time and knowledge in order to bring this book to publication. We are particularly indebted to Vicki Schwartz and Kirk Taylor-Young for their editorial advice; Arnold Miller, whose research first made us aware of the magnitude of the problem; Mickey Ellinger and Jean Livingston, whose insights helped put it into perspective; Lowell Brinson, Richard Beall and Walter Bowman for providing us with information on the Parent Locator Services; Patricia Hoff, who kept us up-to-date on laws and parent support groups; Lorraine Fein and Nancy Waite, our volunteer out-of-state news clipping service; Nolo Press for granting us permission to incorporate their trace forms; Susan Griffin for allowing us to reprint her poem "I Like to Think of Harriet Tubman." And Phyllis and Jerry Gordon.

We offer a special thanks to Bess and Isidore B. Schwartz; to our editor, Dennis Campbell, for his faith and enthusiasm; and to both our families, individually and collectively, without whose love and support this book could not have been written.

Contents

Preface

Part One

Child Snatching — A Case History   3

Part Two

Introduction   105
Why the Problem   109
Child Snatching and Our Law
    Enforcement Agencies   113
Taking the Reins in Your Own Hands   121
Organizations and Support Groups   137
Removal to Another Country   147
Parent Locator Services   149
Private Detectives   161
The Physical and Emotional Aspects
    of Child-Stealing   165

Appendix A: The Parental Kidnapping
Prevention Act of 1980   173

Appendix B: Current Child Stealing
Laws — A State by State
Survey   181

Appendix C: October 1981
Congressional Hearings   221

Appendix D: Hague Convention on
the Civil Aspects of
International Child
Abduction   243

Notes   253
Suggested Reading   257

The Child Snatchers

Part One

Prologue

March 10, 1976
A gray car pulled over to the curb, then stopped, its motor softly throbbing. The driver's hands tightened on the wheel. They were large hands, strong hands . . . and they were shaking now.

The man beside him reached over and grasped his forearm reassuringly. "Stop worrying, Paul. Do you see him?"

The driver shook his head, but didn't speak. His attention had been caught by a group of children laughing and jostling each other as they walked toward the schoolyard. Scrutinizing them one by one, he tried to pick out a redhead amidst the colorful patchwork of jeans, derby jackets and lunchboxes. But Bryan was not among them.

"Damn," he murmured impatiently. "Where is he? School will be starting soon."

"Relax, Paul. At least no one's called the police. I remember one case where—"

But Paul wasn't listening. His mind was on Nancy. In just a short while, he thought with satisfaction, she would discover that their situations had been reversed.

Bryan Andrew Simmons turned the corner of Fifteenth Avenue. "Beat you!" he called over his shoulder to a small Asian boy carrying a sack lunch.

"Not this time." His companion flung the bag into a more comfortable position and shot forward. Intent on their race, neither boy noticed the two men watching and, passing the car without a glance, they ran to join their friends.

"This is it, Paul." The man checked his watch. "Eight fifteen. We've only got a few minutes."

The driver opened the door and got out. He was tall and solidly built with wide shoulders and a thick neck. Shifting uneasily, he examined the schoolyard with hard, deliberate eyes. Good. No one on duty. That would make it easier. As he moved forward, crushing his cigarette to the ground, the other man slid over and took the wheel.

Paul's long strides brought him behind the boy before anyone took notice.

"Bryan?"

The child spun around and, with a flash of recognition, his eyes widened in terror.

"Get in the car, Bryan."

Instinct told the boy to run, but his feet stuck leadenly to the asphalt.

"I said—"

Rough hands grasped his elbow and the touch, painful and alien, set off a frozen scream. Startled, the grasping hands loosened their grip and Bryan broke into a run. Feet flying, chest pounding, he tried to duck between the onlookers who were beginning to gather. But his eyes, blurred by tears, failed to notice a book on the ground. Stumbling over it, he felt a quick snap of his body as the pavement came up to meet him. As if mesmerized, the children watched the heavy footsteps draw nearer the sprawled form.

A few minutes later, the boy lay sobbing on the back floor of his father's car.

The previous scene and the account which follows are based upon the abduction of a real child: "Bryan Simmons." With a few variations, it could just as well be the story of an estimated 99,999 other youngsters who are similarly snatched away each year. Sometimes they are taken at gunpoint, occasionally lives have *been lost and, always, there is a parent left behind struggling with a legal system which prefers to look the other way.*

Until recently, cases of parental kidnapping were viewed as isolated instances. Tragic, of course, but not something likely to touch the lives of ordinary people. As the national divorce rate escalated, however, so did reports of child-stealing. Today, it appears to be a social problem — sometimes termed an epidemic — which cuts into every corner of society.

What causes a parent to steal his or her own child? Psychologists, for the most part, now agree that hostility toward the other parent is a prime factor, as is frustration. Yet they have been unable to come up with a composite personality or environmental profile which would predispose an individual to commit such an act. "Paul Simmons," for instance, (like myself) was a sales representative, college educated and in his early thirties. Had he been twenty or forty, Chairman of the Board or unemployed, however, it would have made little difference. Except for the presence of a past or imminent divorce, the crime is, as a rule, unpredictable.

In my own case, Paul and I may have been incompatible as marriage partners but I thought that, as people, we liked and respected one another. It seems I was wrong. Our actual divorce, in 1969, was referred to by Paul's attorney as "the most amicable" one he'd ever handled. Yet, in the seven years which followed, my life contained one constant: an endless flow of lawyers' letters testifying to the fact that an amiable dissolution is no guarantee of a congenial aftermath.

One

February 3, 1976: The door read *Callan-McCrae, Attorneys at Law*. Smoothing down the blond hair which had a tendency to tumble over my eyes in damp weather, I made my way over to the reception area where a young woman, Lorraine Moore, took down my name.

"Mr. Callan will be with you in a moment." She buzzed the lawyer. "Would you like a cup of coffee while you wait? You looked soaked to the bone."

Gratefully, I sipped the hot liquid and hoped that the rain would stop by Saturday. I'd promised Bryan a trip to Marine World and knew he'd be disappointed if we couldn't go.

"Mrs. Simmons?" A tall man in a three-piece suit joined us in the anteroom. "I'm Michael Callan. Won't you come inside?"

The attorney had dark hair, fashionably cut, and his deep blue eyes seemed at once warm and probing. Ushering me into a private office, he cleared the desk of some papers and motioned for me to sit down across from him.

"You were referred by Rita Ephron, weren't you?" He slid back into a swivel chair. "One of my favorite clients. How is she?"

"Fine." I told him. "In between jobs since her bout with pneumonia, but back to her old cheerful self again."

"Well, when you see her, give her my best. Now, what brings you here?"

I was sorry the small talk ended so quickly because the next topic, I knew from experience, would leave me emotionally drained. "Actually, I'm here on the advice of my Boston attorney," I explained. "I was transferred to San Francisco about eight months ago and he suggested that, once I got settled, I retain legal counsel. You see, my ex-husband has periodically given me some problems with visitation."

"Is that your legal file?" He indicated the manila folder on my lap. "Do you mind if I take a look?"

I watched as he flipped through page after page of correspondence and court documents. Finally, he looked up.

"Your papers seem to be in order. But why don't you tell me a little more about it?"

Tell him, I thought. But how? There were no words.

"Well, after the divorce," I began hesitantly, "Paul . . . seemed different. He took almost no interest in Bryan and getting child support from him was like pulling teeth. At first, I thought we were merely going through a period of readjustment, but when I sent Bryan for a visit that first summer . . . he never returned him."

"Have you any idea why?"

"Just speculation. Do you want to hear that?"

He nodded.

"Okay. This is the only way I've been able to make any sense out of it. At the time of our divorce, it wasn't convenient for Paul to fight for custody. He had just started a new job in a new state and the position required quite a bit of travel. Finding someone to watch Bryan would have been a hassle. By summer, though, his present wife was living with him and he had a built-in babysitter. Why should I have Bryan, and not him?"

"What did you do?"

"What could I do? I flew to Tulsa, where he was now living, and insisted that Bryan come home with me or I'd call the police. Luckily, Paul was out-of-town and SuEllen, his fiancee, was too scared to argue.

"Then, for the next five years, Paul seemed oblivious to Bryan's existence. Maybe it was a case of 'if I can't have things my way, I'll take my marbles and go home.' I don't know. But there were no Christmas or birthday cards and, as you can see, no support unless I dragged him into court. Then, last June, he appeared to have a change of heart. He and SuEllen were married now with a little girl, and he claimed to want a relationship with both of his children. Reluctantly, Bryan went off to Tulsa again, and this time it took an outraged judge to get him back."

"And your son? What does he think of all this?"

"Bryan's basically easy-going, but he's very much afraid of his father. Lately, Paul's been calling and threatening that if Bryan doesn't come for another visit, he'll get a custody order in Oklahoma."

The lawyer looked at me in astonishment. "And you believe that? He's even in arrears. Look, Nancy — may I call you by your first name? Both you and your son live here. Only Bryan's home state or a state that has significant ties to him can make provisions for his custody."

"What about the Massachusetts order?"

"I can't see why California shouldn't agree to honor it. It's a common procedure called foreign judgment. In addition, I'm going to request a restraining order so that it will be illegal to take Bryan out of the state without written permission from either you or the court. So, stop worrying," he admonished me gently. "And Nancy, if those annoying calls continue, I suggest you get an unlisted number."

I had a fleeting feeling of well-being as the weeks went by with no further word from Paul. In late February, a letter arrived from Michael confirming March 11th as our court date and explaining that everything was set except for one technicality. "Judge Livanos, before whom we will appear, declined to issue a temporary restraining order. It was his feeling, upon reviewing the case, that your son is in no imminent danger. However," Michael had added, "upon a hearing in open court, this should be rectified to our satisfaction."

March 1st, March 2nd, March 3rd . . . the days passed evenly. Bryan tried out for, and made, the baseball team but lost the bat my father had given him. I concentrated on my job, my home and my social life, determined — perhaps unrealistically — that we were going to lead normal lives. March 7th, March 8th . . . we had dinner out to celebrate my landing a new account; I worked on my income tax; and Bryan's bicycle, now too small for him, was given to his friend, Rusty, in exchange for a ticket to the local showing of *Godzilla vs. King Kong*. March 10th.

4:00 p.m. The clock on the wall ticked mockingly as I wondered what had become of my son. Could he have gotten his dates mixed up and gone over to a friend's house?

With a quick tug, I pulled aside the curtains and scanned the streets below. Fog, thick and clammy, had engulfed the city in a white shroud and, from the blurred pavement, a small figure waved up at me.

"I thought you were buying Bryan a new bike today," my neighbor, Emily Rossi, called out.

"If he ever gets home," I shrugged. "It's not like him to forget something like this."

"Well," she gave an exaggerated sigh. "I guess that's kids for you."

4:35. I stopped my vigil by the window long enough to put dinner in the oven. The stores would be closing soon. Where was he? Could he have been in an accident? I allowed one of my fears to surface. But, no. Surely, someone would have called me by now.

4:45. Soft footsteps sounded on the staircase. "Bryan, is that you?" I rushed to the door, snapping back the chain lock, and Dianna Foster of 3A continued her spiral climb. The minutes passed with agonizing slowness as I made a few useless calls to Bryan's friends. Then, unable to relax, I grabbed my coat and drove the few short blocks to Viscennes School.

It was an outmoded building, circa 1920, soon scheduled for remodeling to meet present earthquake standards. As my eyes swept over the sign, "Visitors, Please Register at the Office," a sick dread welled up in the pit of my stomach. The schoolyard was empty!

With trembling hands, I wove in and out of traffic.

The library?

"I'm sorry, Mrs. Simmons. He hasn't been in today."

The Donut Shoppe?

"A redhead? Eleven-years-old? No. I don't think so."

The coin store?

Closed.

How long I sat transfixed, I couldn't say. It was probably less than a minute. But, in that instant, I knew. Careening against waves of nausea, I tried to exorcise the dark thought from my mind. Driving back to the apartment, I clung desperately to the image of my son at home, waiting for his dinner.

A thin veil of silence greeted me.

"Hello, Larry?" I began phoning again. "Is Bryan there?"
"No, Mrs. Simmons. I have the flu."
"Kevin, have you seen Bryan?"
"Didn't Miss Neely tell you?" He sounded surprised. "A tall man with glasses took him out of the schoolyard this morning. I thought—"

Blood surged to my head as teeth, clamped over my lower lip, barely stifled the screams in my throat. Paul!

Bracing myself against the kitchen table, I thanked Kevin and dialed the operator. "Please, please get me the police," I screamed hysterically. "And my attorney, Michael Callan . . . I can't remember . . . C-a-l-l-a-n . . . I think there's only one in San Francisco . . "

5:30. I paced the apartment like a caged beast, the ticking of the clock a metronome of terror. Where was everybody? Why were they taking so long?

Then flashing red lights, reflecting in the driveway, signalled the arrival of the police. There were dreamlike overtones to the next half hour and my recollection, though burnt upon memory, has the hazy quality of a sleepwalker's.

Sergeant Burns, tall, gaunt, sitting hunched over the phone. Rita rushing in, her long chestnut hair in rollers. A second officer, Patrolwoman Reed, asking questions in a soft, precise voice.

"Would you please state your full name, age and occupation?"

"Thirty-two . . . sales representative for a sportswear manufacturer." In the background, I could hear Bryan's description going out over the wire. "Red hair . . . freckles . . . 90 pounds . . . blue derby jacket . . . possible child snatch."

For a moment, there was a glimmer of hope. Sergeant Burns discovered that Paul had rented a Budget car in San Francisco that morning, giving the Airport Hilton as his local address. A quick call to the hotel, though, revealed that the information had been misleading. "I'll check with Budget again." The officer frowned. "Maybe there's a second address."

While this was being verified, the doorbell rang. "I'm sorry for taking so long," Michael apologized, "but I stopped by Judge Arnstein's to get that restraining order."

He handed the document to Sergeant Burns, who regarded it with skepticism.

"What's wrong!" I panicked.

"Mrs. Simmons," the officer explained, "a restraining order can only be enforced if the child's not yet been taken out of state."

"Are you saying there's a catch-22?" My mind was suddenly clear. "The order prevents Bryan's removal from California. But if Paul removes him, the order is useless?"

Their silence was answer enough.

I sat back, numbed, while Rita poured me a drink. Minutes later, Budget phoned back with a report: Paul's car had been abandoned in Reno.

The night dragged on. The police left, and Michael replaced Sergeant Burns at the telephone. He repeatedly called Paul's house, only to be met by a dial tone. Vincent Morrell, my ex-husband's lawyer, was also "out-of-town" according to his answering service.

"Will she have to go to Tulsa again?" Rita asked.

Michael opened his mouth, seemed about to speak, then closed it without having said anything. For the next few minutes, he seemed lost in thought as he nervously twisted a wine glass.

"No," he replied at length. "What we'll do is go from A to B to C. Tomorrow morning, since we're already going to court, I'll petition the judge for a writ of habeas corpus—"

"But—"

"—for Bryan's return. And, if that doesn't work," he lit a cigarette and took a long drag, "we'll head straight for the District Attorney's office and file a complaint of criminal child-stealing . . . and . . . if that doesn't . . ."

My God, he was groping!

". . . we'll investigate the possibilities of going through the federal courts."

By 8:15, Michael had realized that any further efforts to contact Paul or his attorney that night were futile. As I watched him walk out the door, I felt lost. Abandoned. Like a child, I had fantasized that he would make everything right again before leaving.

Fortunately, Rita's presence spared me some of the pain of being alone. Offering to stay over, she listened with infinite patience to my steady stream of "what-ifs" and "if-onlys." In retrospect, I realize that being a single mother of three boys, the youngest around Bryan's age, she must have been feeling her own vulnerability that evening. But for my sake, she remained doggedly optimistic.

Somewhere between the discussion of Rita's driving me to court the next morning and reassurances that Michael was a good lawyer, I remembered that there was a three hour time difference between Massachusetts and California. The task I'd hoped wouldn't be necessary could no longer be put off. Picking up the phone, I dialed my home town of Springfield and grimly wondered how you told people 3000 miles away that their only grandchild had been kidnapped.

By midnight, fortified by countless cups of coffee, Rita and I were still piecing things together.

"It doesn't make sense." Her eyes were thoughtful. "Why didn't the kids say anything? It takes five hours to drive to Reno. If you'd been able to contact the police right away, maybe they could have stopped Paul."

"But they did say something!" Memory flooded back. "Kevin said, 'A man took Bryan out of the schoolyard. *Didn't Miss Neely tell you?*'" Grabbing a phone book, I scanned the listings. It was late, but emergencies don't always happen at convenient times. I had to talk to Brian's teacher. Now.

The phone rang for several minutes before a sleepy voice answered, "Yes?"

"Miss Neely? This is Nancy Simmons. . . ."

Sondra Neely's reaction to my story was a prolonged silence. "Then . . . it's true?" She finally whispered.

"You mean you knew?"

"Well, when I was calling the roll this morning and got to Bryan's name, Kevin Leong and Jonathan Murphy told me that a man had grabbed him from the schoolyard . . . but . . . they were smiling . . . it seemed like a joke . . . and then a fight broke out amongst the kids . . . and . . . I forgot." In a hushed tone, she added, "Sorry."

Two

When the world as you perceive it suddenly collapses at your feet, you are left with no point of view, no stance from which to organize the influx of material besieging your senses.

In the days and weeks which followed, I found myself an alien in a topsy-turvy universe which took little notice of my presence, and seemed to care even less. The people I met who, through a twist of circumstance, came to play such a vital role in my life were unaware, I'm sure, of their importance. To them, I was merely a part of the human file which marched past them every day. Presenting problems. Demanding answers. Yet, from my side of the desk, they loomed as Almighty Beings. Saviors or demons who could put my world back in order or toss it to the winds. If, perhaps, some of them appear monochromatic, or even a little caricatured in the retelling, it's not because the events are untrue. Rather, in a land of one dimension, where my son and I became numbers, our dehumanizers lost their humanity as well.

Judge Theodore Livanos stepped into the courtroom at precisely 9:02 a.m. He was a florid-faced man, about seventy, with loose jowls and small, shrewd eyes.

"All rise!" commanded the Clerk of Court.

We stood respectfully as the magistrate slowly walked to the podium.

"You may be seated."

The first case, Miller vs. Miller, was by-passed because the petitioner's lawyer, who was also my own, had been detained at a meeting with the presiding judge.

"Call the next case," the judge instructed, as Michael entered the room.

"Excuse me, Your Honor," he protested. "But I represent Mr. Miller." With long, even strides, he appeared before the bench. "I'm sorry, but I got here as soon as I could. May we continue?"

There was something unsettling in Livanos' narrowed eyes. "Your case has already passed, Mr. Callan." He banged the gavel down. "Postponed until next week."

A few stunned moments went by while Michael conferred with his unfortunate client. Then, as he took the seat next to Rita's, I handed him a scribbled note: *The judge seems openly hostile. Will that affect our case?*

"No way!"

Wanting to believe him, I sank back in my chair and sweated out the next four hearings.

"Case number six. Simmons vs. Simmons."

I made my way to the stand on rubbery legs. The clerk solemnly placed a bible under my hand and recited the familiar oath.

"Do you swear to tell the truth, the whole truth, and nothing but the truth?"

"I do."

"You may be seated."

Looking down at the sea of anonymous faces, I suddenly felt intimidated. What if I said or did the wrong thing? Would the judge allow Paul to keep Bryan?

The initial proceedings were routine, however, and Vincent Morrell, in a classic understatement, had filed notice that his client "would not appear." Within five minutes, my child support was upheld and the California court agreed to honor the Massachusetts decree.

In a subdued voice, Michael continued the questioning. "Mrs. Simmons, will you please tell the court what happened yesterday?"

I responded as best I could, acutely aware of Judge Livanos

seated nearby. Possibly, for an instant, he felt a touch of compassion but, if so, he kept it well hidden. At the end of my testimony, he added a rider to his previous order, though, stating:

"The minor child of the parties may not be removed from the City and County of San Francisco without the written consent of the custodial mother or of this Court."

Eyes tensely fixed upon the magistrate, Michael then came to the most urgent point. "Your Honor, in view of the boy's forcible removal from California, will you issue a writ of habeas corpus?"

An endless pause ensued as Judge Livanos looked at the attorney with ill-concealed distaste. Then, his voice deceptively soft, he replied, "You got what you wanted, Mr. Callan. Let Oklahoma take care of the rest."

"But my son's been kidnapped!" I burst out, losing all control.

"Be quiet!" the judge snapped back, his eyes smoldering. "Now, both of you get out of here. Case dismissed!"

Sobbing wildly, I ran from the courtroom. As Rita and Michael followed, all my thoughts abbreviated into a single sentence. "I... just . . . want . . . you to know," I managed to choke out, "that the Honorable Judge is a fucking bastard!"

Later, Michael explained that he'd overturned three of Livanos' decisions that year, and a fourth was pending. But, at the moment, any speculations regarding the judge's motives or competence were irrelevant. He had failed my son, and I took it personally.

Stopping in the lobby, I phoned my parents. My mother's voice, muffled with tears, answered before the first full ring. "Nan . . . will they help?"

I repeated the details, trying to make it seem like a temporary set-back.

"Daddy and I will do everything we can." She tried to reassure the both of us. "Even if the District Attorney won't help—"

"He's got to, Mom." My protest sounded more like a plea. "Michael's making an appointment for us as soon as he gets back to the office."

"We won't give up. Whatever it takes, we'll get Bryan back."

"Oh, Mom . . . I . . ."

"We'll even sell the house if we have to."

Half an hour later, riveted to the spot in front of Michael's desk, my eyes were irresistibly drawn to a picture of his children. One was about Bryan's age, a cute freckle-faced boy with an impish grin. He was probably in school right now . . . perhaps, doing a project for his science class.

". . . and it seems it's policy to file a report with the juvenile authorities before the District Attorney's office can become involved." Michael brought me back to reality.

"But we filed a police report last night!"

"I'm sorry, Nan." He absently tapped the bowl of his pipe. "Apparently, that only partially fulfills the requirements. You've got to file a duplicate with Juvenile Division."

"I understand." But I didn't. Not really.

Rita shrugged helplessly. "Well, let's get down there right now. That way the D.A. can have it on his desk before he leaves for lunch."

"I'm afraid you'll have to wait until four o'clock." The lawyer avoided our eyes. "I tried to arrange an earlier appointment, but they can't see you until then."

There are those people who seem to possess that elusive quality of grace under pressure, who can maintain a cool countenance while drowning in pain. Unfortunately, I was not one of them. Feeling too tense, too keyed up to sit still, I asked Rita if she'd come with me to Viscennes School.

Sondra Neely appeared nervous as she invited us into her classroom. Evading any reference to last night's conversation, she quickly pulled a snapshot of Bryan from her files and agreed to accompany us while we questioned the students.

She held up the picture, "Children, this is Bryan Simmons. Some of you know him. He's in my class. Yesterday a man took him out of the schoolyard and I want to know if anybody saw what happened."

In every room eager hands shot up and childish voices called out.

"That's our first baseman."

"A man punched him in the stomach."

"He was holding his stomach in the back seat of a car."

"He was fighting with his father. Was he going to the dentist?"

Nobody had seen the entire episode, but from blurted out details, the puzzle fell rapidly into place: a man fitting Paul's description had come into the schoolyard and dragged Bryan, kicking and screaming, toward a waiting gray Camaro.

One little boy, frightened by what he saw, had copied the license down on his hand. Typical of ten-year-olds, he hadn't washed it since yesterday and now proudly displayed an ink-smeared palm with the numbers 952-ARX.

"There was another man too," a curly-haired girl named Carrie Knoll said eagerly. "He plays pool with my father at the Billiard Barn."

"What did he look like?"

"Oh, he's got black hair and was wearing a sweatshirt with a tiger on it." She thought for a few seconds, then added, "He was also kinda fat."

Another girl seemed about to speak, but stopped herself. She was shy, Sondra confided as she asked the child, "Charlene, is there something you want to tell us?"

"The man in the sweatshirt had a rope in his hand."

My voice trembled as I asked the next words. "Was . . . Bryan *tied up?*"

"Yes."

The knot in my stomach tightened. "Does anybody else remember that?"

No one else appeared to, but several children had heard the second man say, "Do you need any help?"

My poor baby. He must have fought like hell. Paul was 6'3", yet he needed someone to assist him. Did it take two grown men to subdue an eleven-year-old boy?

"Who was the teacher on yard duty?" Rita was asking. No one was sure. "Did anyone see a teacher in the yard?"

Silence.

"I don't understand why they didn't report it." Sondra gestured toward the children. "Why do they accept violence so easily?"

In a flat impersonal voice, she theorized, "T.V. could be a factor . . . or maybe they come from abusive homes."

At least one teacher had been told, I wanted to confront her, but fearing a loss of cooperation, continued questioning the children instead.

"Didn't you tell Mrs. Dawson?" I asked a fifth grade class.

"I did." A young boy piped up.

"What did she say?"

"She said she'd already heard the story, and twice was enough."

"You know how it is," the teacher blurted in self-defense. "We hear so many stories. You just believe some kids and not others."

It was recess by the time we walked outside. Bryan's friends were in a far corner of the yard tossing a ball around. The children looked happy, everything seemed normal; yet, it was a parody. Twenty-four hours after my son had been tied up, thrown into a car, and dragged from this very spot, the gates remained wide open with not a single adult in sight.

At 3:30 we drove to the Hall of Justice. The front door was guarded by security police and, as we emptied our purses, Rita remarked that it reminded her of the night she'd seen Golda Meir.

Upstairs, Juvenile Division was a bleak gray rectangle, lined with file cabinets and cold, metallic desks. A wooden bench, apparently for visitors, stood in one corner but Rita and I chose to wait in front of the central counter where we could be seen easily. Everyone looked preoccupied — I watched as they shuffled papers or blankly stared out the window. One inspector was intently shooting paper clips across the room, while another blew smoke rings at the ceiling.

Finally, a swarthy-complexioned man with a gun on his hip wandered over.

"Weren't you in my history class last year?" He smiled at Rita.

"Why, yes." She seemed surprised. "Hi."

"What are you doing down here?"

Putting her hand on my arm, she explained. "This is my friend. Her son's been kidnapped."

"Oh? Well, it's nice seeing you again," he replied, still smiling, and walked away.

The whole scene was bizarre, almost surrealistic. Was my life turning into a Kafka novel? Eventually, a gray haired woman in a dark print dress confronted me. It was Inspector Halsey.

"I remember you," she said harshly. "You were here last summer when your son was missing. Didn't I tell you to grab him back yourself?" Shrugging, she added, "I've already thrown out the file. Is he gone again?"

"Yes. This time he's been kidnapped. My lawyer made an appointment for me. Mr. Callan?"

Somebody please listen, I silently pleaded as she turned her back and walked to her desk. Wait a minute! Why are you leaving? I'm over here! For the second time in less than two hours I made a determined effort to remain quiet rather than antagonize somebody who could be of help.

Five minutes passed while Ms. Halsey lit a cigarette and appeared to be studying an oblong smudge on the wall.

"Nancy, just stay right here," Rita said in a deliberately controlled voice. "I'll phone Michael."

She left and I sat down, feeling small and vulnerable. A bulletin board in the corner caught my attention and I leaned over to have a closer look. Tacked to it was a cartoon showing a small girl peeking down a young boy's pants. The caption read: "Boys run faster than girls because they have built-in ball bearings and a stick shift."

"Michael's going to call here. He's furious," Rita whispered a few minutes later. The phone rang on Ms. Halsey's desk. Reluctantly, the inspector put down her coffee and returned to the counter.

"You sit down." She glared at Rita. "I want to talk to Mrs. Simmons. Your lawyer just called, but before we do anything else, I've got to see your divorce papers."

"Divorce papers? But my son's been kidnapped!"

"First things first." She sounded as if she were speaking to a child. "Now go on home and be back tomorrow at 10:30. Mr. Callan will meet you here." Dismissing me, she turned on her heels and walked away.

There was nothing to do. It wasn't Kafka after all, I realized. It was Kesey! After creating Nurse Ratchetd, he'd forgotten to destroy the mold.

Back at the apartment, I mixed a shaker of martinis and downed a tranquillizer while Rita called her kids.

Bryan, I hope you know I'm doing everything I can. You must know. Just please don't give up, please don't give up. I closed my eyes and willed this thought to him.

Just then, there was a soft rap on the door and Dianna Foster came in carrying a large, flat box. My neighbor was a slim woman with intense dark eyes and silky brunette hair pulled high in a topknot. Trying to smile, she uncovered a steaming pizza. "Half mushroom, half meatball," she remarked. "I thought we all deserved a break from cooking."

Suddenly, I realized how long it had been since I'd eaten, and the food looked tempting.

We exchanged news during dinner, and Dianna mentioned having spoken to the pastor at her son Rusty's school. He'd given her the name of a Reverend Frederick Gage in Tulsa, an old friend, and the kind of person who would help if he could.

"I'll call him tomorrow," I told her gratefully. "Maybe I'll have a better picture by then."

After my friends had gone, I stared into the darkness. Bryan's presence seemed to haunt the apartment. "Would you kiss me goodnight?" he'd be saying about now, as I turned off the television and tucked him in. "And be sure to set the alarm." What would happen to him now? What would happen to me? What was happening to the life I'd built?

The unexpected sound of the doorbell startled me and I ran to answer it. Kevin stood there looking shy and uncomfortable. Without a word, he handed me a small bouquet of flowers and a childlike card fashioned from pink construction paper. Thanking him, I opened the poignant message created and signed by Bryan's classmates:

Dear Mrs. Simmons,

We understand how you feel about what happened to Bryan. We feel sad and we miss him, too. We hope that all your worries and troubles will soon be over. God will take care of you both because He understands.

Three

The dream had come back to taunt him again, hurtling him into the cold, churning waters. He tried to twist free but concrete blocks, heavy on his feet, compelled him downward. Slowly, slowly, he sank. Until, at last, he was lost in a dark labyrinth of slime.

He'd cried all the way to Reno. The hard floor bumped against his cheek as great, wrenching sobs shook his whole body. They'd taken three planes. A blur of people. "Chew gum so your ears won't hurt." He'd cowered in his seat as voices ordered him not to make a fuss. I don't want to die! I want my mommy! Then, Tulsa. Paul bolting the door. A very pregnant woman coming forward to embrace him. "Welcome home, Bryan. Isn't it nice that the courts gave you to us?"

Stunned, I put down the decree that had arrived with the morning mail.

"THE SUPERIOR COURT OF THE STATE OF OKLAHOMA" it began: "Honorable Martin F. Bernhardt presiding:

> Bryan Andrew Simmons should establish a relationship with his natural father, the Defendant herein; therefore, the ex-

clusive care, custody and control of said minor child should now vest in the Defendant Paul Stuart Simmons, subject to rights of reasonable visitation to the Plaintiff."

"It's impossible!" I shuddered violently, putting through a call to the Tulsa courts. "When was there a hearing . . . and why wasn't I served for it?"

Nowhere did it claim that I was unfit. Or that Bryan would be better off with Paul. Even criminals have a right to know the charges, I reasoned, as the clerk looked up my file. Weren't parents entitled to the same equality?

"I'm sorry." She was back on the line. "I have no record of any proceedings. I suggest you call Vincent Morrell."

"It's a fluke," Rita insisted when she came to pick me up. "They can't hold hearings without you! Either someone was paid off or they didn't know the law."

"Marriage and divorce decrees are honored in every state." I was still wrapped up in useless speculation. "Is it possible that custody is exempt from full faith and credit?"

"No. It's not possible. Nan, be reasonable. People can't be expected to see a judge every time they cross a state line. You and Bryan have never lived in Oklahoma. It simply has no jurisdiction."

"Well, jurisdiction or not," I told her bitterly, "Oklahoma has Bryan."

Traffic seemed to be with us and we arrived early at the Hall of Justice. Once more, the guard looked with interest at the contents of my purse, then indifferently handed it back. I knew I couldn't face Inspector Halsey again without Michael, so Rita and I decided to wait for him in the hallway.

"What's this, a sit-in?" an amused detective smiled down at us.

"No chairs," I shrugged. "Would you like to join us?"

Declining the offer with mock regret, he walked on and I turned to Rita.

"Something else doesn't add up. How long did it take you to get a copy of your divorce decree?"

"Oh, a month, six weeks maybe."

"Did you ever hear of anybody getting a copy mailed out the same day?"

"No. Why?"

"Well, it's occurred to me that, aside from not keeping records or notifying people, the Tulsa courts are incredibly efficient."

Just then two uniformed officers passed by. "What's this, a sit-in?" they echoed. But before either of us could answer, Michael had turned the corner and innocently asked if we were holding a sit-in.

As he headed toward the door, I put a restraining hand on his arm. "Paul has custody in Oklahoma. I was hit with the news this morning."

"I received a copy of the order too. But please, Nan, don't worry about it. It's not legal."

There was a marked change in Erma Halsey this morning. Her eyes flickered with interest when she met Michael and her manner became demure. "How terrible, Mr. Callan." She shook her head as he explained our case. "Would you mind if I peeked at the file?"

We watched in silence as she scrutinized each document. Divorce decree from Massachusetts, 1969. Suit against Paul for non-support, 1970. Letters between lawyers regarding arrearages, 1972. Suit against Paul for non-support, 1974. On and on the papers were microscopically inspected. She lifted her head only to ask Michael an occasional question, or to complain to him about her heavy caseload. Her caseload was irrelevant, I thought with irritation. So were these papers. What did the fact that Paul owed me money in 1970 have to do with his kidnapping my son in 1976? Why wasn't she asking about Bryan?

I had become stiff from sitting by the time Ms. Halsey finally glanced up from her desk. Fluffing her hair, she smiled at Michael. "This file looks like a Sears catalogue, but we're almost through now. I just have to locate a typewriter."

"What's taking so long?" I asked him after she'd walked away.

"I don't know." Michael shrugged helplessly. "But this is ridiculous. Let me see if there's anyone else I can speak to."

Ms. Halsey returned a few minutes later carrying an over-age Smith Corona.

"Where's Mr. Callan?" she snapped.

"He'll be back in a minute."

She banged the typewriter down, hardly bothering to hide her annoyance.

"He's probably making a luncheon date." Her voice appeared sullen. "Well, we can't wait around all day for him." She grabbed a piece of paper and stuck it into the typewriter. "Now, let's see if we can finish this up. We've already wasted most of the morning."

I sank back in my chair as she started typing Bryan's name with two fingers.

Fifteen minutes later, Ms. Halsey reached for the phone. "One more thing. I have to check out the story with the children at Viscennes."

"Wait," I tried to tell her after she'd spoken to Kevin and Jonathan. "There are others."

"I have all the information I need," she replied brusquely and hung up.

"But we found out Paul had an accomplice. One child said she saw a rope in his hand and insisted that Bryan was tied up. Another is positive the man plays pool with her father at the Billiard Barn."

Eyes narrowing, the inspector reluctantly pulled a street directory from her desk. "Where is that located?" she asked abruptly.

"On McAllister."

She ran her finger down the page of cross streets. "It's a bad neighborhood. You wouldn't want to go there."

"I wasn't thinking of going there. I thought the police were supposed to do that."

She stared at me wordlessly.

"I don't understand." I pleaded. "You've seen my papers, spoken to witnesses and already know Paul's past actions. How long does it take to write up a writ?"

"We'll have to see," she replied, unperturbed. "Anyhow, I'm sure the boy's all right. He's with his father."

Rita looked unable to keep still any longer. Leaning forward, she reminded the inspector, "That's still circumstantial. No one's actually proven that Paul Simmons is the man who kidnapped Bryan. And what about the second man? Can't charges be brought against him?"

"No. He had parental permission."

"To do what?" I demanded. "To tie Bryan with a rope? To drag him to another state? I didn't give my permission!" I closed my eyes and drew a deep breath in an effort to keep calm.

"How can you assume he's safe just because he's with his father?" Rita was saying. "Doesn't your office handle cases of child abuse? I remember reading about parents who chained their children to a freeway."

My eyes blinked open as the inspector waved a frantic hand across the desk in an effort to quiet us. "You're both getting excited," she observed correctly. "I'm sure he's fine."

"Will you put that in writing?"

Her body stiffened as she was momentarily thrown off guard.

"I want it in writing that you are guaranteeing my son's safety," I repeated.

"I—I can't do that." She sputtered. "It's—"

"Then call the Tulsa police and have them check on him."

"I'll send out a telex," she replied, quickly regaining her composure. "But I'm sure you're worried over nothing."

"Nothing? Tell me, Ms. Halsey. If you had to get an hysterical, possibly bound child out of the city, how would you keep him quiet through the toll booth? Would you put him under a blanket, tranquillize him, or use the trunk of a car like they did with Patty Hearst?"

"Oh, those people on the bridge see screaming kids all the time." She dismissed my words. "Parents just turn around and slap them. I've got five kids of my own."

Michael came back just then and our conversation stopped.

"I don't know if the District Attorney's office will want to issue a writ," Inspector Halsey told him without her former friendliness. "There's got to be evidence of criminal intent."

"But stealing a car is a crime," I insisted. "How can there even be a question. Isn't Bryan as important as a Volkswagon?"

Ignoring me, she continued to Michael, "I'll need to see Mr. Simmons' custody order before I can recommend anything to the District Attorney."

"Mr. Simmons' custody order is meaningless, you know that. California has the only legal jurisdiction."

"I'm sorry. I cannot proceed until I see the Oklahoma order."

Michael, my thoughts were racing, do something . . . anything. She was flirting with you before, maybe if you took her to lunch or to bed. "Ms. Halsey, if the order were valid," I tried to reason with her, "why didn't Paul just present it to the California courts? Why did he have to grab Bryan and run?"

"I can't do anything until I see the order."

"All right," Michael said with resignation. "I'll have my secretary bring it down this afternoon."

"Why is she confusing the issue?" I asked numbly as we walked to the elevator. "It's not custody. It's kidnapping. She's spent all morning trying to decide whose parental rights have been violated. What about Bryan? Doesn't he have any rights?"

"I'm sorry, Nan." Michael put his arm around me. "Unfortunately, our laws protecting children from members of their own families are grossly inadequate."

"What an emotional wringer they dragged you through," Rita was saying as Michael left us in the lobby, "and I can't help but feel it's on purpose." Of course, it's deliberate, I thought tiredly. If they make things unpleasant enough, maybe I won't bother coming back.

"Well, that's enough for one morning," she continued gently. "There must be a cafeteria in the building. Come on, I'll buy you some lunch."

I thanked her for the offer, adding, "But I should warn you about the food in this building. It's on a par with the service. I used to eat here occasionally when I was seeing John."

"Oh, that's right," she replied. "I'd forgotten all about him. Nan, did you ever think when you were dating a prosecuting attorney that you'd wind up as a case?"

"Never, but right now I want to talk to him very much."

Downstairs, the cafeteria was crowded and thick with the smell of french fries. Rita went to look for a table while I headed for the phone booths outside. First, I couldn't find a dime, then I couldn't find John's card. I was looking up his number when someone started pounding on the glass. "Oh, go away," I muttered. "I'll be out in a minute. This is an emergency!" He must have found another booth, because the banging had stopped by the time the familiar voice answered "John Elliot."

"Hi. It's Nancy."

"Well, hi." He greeted me warmly. "I've tried to call you a few times, but you weren't home."

"I'm downstairs in the cafeteria now, John," I said softly, not wanting to sound dramatic, "Paul's taken Bryan again."

"Oh, my God." His voice trailed off into a whisper. "I'll meet you there in five minutes."

I also called Oklahoma before joining Rita. Like yesterday, Paul wasn't home and his answering service didn't know how to reach him.

John spotted us as soon as he walked in the door. He looks different, I mused, as he walked past the rows of institutional tables. He's still got his mustache, and he hasn't cut his hair but . . . John kissed me lightly on the forehead and pulled over a chair. "I'm glad you're with her," he nodded at Rita. "Now tell me. What in God's name is going on?"

I repeated all the details, Rita filling in whenever it became painful.

"Who's the inspector on the case?" was John's first question.

"Erma Halsey."

"Oh shit." He scowled, "Good old Ballsey Halsey! You'll have to keep after her if you want anything done."

"If she's such an incompetent," Rita said angrily, as I grew progressively more upset, "what the hell is she doing here?"

"It's not like *Streets of San Francisco*. The longer people work in this environment, the more callous they seem to become. Anyhow, she's near retirement. They just leave her alone."

They continued talking while I picked at my lunch. John swore a couple of times and, at one point, commented that working here had taken the edge off some of his former idealism. Finally, he got up to leave.

"I'm sorry, I've got to get back now," he apologized, "but I promise to do everything I can. It's not my division, but I'm going to request Bryan's case file anyway." In a tender voice he added, "I'll call you."

"That must have been some ski trip," Rita remarked as she watched him leave. "He'll be in that cast for weeks!"

"What cast?"

"Nancy, I don't believe it!" She started to laugh. "That was the guy you were so crazy about, and you didn't even notice that he had a broken ankle."

Throughout the morning, I'd felt a tightening in my chest but had forced myself to ignore it. Now, as we left the building, I could no longer speak without wheezing. "Damn!" I tried to clear my throat. "What lousy timing!"

"Do you want to see a doctor?" Rita looked worried.

"It sounds worse than it is," I tried to reassure her, "but maybe I'd better get a shot of penicillin. I hate to waste the time, but Dr. Carlisle knows about Bryan, so it shouldn't take too long."

Rita dropped me off in front of U.C. Medical Center and went to look for a parking space while I took the elevator upstairs. Five minutes later, bewildered and angry, I was back at the elevator. It had been another in a series of fiascos. The doctor wouldn't see me without an appointment, and the nurse had shoved a useless packet of pills in my hand with terse instructions to relax.

"Nice day," the man next to me remarked. "The view is beautiful from here."

I answered him by bursting into tears,

"What's the matter?" he asked and, suddenly, I found myself blurting out all the horrors of the past few days to a perfect stranger.

"My God. Can't the police help you?"

"They don't even seem to be trying," I sobbed. "And to top it off, now my doctor won't see me without an appointment. How am I going to help Bryan if I can't even breathe?"

"Jesus, it doesn't take a genius to tell you're wheezing. Is there another doctor you could see?"

"No. He's the only one with my records from back East. It's right down there in black and white that penicillin works best. But he doesn't care. Nobody cares." I went on in a flood of despair. "I guess I'll try the emergency room."

"That won't do any good. Since it's not the usual remedy, all you'll get is another hassle." He put his hand on my arm and continued, "Look, I'm a resident here. Want some advice? If you need penicillin, just go to a VD clinic and tell them you've been exposed. You'll get your shot, no questions asked."

"I never thought I'd be better off with VD," I managed to smile.

"Believe me, you wouldn't," he smiled back. "It's just been my experience that, if you need help, it doesn't always pay to be honest."

My mood was lighter as I walked outside. How many people could claim they'd been rescued by Sir Galahad of Gonorrhea! It wasn't necessary to follow his instructions though. Rita remembered she could refill her son's prescription for strep throat, and pills would work just as well.

As we drove to her pharmacy, I absently glanced at the samples I'd been given in lieu of an appointment. Printed on the label, beneath the instructions, was a warning: This medication should not be taken by people under stress.

"You know, I've been thinking," I told Rita when we left the drugstore. "KGO did a T.V. show last week on a fourteen-year-old's right to have sex. Don't you think they'd also be interested in an eleven-year-old's right not to be kidnapped?"

"I'm not sure they would. But, in any case, are you up to handling the publicity?"

"Frankly, no. I don't want my problems broadcast all over San Francisco. But Bryan hasn't been heard from in two days, and maybe it would get Erma Halsey off her ass."

"That would take a bulldozer," Rita remarked dryly. "But if you're feeling well enough, let's go down there. Maybe we can get it on the six o'clock news."

"Why didn't you let us know Wednesday afternoon?" the reporter asked as we sat in the plush lobby of Channel 7. "We could have sent our mobile units out to interview the kids."

"But I didn't know it then either," I told her. "That's part of the story."

"Since it happened two days ago, it's not considered news anymore."

"But there's a different angle here," Rita persisted. "A child's been kidnapped and the authorities have doubts that a crime's been committed."

"I sympathize," she answered in a voice that made me believe her. "But we've got another problem now. All our units are tied up at the Patty Hearst trial and we don't have any to spare."

What irony, I thought, as we walked out the door. The Hearsts were probably dying to be left alone. I bet they'd give their right arms if the situations were reversed and no one was available to cover their story.

Four

"They also serve who only stand and wait." I visualized the poet Milton's words as I crawled out of bed Saturday morning. He really was blind, I concluded as the endless weekend loomed before me. What possible purpose could waiting serve? While the wheels of justice observed the Sabbath, I had to do something, anything, to cope with the anxiety. In desperation, I decided to search for the second man.

Dianna and I drove down McAllister until we spotted a torn sign reading "Billiard Barn." The neighborhood was unkempt and peeling Victorian houses looked onto the street through broken windows.

"It's not safe to get out of the car," Dianna shuddered.

"It'll be okay. Just stop right in front."

Stepping over discarded beer cans, I peered into the dimly lit room. Two men stopped their game to stare suspiciously at me, but neither fit Carrie's description. Disappointed, I hurried back to the car and locked the door.

"Dianna!" I froze in memory of the poolhall, "What would I have done had I found him?"

Later that morning we drove to the airport. "On March 10th you rented a car to Paul Simmons," I told the agent at Budget. "It was used in a kidnapping. Could you please check your files to see who handled the transactions?" He shook his head.

"I'm sorry. I can't give you that information."

"But it was my son who was taken. I want to know if someone remembers a second man being there or if the car showed signs of a struggle. Please help me. You can check with Officer Burns at the Taraval station."

His head continued shaking as if he were a wind-up toy. "I really don't have that information. Maybe the manager can help on Monday."

"Starsky and Hutch would've found out something by now." Rusty looked accusingly at us when we returned to Dianna's.

"This is real life," his mother explained. She tossed together a few sandwiches and we ate in silence.

"Maybe I can help," he offered, chewing thoughtfully. "The kids might know something they'd only tell another kid."

I handed Rusty the list of names Rita had copied down and he picked up the phone with an air of importance.

"I'm a friend of Bryan Simmons. . . ." He went down the list one by one. Nobody offered anything new and Carrie Knoll's father said he didn't know what his daughter was talking about.

"It's not so easy," Rusty acknowledged as he put down the paper and walked towards his room.

Dianna had been sitting there, quietly studying an empty coffee cup. "Maybe we're on the wrong track," she suggested. "Carrie might only think she knows the man. Can you remember anyone Paul knows who would fit the description?"

"His lawyer, Vincent Morrell!" I laughed.

She raised an eyebrow. "That might not be as farfetched as you think. He wasn't home that night and you've said a thousand times that he's unethical."

I stopped laughing. "He'd be disbarred."

"Let's hope it's him for that reason. Once this is over, Paul will have trouble finding another attorney who fights so dirty."

It was hard to believe, but nothing was impossible. I checked the Reno airport. There were only two flights that went from there to Tulsa, but neither "Paul Simmons" nor "Vincent Morrell" were on them.

"Morrell has a private plane," I remembered. "My lawyer in Oklahoma joked about his being the 'Evel Knievel of the skies.' Maybe that's why they went to Reno. They might have been afraid to take Bryan on a commercial flight." But why should he risk his career for Paul? To prove a point? "No." I changed my mind. "That can't be it. Paul can't pay him enough money to take that kind of chance."

"What chance? If Paul had papers and Morrell brought the plane into California, what law was he breaking? He was just 'taking a client for a ride'!"

I called the Reno airport again, this time asking for the names of private landing fields. I was given two.

"What's the number of the plane?" the receptionist asked at Glenwood Landing. I didn't know.

"Well, I'll check around and see if I can find out anything for you, but we log by number, not name. Besides," she added, "it's not mandatory for private aircraft to file a flight plan."

I thanked her and dialed the FAA. They informed me that central registration on all private planes was located in Oklahoma. Shuddering at the coincidence, I had Dianna make the next call.

"No information on a plane registered to Vincent Morrell," she reported. "It's not unusual, though, to register planes under the names of businesses or corporations."

We were back where we started. Three o'clock and nothing had been accomplished.

I went home and tried to take a nap but sleep was fitful. Visions of ropes kept taunting me with coarse, scratchy strands weaving a pattern on my eyelids. Shaking myself awake, I sat straight up in bed. "Bales of hay. Bales of cotton," I thought angrily. "That's what ropes should bind, not children."

Still half-dazed, I realized that the phone was ringing.

My neighbor, Emily Rossi, greeted me in a low voice. "I'm sorry I couldn't call sooner. Have you heard anything yet?"

She sounded funny — depressed — and I asked what was wrong.

"Oh, I'm just working through a few personal problems. I was hoping to hear from Rick — you know, the guy I met a couple of weeks ago — but he hasn't called. Listen I know you're not crazy about singles bars, but would you like to go down to Perry's with me tonight? It might be good for you to get out of the house."

"You must be kidding! That's the last place I'd want to be right now."

"Well, I thought if you met somebody, it might take your mind off Bryan for a while."

Stunned by her suggestion, I wondered if she thought taking my mind off of Bryan was as simple as getting hers off of Rick.

"I'm afraid not, Emily. You'll have to find someone else to go with."

"I understand. It's a bad time for you. But have you thought of what you'll do if you don't get Bryan back?"

"What do you mean?" I became frightened. "What makes you think I won't?"

"Well, when the courts awarded my cousin custody, his ex-wife grabbed their little girl and ran off to another state. Unfortunately, the courts there decided a girl should be with her mother."

"They gave custody to the kidnapper!"

"I didn't want to upset you, but I thought you should be prepared for the worst. Nan, how many times can you fight for Bryan? It's got to take something out of you each time, and you have to think of yourself. Have you considered letting Paul keep him? It would stop the harassment and, even if you don't think so now, life will go on." Apparently unaware of my silence, she continued, "I've learned that we all have to make accommodations somewhere, and I'm sure Bryan will grow up all right."

"Well, I'm not sure of that." I was adamant. "What's 'all right'? Accommodating to violence for survival? Being afraid to form attachments because they won't last? What kind of self-image can he possibly grow up with? All situations are not the same. Some you accommodate and some you fight. There's a fine line, Emily. But my son's life is not open for negotiation!"

I made my excuses and hung up.

Five

Sunday passed with still no answer at Paul's house. My mind sought to drown out the soliloquy of the ticking clock but the sound was merely replaced by an incessant interior monologue.

"Why, Paul?" I pleaded with the man I'd once known. "Why are you doing this? Bryan hasn't existed for you in years . . . is it revenge? Money? Blame for a shattered dream?"

I opened the door to Bryan's room. The air was strangely quiet as I stared wistfully at the array of unused toys.

It reminded me of a childhood poem:

"Ay, faithful to little Boy Blue they stand
Each in the same old place
Awaiting the touch of a little hand,
The smile of a little face. . . . "

"Damn it, Paul," I cried out to the empty surroundings. "Why don't you grow up?"

On Monday morning, I called Erma Halsey.
"Has there been any word on my son?"
"No."

"But it's been over seventy-two hours . . . have you sent out the telex yet?"

"Look, Mrs. Simmons," she told me curtly, before the phone went dead, "you're not my only case."

While her words were still ringing in my ears, two reporters phoned to tell me that Dianna had just contacted their newspapers. Both were interested in writing Bryan's story and, hopefully, I set up appointments for the following day.

The most important call came at dinnertime. "Mrs. Simmons? This is Reverend Gage. I was at your husband's house this evening. He's a difficult man to talk to."

Thank God . . . at least they were there. "Did you see Bryan?"

"Well, I was able to see his wife and little girl," he answered slowly. "But when I requested to speak with your son, he flatly refused. I tried everything I could," the minister seemed to apologize. "I even peeked in the window. There were furnishings and boxes all over the living room, but it was impossible to see beyond that."

"What do you think was going on?"

"I don't know," he answered quietly. "But it's my personal opinion that the boy isn't even there."

I couldn't allow myself to think. Thanking Reverend Gage, I hung up and dialed Paul's number. SuEllen answered in a sugary drawl.

"I want to speak to Bryan," I told her, relieved that at least they were answering their phone now. There was a pause and, for a split second, hope.

"Who is this?" Paul was suddenly on the line.

"Bryan's mother. Put him on."

"On the advice of my attorney," he replied, "Bryan can't speak to you."

He slammed the phone down and, for the second time that day, I stood there listening to a dial tone. First they take away your child, then everyone hangs up on you!

Bryan can't speak to you. Bryan can't speak to *you* . . . over and over the words repeated themselves like a broken record . . . but, maybe. . . .

"Why are you calling?" Paul was screaming at Rita half an hour later. "On the advice of my attorney, Bryan can't come to the phone and, if his mother wasn't such an hysteric, she'd tell you the truth."

"And what is that, Mr. Simmons?" she replied coldly while I held my breath on the extension.

"There's been a simple change of custody. That's all. Just a simple change of custody." Before hanging up he added "And tell that woman to have her lawyer answer Mr. Morrell's calls for a change. Vinnie's been trying to get hold of Callan all week."

The conversation, such as it was, ended and I stomped out of the bedroom hysterically screaming, "How dare he call me an hysteric?" Rita and I stared at each other, then burst into nervous laughter.

"Nan." She smiled as the tension eased. "My father always said you can survive anything if you keep your sense of humor."

The next few hours were a nightmare, with everyone trying to contact Bryan in their own way. Kevin, Rusty, my family, Greg Ephron impersonating a police officer. All were given the same words: "On the advice of my attorney . . . " SuEllen had a few words of her own to add: "His mother's a bitch to make you waste your money," she informed Rita's eight-year-old son Mark.

When Rita left, the dam burst. A strangled cry came from somewhere in my throat and I flung myself on the bed. Nobody could speak to Bryan. Why? What harm could Reverend Gage have done except report an abused child to the police? Was my baby even alive? I writhed and clutched at the blankets till the green pile came up in my hands. What about the boxes all over the house? Were they redecorating or planning to disappear? How would I locate them? Maybe we were working on a Writ for Oklahoma while Bryan was stashed away with Paul's father in Boston or SuEllen's mother in Tennessee. Why wasn't anybody helping us? Didn't anybody care? I cried uncontrollably until at last I was drained and fell asleep.

"Bullshit" was Michael's reply when I relayed Paul's message the following morning. "I've been phoning Morrell since Wednesday and the man's more elusive than a greased pig. I'll keep trying, though," he reassured me. "Meanwhile, have you received my news yet?"

"What news?"

"I've been doing some research on Oklahoma law and everything corroborates what I've been saying. They have no jurisdiction. I've had Lorraine mail out copies of the precedents. You should have them by today or tomorrow."

Feeling strangely detached from points of law, I asked Michael to read the precedents anyhow.

"Well, two conditions must exist in order for a custody change: there has to have been a change of circumstances affecting the child's welfare since the last order was granted; and the child must be lawfully domiciled in Oklahoma at the time of the hearing."

"Paul's order didn't even allege those circumstances. How could they have given him custody there?"

"I don't know." My lawyer sounded genuinely puzzled. "And I don't want to guess. But it doesn't matter now. I have an appointment with the District Attorney's office tomorrow and can show it to them in black and white. California is the state of jurisdiction."

"Well, let's hope California will exercise it."

Checking the morning's mail, I found the envelope from Callan-McCrae in the box and ripped it open:

> We must hold that the judgement of a court of a sister state awarding the custody of a child will be sustained by the courts of this state unless it is shown that the conditions affecting the welfare of the child have changed since the judgement of the court of the sister state and that the child is lawfully domiciled within this state. If the conditions have not so changed, then the judgement of the sister state will be sustained. If the child is not lawfully domiciled within this state, the judgement of the sister state will be sustained.

Further, regarding the state in which the child is legally domiciled:

> In Oklahoma as well as in other jurisdictions, it is a well recognized principle of law that the domicile or residence of a minor child whose parents have been divorced is the domicile of the parent to whose custody the child has been legally given. The doctrine of comity and full faith and credit requires that the courts of Oklahoma recognize the decree of a sister state.

Cox v. Paulson, Clampitt v. Johnson, Wilkerson v. Davila. On and on the cases supported Michael's contention. Even if the issue were custody, Paul was clearly in possession of an illegal order.

I was feeling slightly better by the time Michael called back to say that he'd contacted Morrell, only to be cursed out. "He also told me that there's a warrant out for your arrest in Oklahoma."

"My arrest? I didn't know that Macon County line was in Tulsa!"

"Don't let it throw you. He's obviously using scare tactics because he's worried. By the way, did you get the precedents?"

"Yes, and thank you. They're beautiful. The first solid hope I've had since Bryan was taken. But Michael," I hesitated, "if you don't mind my asking, what did you say to Morrell?"

"You would have been proud of me. I kept my cool for the longest time and tried to reason with him. Then, with a great deal of dignity, I finally screamed, 'Look, sir, you are not talking to some fuckin' Okie. You are speaking to a lawyer!'"

My sister Laurel phoned from Connecticut while I was waiting for the reporters. I filled her in on my latest legal hopes, but she was unimpressed. "Matt and I are very worried," she told me. "We're starting to see a pattern in the way Bryan's case is being handled."

"What is it?" I asked with a growing sense of apprehension.

"Well, you're counting on law enforcement agencies to pursue a kidnapping and it seems to us that they're just looking for a legal loophole to avoid doing anything."

"But they've eventually got to do something. It's not a matter of complaining about a barking dog. A child's been kidnapped."

"That's just it. Bryan was kidnapped as surely as the Lindbergh baby or Bobby Breen, but were those cases thrown into Domestic Relations? Did anybody question criminal intent? Hell," she pointed out disgustedly, "they're not even calling it 'kidnapping' but 'child stealing'. Remember your Greek history? Give something a different name and you can treat it differently."

"You said you saw a pattern," I reminded her. "What kind?"

"It seems to me that Bryan's almost irrelevant to the issue. Instead of the authorities being concerned about his welfare or outraged at Paul's behavior, I think they're looking at the whole thing as a domestic spat. In other words," she concluded, "mainly a women's problem."

"But legally . . ."

"Nan, think about it. If this were being treated as a serious crime, there'd already be a warrant out for Paul's arrest. It's not as though they don't know who the kidnapper is. Instead, you're having to prove you have valid custody while the authorities leave him alone." She paused. "Doesn't that sound like a rape victim to you? Or a battered wife?" A chill went through me. Matt was on the extension now, and I asked if he agreed.

"Yes, Hon, I do. Women generally have custody of their kids so they would be the primary target for this sort of thing."

"What about a man with custody? Do you think he'd receive better treatment?"

"Probably not," he guessed. "If the policy's already been established, he'd be subject to the backlash. Nan, whenever women are the main victims of a class of crimes, the onus is on them to show that they didn't provoke or deserve it. I see so-called 'child-stealing' in the same light. After all, how could a nice lady have something like that happen to her?"

I was pouring Howard Olsen a cup of coffee when Marion Ross arrived. Good. I could combine both appointments. The reporters seemed friendly and, to my relief, the interview came off quite well.

The next morning Mr. Olsen phoned to say his editor had thought the story "too messy." Bryan's picture returned by mail with no comment was the verdict of his competitor.

"What do I have to do to get this story told?" I called Laurel in frustration. "Run naked down Montgomery Street with a sign saying *Help! My child's been stolen.*"

"Well, it might do the trick," she laughed half-heartedly. "But they'd probably focus on the nutty nudie and not the kidnap victim."

"I can't understand it. A child's life is in question. No one knows how he is, or even where he is, and it's not considered newsworthy."

"Nan," she replied, "if you were famous you'd probably have no trouble getting media attention, but I'm still not sure that would accomplish anything. Remember Yoko Ono, John Lennon's wife? In spite of all the publicity, the authorities have still done nothing to help them locate her little girl."

Six

The eyes peered down at him. Always watching. He turned over in his bed and tried to hide his head under the pillow, but it was no use. They always found him. When he'd summoned up enough courage to call his mother, he'd gotten no further than half the number before his father had crept up behind him and replaced the receiver on the hook.

"Bryan," the stern voice had ordered, "you're not to try that again. What's wrong with you anyway?"

For the most part, they watched from a distance. Shadowy phantoms wiggling in and out of his consciousness. Huge, hulking, menacing. Ready to pounce if he said or did the wrong thing. Sometimes Paul had little talks with him. Wheedling, pleading, then, in frustration, threatening. The tone was always the same. We can give you everything a boy your age needs. Damn it, why don't you respond?

He tried to take refuge in the television set, the familiar patterns a link between past and present. If he could just endure, his mother would come. She always had. But, where was she?

"You all right, boy?"

Bright lights jolting him into wakefulness now, Bryan removed the pillow from his head, and stared into the ruddy face of a police sergeant.

"Of course, he's all right," SuEllen snapped, as his father threw him a silencing glance. "How dare you wake us up in the middle of the night like common criminals!"

"I don't understand." Paul tried to suppress the fury in his voice. "An hysterical woman in San Francisco screams that her kid's been hurt and we have to go through the embarrassment of having three patrol cars block our driveway and our son disturbed so you can check on him. Why is all this necessary? I've already shown you my custody papers."

"Okay, Mac. Calm down. If the boy's not bruised, you have nothing to worry about."

Bryan felt his face flush as he was asked to strip and turn around. Apparently, the officers were satisfied because they wrote something down and turned to leave.

"Aren't you going to take me with you?" Bryan pleaded.

The sergeant returned, a sympathetic look betraying his brusque manner. Tousling the child's hair, he said, "I'm sorry, son."

It was now a full week since I'd heard from Bryan. Too restless to sit in the house any longer, I drove aimlessly down the street. The familiar surroundings seemed strange and ethereal as my basic beliefs were being undermined.

Who were these people, I wondered, whose job it was to interpret the law? Where were our procedures to monitor their competence . . . to remove them if necessary? Was expecting justice like throwing yourself on the mercy of a roulette wheel? Anxiety unrelieved, I came home to wait again.

"Mrs. Simmons?"

My stomach tightened as I recognized Erma Halsey's voice.

"I've been trying to call you for fifteen minutes. We've received a report from the Tulsa police and they say the boy is fine."

"Oh, thank God! Did they talk to him alone? Are they sure it was Bryan?"

"I haven't any other details," she cut me short. "But Mr. Cattano, the deputy in charge of your case, has just turned it down."

My mind reeled. Bryan and I needed each other. We loved each other. How could Mr. Cattano take him away? My lips tried to form words but no sound came out. It didn't matter. There was no longer anyone on the other end. Michael. I had to get through to Michael. Blinded by tears, I fumbled with the phone until I heard the familiar "Law Offices."

Michael was in court but Lorraine put me on hold while she contacted the District Attorney's office. A few minutes later she reported with satisfaction that Erma Halsey was mistaken. No decision had been made as yet and Michael was to see Cattano in the morning. Joyfully, I hung up. We'd been granted a reprieve!

I woke up the next morning and searched through the paper for my horoscope. "A good day for getting chores done around the house," it advised. Nothing significant. Quickly, I scanned Bryan's sign, Paul's, Michael's, and would have looked up Cattano's had I known his birthday. Not usually superstitious, today I was willing to believe in anything that would give me some knowledge of the future.

At ten o'clock the phone rang. "I'm sorry," Michael said with hesitation. "Mr. Cattano felt that Paul's papers were in order."

Oddly enough I reacted calmly to his words. I'd been through the shock of a turn-down yesterday and at least was out of limbo now. It looked like we'd have to go to Tulsa after all.

We made plans to meet at Michael's office on Saturday and, as I hung up, I forced myself to focus on the details for the trip. Clothes to pack. Reservations to make. Someone to work the answering service.

"Bryan," I silently instructed my son. "Mommy's coming. Please, please you be there."

I called Laurel who cried in spite of her premonitions. Then Rita, who numbly promised to be right over. Dianna, furiously cursing, told me she'd stay late at the office that night and flood the government with letters asking for help. Nobody could seem to believe it had really happened.

"Nan, I'd like you to read something," Rita told me when she arrived. "It's from one of my courses and, somehow, seems appropriate."

> The fundamental conflicts in human life are not between competing ideas — one of which is true and the other false — but, rather, between those who hold power and use it to oppress others, and those who are oppressed by power and seek to free themselves of it.

"That's from Thomas Szasz." She came to the point. "We've got to protest this decision."

"Protest? I'd scream from the top of Sutro Tower if I thought it would do any good."

"I'm talking about organized protest," she went on. "Plenty of people are going to be outraged by this decision."

I felt a sudden surge of hope. "Do you think it would work?"

"Remember the Saturday Night Massacre? The whole country was up in arms and flooded Washington with cables and letters. It was the turning point in Watergate. The District Attorney is an elected official. He'll have to react to a stack of telegrams informing him that his decision is being challenged. I was thinking about it on the way over. We both have friends and relatives all over the country. I'm sure they'd be willing to help."

We took turns calling and a chain reaction started: California, Massachusetts, Illinois, New York. Friends, past and present, promising to wire San Francisco and ask their friends to do the same. In spite of the situation, I managed to laugh at Bonnie Whitman's reaction. "Do you want a telegram from me or an organization?" my Boston neighbor asked. "In fact, name any organization. You want it, I'm it."

Bill Steele, now living in Florida, thought his Congressman was sponsoring legislation against child-stealing. "I work for a local paper," he told me, "and I'm sure we've got something on file. I'll send you all the information I can and, of course, Marge and I will send a telegram."

The hardest call was to Springfield. My parents. My father wasn't home and my mother's anxious "Have you heard from Bryan?" broke my heart. Her deliberate calm in hearing the verdict, though, was strangely reflective of my own.

"I'll tell Daddy," she said quietly. "But I don't know how he'll take it. You know what Bryan means to him. Nan dear, do whatever you think is best. We're behind you all the way . . . but I can't help wondering. There are no details. How do we know Paul didn't show some friend's child to the police and claim that it was Bryan? If we could only hear his voice."

We tried to console each other. Then, promising to phone as soon as I'd seen Michael, I hung up.

Rita poured me a glass of wine as I drafted my own telegram. It was to go to Julian Garth, the District Attorney, with copies to the newspapers. Western Union asked, "Will you read the message?"

"RE: Bryan Andrew Simmons," I replied. "Can you and Mr. Cattano face me personally, parent-to-parent, and explain how my child can be beaten, bound, kidnapped and held incommunicado and receive no help or protection from your office. As of today it has been nine days since I heard from him. Will you also explain how your office will honor an illegally obtained custody order from a state in which my son and I never lived, at a hearing for which I was never served. A clergyman in Tulsa informs me that he was not allowed to see my son, neither is Bryan allowed to the telephone. Will you guarantee me in writing that my son is alive as a result of what you consider a civil matter? I beg you as a human being and a parent to reconsider your decision. This is not a fight between states. This is my son's life."

Seven

"Hey, you're really a tiger." John's call woke me the next day. "This office hasn't been so lively in years. I'm sorry about Bryan, Nan." His voice softened. "I did everything I could. All I managed to achieve, though, was a pointed warning to keep my nose in my own division."

"I appreciate your trying," I thanked him, knowing there were no adequate words. "But what about the telegrams? Do you think they'll do any good?"

"I wish I could be more encouraging. But there's no way of telling. Changing a decision is admitting a mistake. And with public officials, that's tantamount to treason. Besides," he added disgustedly, "their way of handling Bryan's case was in keeping with years of policy."

"Policy towards what?"

"Family crimes. Look, if I were to grab some random child off the street and drag him to Oklahoma, there'd be hell to pay. Even if I left him where he was but knocked him around a little, I'd be looking at some pretty stiff charges. But, if that same kid wound up in the hospital because one of his parents beat the shit out of him, the law enforcement agencies would probably suggest therapy to see why the abuser couldn't handle his or her frustrations."

"Nothing would happen to you either if you had parental permission."

"I'm really sorry," John apologized. "I didn't mean to hit so close to home. But the fact is, no one is trying to punish Paul, are they?"

My silence was answer enough.

"Paul's not even unusual." He continued. "Child abuse is only reported in the smallest percentage of cases, and then prosecuted in even fewer. And the problem isn't limited to parent-child. Can you handle a mind-blowing statistic?"

"I'm getting used to having my mind boggled. Go ahead."

"Well, as you know, many women are afraid to go out alone at night because they may be attacked. Yet nearly one-third of the female homicide victims in California are murdered by their own husbands and, in most cases, the police were aware of previous battery. Unfortunately, when the initial incidents happen, the victims are usually discouraged from filing charges. Most often they're advised to seek counselling or simply to go home and try to work things out."

"That's like telling a rape victim to befriend her assailant. How can it be justified?"

"Nancy, you justify yourself to the legal system. It doesn't work the other way around. Besides, we're dealing with that age-old saw: the Sanctity of the Family. Or, in other words, a legal viewpoint which considers anything to do with spouses, ex-spouses or their children as somewhere between sainthood and a damned nuisance. So-called family cases are even handled by a different division. You know that."

"I know I was heard in Domestic Relations, but I didn't give it a second thought. I was under the impression that all courts had the same objective."

"No way. In criminal court the objective is punishment upon conviction. Domestic Relations often operates on the premise that there is no guilty party, just some nice folks having a hard time getting along. The aim, then, becomes reconciliation . . . to keep the family together. Except," he hastily added, "in the case of murder."

"That sounds pragmatic, John. It's pretty difficult to reconcile with a corpse!"

"Well, whatever turns you on." He burst out laughing despite himself, and so did I. "You know," his tone became reflective, "there's more truth to that than you might realize. There was a recent case in Georgia where a lower court ruled that it could be considered 'justifiable homicide' if you murdered your spouse's lover to protect your marriage, but killing the adulterous spouse was taboo because that would terminate the marriage."

I found myself growing impatient. "But how does Bryan fit into the picture? Paul and I have been divorced for years. Surely, no one's pushing for a reconciliation."

"No. But we're still dealing with the Sanctity of the Family. In this case, parenthood. Since the biological father did the kidnapping, the act reverts to a minor skirmish between two parents, both of whom, of course, love the child."

"That's unmitigated bullshit!"

"I agree with you."

"And how can anyone consider kidnapping—even by a parent—a domestic issue?"

"But it's not considered kidnapping, Nan. The term is *child-stealing*, and that's another category entirely."

"Nothing but semantics," I muttered, as Laurel's words came back to haunt me. *Give something a different name and you can treat it differently.* "I hate to sound trite but 'a rose by any other name'. . . . "

"Would still smell! Actually, I believe two crimes have been committed. Kidnapping against Bryan and child-stealing against you. Also, anyone who willfully causes a child to suffer either physically or mentally is liable under the child abuse statute. The trouble with filial crime though, as I've been telling you, is in getting the laws enforced. Even with my attempts at intervention, Bryan's case wound up back in the civil courts."

"Ironic, isn't it?" I thought of Livanos' refusal to issue a writ. "It was thrown out of there in the first place. It's like a game of hot potato."

"Yes," John agreed. "Half-baked. But at least you've got the financial backing to go to Oklahoma and fight for Bryan."

"I know. I'm making plans with my attorney tomorrow. But, damn it, if there are laws on the books, Bryan and I shouldn't have to go through all this. And what about the people who can't get hold of the money? Do they simply lose their children?"

There was a subdued pause. "Don't worry about that right now, Nan. Just be grateful you've got help. You're in better shape than most."

I opened the door to Michael's law firm on Saturday morning to find him bent over the coffee machine in jeans and a "St. Andrews" sweat shirt.

"Doing penance?"

"Coaching baseball this afternoon," he grinned. "How do you think this outfit would go over in court?"

"You're missing your vest," I reminded him as we stepped into his private office. It was a richly panelled room with deep red carpeting, and the prominent display of family photographs was a relief from the judicial atmosphere of books and diplomas. As Michael seated himself behind a massive oak desk, I drew up a chair and waited.

"I've read and re-read the precedents," he began slowly, flipping through my files, "and I'm convinced that your case isn't difficult. We have one problem, though. I've learned that child-stealing isn't a federal matter, so we'll need a local associate to present it to the Oklahoma court."

Before I could react, he asked, "Do you want me to contact Art Alpert? You liked him."

"He's retired now," I heard myself mumble as the impact of his words sank in.

"Can you think of anyone else?"

"Michael, it's hard enough finding a good attorney in the same city, but from 1800 miles away, it's sheer Blind Man's Bluff. You know what my experience has been." Suddenly I found myself in a cold sweat as my mind flashed back to the image of Jerome Pollock.

Jerome Pollock had been a "mail order" attorney, selected by virtue of being the first to respond to my Massachusetts lawyer's plea for an Oklahoma counterpart. After spending two fruitless years trying to negotiate with Morrell about child support, he'd contacted me in the summer of 1974 to relate that he'd "settled the case." In fact, he told me excitedly, Paul had even decided that he wanted to re-establish a relationship with Bryan. "Mr. Simmons is ashamed of having restrained the boy after visitation," he repeated, referring to the first fiasco, five years earlier, "and now wants a second chance to have his son spend some time with him." With Bryan's safe return guaranteed by both lawyers, I hopefully agreed to the reunion. It was a naive decision and, smarter this time, Paul had disappeared with Bryan.

"You handed the boy over," Erma Halsey stated flatly when, having just moved to San Francisco, I reported the incident to her office. "Now, our hands are tied. Why don't you just kidnap him back?" The idea, surprising from a police official, was an impossibility in any case. I didn't know where to start searching.

Taking an immediate leave of absence, I flew to Tulsa to consult with Mr. Pollock. "Oh, they'll turn up," he said unconvincingly. "Vinnie gave his word, didn't he?"

What turned up instead, however, were several discrepancies in my legal file. With no power of attorney, my lawyer had apparently taken it upon himself to sign papers modifying the financial portions of my divorce decree. Firing him on the spot, I walked out grateful that at least he'd been kind enough to leave the custody arrangement intact.

In a strange city, the phone book can become a much needed friend; that night, I combed its pages in search of a legal advisor. The first name I called turned out to be an officer of the Tulsa Bar who was unable to take over the case because "it would constitute an official reprimand to a colleague." He wanted to be of help, though, and suggested I contact a feisty, semi-retired lawyer by the name of Art Alpert, whose reputation was above reproach. A month later, with Art's help and that of a local detective, a withdrawn Bryan was found at Paul's new address and returned by order of a sympathetic judge. I received a bill from Jerome Pollock for services rendered.

"Michael, I trust you," I was saying now. "Maybe my father's friends in Tulsa can find us a passport into the courts, but please, please come with me."

The lawyer shifted uncomfortably in his chair. "Do you know what that would cost, Nan?"

"No," I admitted. "I have no idea."

"Well, it would be $500 a day for my fee alone, and that would have to be in advance, plus plane fare for the three of us, hotel bills, meals and, of course, there'd still be 'Mr. Passport' to pay."

For a brief, terrifying moment I wondered if my parents could raise that kind of money. Michael's eyes seemed to penetrate my thoughts as a frown creased his eyebrows.

"My car," I realized out loud. It was fairly new and in good condition. "I can always sell my car." Hastily, I composed myself to assure the attorney that money was no object.

Michael suggested the alternative I was dreading. "If finances are a problem, an Oklahoma attorney could handle the whole case, with my preparing it before you go."

"No. Bryan's life is too important to risk in the hands of a stranger. I'll come up with the money . . . but, please, I need you there."

Michael gave me a searching look, then nodded his assent. Closing my eyes in relief, I silently thanked my parents for making the choice possible.

Breaking the tension, Michael got up to refill our coffee cups and, when he returned, began to outline details for the trip.

"First, we'll get a writ of habeas corpus," he explained, "and Mr. Simmons and/or his lovely wife will be ordered to bring Bryan before a judge within forty-eight hours."

Forty-eight hours. To appear . . . or disappear.

"And if they don't?"

"They'll be in contempt of court."

"But what does that mean realistically?" I pressed. "That I'll be left holding another paper victory?"

"Nan. I can't promise you they won't fade into the night," Michael relented, "but it isn't that simple on such short notice. We'll take extra precautions and, once the matter goes before a judge, Mr. Simmons' order will be vacated. In other words, it will never have existed."

"Are you sure that's what will happen?" I wanted so much to believe him. "Mr. Cattano saw the same papers and he was unimpressed."

"Yes. But we're not asking for criminal charges now."

"Then what's to stop Paul from doing it again?"

Michael took a long time before replying. "He's been made to give Bryan back each time," he said softly. "How pig-headed can he be?"

I left the question unanswered as I privately realized that Paul could keep playing his game until I either fell apart or ran out of money. And what about Bryan? What protection did he have?

"Michael," I finally spoke. "It's a poor system that has to depend on the criminal's good will for its effectiveness."

Leaning forward, he almost seemed to be pleading. "The law is my life's work, Nan. I have to believe in it."

Absently, I noticed that the sun was cutting through the noonday fog. It would be a good day for baseball after all.

"Is that it?" I stood up.

"For now." Michael helped me on with my coat. "There's just one more thing I want you to do. It might not be a bad idea to get some letters of reference. You know. Clergy, professional people, friends. People who can testify to your relationship with Bryan."

Slowly I sank back into the chair. "You mean to prove I'm fit? That sounds like a custody battle. You said it was just a simple matter of jurisdiction."

"It is." He tried to smile reassuringly. "I just want to make sure all bases are covered."

Alone in my car, I wondered if it wouldn't be easier to just kidnap Bryan back myself. I no longer shared Michael's unwavering faith in the legal system. And I longed for the the return of innocence.

Eight

New York—Police said they still did not know the whereabouts of 7-year-old Catherine Leigh Mellon and her 5-year-old sister Constance Elizabeth, "though we have been assured by Pittsburgh banker Seward Prosser Mellon that the children are safe and that this is a custody dispute."

Mellon and the children's mother, Karen Boyd Mellon, were divorced in 1974 after eight years of marriage. Mellon was awarded custody of the girls in Pennsylvania courts, but Mrs. Mellon won a custody action February 3 in New York state.

The girls were abducted from outside their mother's home Friday.

The abductions have posed a problem for the police here and for the Brooklyn District Attorney, Eugene Gold, in whose jurisdiction yesterday's abduction took place. Deputy Commissioner Frank McLaughlin said that if the three men who took the girls—after identifying themselves as F.B.I. agents—had been caught before they left the state they "would have been bagged for kidnapping, but now we don't know."

And Mr. Gold is equally unsure. Both he and the police agreed, however, that a crime had been committed, if only the robbery of a private detective.

The bodyguard, Lester Carew, 59, was relieved of his .38-caliber revolver in the abduction. . .

"Why are you harassing the District Attorney? What's the purpose of the telegrams?"

A reporter, identifying herself as Kay Wickert, started the week off on a discordant note.

"I'm not trying to badger him. It's just that my son's been kidnapped and I want something done about it," I repeated for the hundredth time.

Rita, who'd stopped by earlier, looked up from the newspaper account to eye the phone quizzically.

"As I understand it," Ms. Wickert continued, "Mr. Cattano has decided that you have no case."

"Why are *you* trying to harass *me*, Ms. Wickert?"

"I'm merely doing my job," she replied in a businesslike tone. "You once contacted Mr. Olsen about writing your story and now, with the Mellon heiresses taken too, there's an angle. Howard's busy but I'd like to come down and interview you."

Torn between the desire to get Bryan's story in the paper and an instinctive fear of Ms. Wickert, I asked for some time to think about it.

"All right," she agreed reluctantly. "I'll speak to you later."

Not ready to make a decision, I turned on my answering service to ward off further calls.

"JoAnne, I'm home." I picked up the phone as a friend from Parents Without Partners was about to leave a message. "I'm just trying to avoid a reporter who equates the telegrams with rabble-rousing."

"Well, that makes all of us trouble-makers then," the club's energetic secretary replied. "But, what the hell, it's about time respectable citizens came out of the closet. Nan, the reason I'm calling is that the Board of PWP has voted to establish a Bryan Simmons Fund to help pay some of your legal expenses. We plan to have a kick-off at my house next Friday and I'd like you to be there."

"JoAnne, I couldn't take other people's—"

"It's a start toward humanitarian purposes," she said over my objections, "and that's what I think this organization should be all about. You'll just be the first, and what you don't need can be saved for someone else. Look at it this way. No one is being asked to make a personal sacrifice and contributions will be strictly voluntary."

"I guess you've made me an offer I can't refuse," I replied with a lump in my throat. "You know, I'm really touched by everyone's thoughtfulness but, between you and me, Jo, I feel like that poster we saw down by the wharf."

"Which one?"

"A Friend in Need is a Pain in the Ass!"

A few days later, members of the San Francisco chapter of Parents Without Partners were to receive the following flyer:

EMERGENCY—ALL OUR CHILDREN ARE IN DANGER!

On March 10, 1976, the eleven-year-old son of one of our members was abducted from his schoolyard by two men. He has not been heard from since. Children who witnessed the tragedy have described a tale of horror and brutality, but since one of the abductors was apparently the boy's father, the district attorney's office will not get involved.

The children of single parent families are discriminated against by law enforcement agencies. Child abuse and child-stealing by a "natural" parent are obviously not considered criminal.

Bryan's mother, Nancy, and several other members of our chapter have tried to speak to Bryan, presumably being held by his father in Oklahoma, but to no avail.

Nancy must now face the financial hardship of a cross-country legal battle for a child who has always been in her care and custody. She is a victim of legal indifference toward the single parent. Nancy is one of our members. Bryan, one of our children. If the authorities do not consider his abduction a criminal matter, none of our children are safe! We must be involved!

First of all, we can help by contributing whatever we can toward the legal battle against Bryan's abductors. Secondly, we must organize on local, regional and national levels for the purpose of legislation to prevent other members, and all children, from being so victimized.

ON FRIDAY, MARCH 26, JoAnne Metzger will be having a "wine and cheese" party. On that night, we will initiate an emergency fund drive to help meet the legal expenses in the fight for Bryan Simmons' freedom. Contributions of any size will be gratefully accepted. From that night on, until further notice, donations will be accepted at every gathering of the San Francisco Chapter of Parents Without Partners.

Checks made out to "Parents Without Partners, Bryan Simmons Fund" are tax deductible. So are cash contributions. If you can't attend any functions, please consider mailing whatever you can.

Please help Bryan and Nancy: In the long run, we alone must fight the battle of justice for the single parent family and the safety of our children!!

Swallowing with difficulty, I thanked JoAnne and hung up, forgetting to re-hook the answering service. Half an hour later, Ms. Wickert was back on the line.

"I've just spoken to Mr. Simmons," she announced without preliminaries. "And, if you can't see me, I suppose I'll just have to make do with the information I have."

For a moment I was too shocked to answer. "You spoke to Paul? What did he say?"

"He gave me a very nice interview, but I know there are always two sides to every story. May I come over now?"

"All right, Ms. Wickert," I relented. "Can you be here this morning?"

"In twenty minutes."

"Why did you agree to see her?" Rita looked puzzled.

"Because I've been intimidated." My voice faltered. "She's already spoken to Paul and will print it without me."

"Paul said something?" Her eyes widened. "I thought the only words he knew were 'on the advice of my attorney.' What do you think she did to make him cooperate?"

"Maybe the same thing she just did to me." I smiled weakly. "Will you stay for the interview? I don't think I can hack it alone."

Rita agreed but was concerned about appearing in jeans and a sweatshirt. Offering to lend her some clothes, I ransacked my closet for a suitable outfit.

"I'm going to stick to the larger issues and avoid any personal attacks," I told her, buttoning my cuffs. "Do you think this is appropriate or would the green dress have been better?"

"You look just fine." She nodded, pulling on a pair of plaid slacks. "And I think it's a good idea to accentuate the legalities. She can't very well zonk you if you're speaking about conflicts of law rather than conflicts of Simmons—damn, these don't zip."

The bell rang, Rita breathed deep enough to get the outfit

together, and we threw the pile of unused clothes into a heap in the closet. How many times, I wondered, had I threatened Bryan with no T.V. for doing exactly the same thing?

"Mrs. Simmons?" The buxom woman in a stylish suit made no effort to hide her surprise. "You don't look anything like I pictured. You're so tiny."

She quickly brushed past me as I tried to introduce Rita and walked briskly toward the couch. A lanky photographer followed meekly in her wake.

"Now," she pulled out a pad and pencil, "what's your side of this custody battle?"

I tried to explain that it wasn't a custody battle, but she indicated that the word "kidnapping" was offensive to her. "After all, Mr. Simmons had an order, didn't he?"

"Yes. But it was a duplicate from a state without jurisdiction, and clearly illegal.

"Ostensibly," I pointed out, "every child could have fifty alternate orders on its custody and there'd be little recourse but to challenge each one separately. Obviously, our domestic laws are in disarray and I think you could help the situation by bringing it to public attention."

"Are you denying State's Rights?"

"No." I was taken aback. "I'm focusing in on an issue. Ms. Wickert, unless child-stealing and custody matters are federalized, or there are uniform reciprocal laws between states, parents will continue to suffer and children to be uprooted from their homes."

She looked slightly bored by my remarks and brought the conversation back to an emotional level.

"What if your son is happy with his father. Don't you think he should have the choice to stay?"

"What choice did he have to go?"

"But if he's adjusted now?"

"Adjusted to what?"

"Oh, then you're determined to fight under any circumstances?"

"If Bryan wanted to stay, I'd give him the opportunity," I said softly, my heart pounding. "But he'd have to tell me that privately in an atmosphere free from duress. Don't forget, child-snatch victims are traumatized. God knows what they're told or thinking. Look, if you want, I can give you the name of a child psychologist I've spoken to who called this crime an atrocity."

She jotted down the information, then sighed deeply. "My husband's a social worker and I hear stories about parental disputes all the time. Hard as I try, I just can't get used to the idea that two people can't stop their fighting long enough to consider the children. Sometimes I think if they're that immature, they shouldn't have kids at all."

"Now wait a minute." Rita stopped her. "When one parent is intent on harassment, or refuses to abide by court orders, I think it's unfair to hold the other one equally responsible. Please remember one thing. It wasn't Nancy who stole her child."

"Isn't it true that you're representing Parents Without Partners on this matter?" She suddenly switched her attention to Rita.

"No. I'm not even an officer."

"Then why are you here?"

"Mrs. Simmons is one of my closest friends."

Rita looked bewildered as Ms. Wickert proceeded to ask her for a statement.

"I don't know why you want one from me," she hesitated. "But okay. I think the local authorities have outrageous priorities. We've got a newly elected District Attorney who babbles about the rights of hookers—and please don't get me wrong, I think they have rights—but blatantly ignores the rights of children not to be snatched off the street. The District Attorney is fully aware that Mr. Simmons' custody order defies all legal precedents. Mr. Callan showed him the same documents he sent to Nancy . . . perhaps, what he was really saying in his campaign speech is that his office can't be bothered with prosecution at all."

"Well, that about wraps it up." The reporter stuffed her notes into a large leather bag. "Watch for the story. It should be out either Wednesday or Thursday."

My head still spinning, I walked Ms. Wickert to the door. To my astonishment, she stopped for a moment and engulfed me in an awkward bear hug. "You poor thing." She shook her head. "I don't know how you can take it. Have you tried hypnosis or meditation?"

Nine

The cry was eerie. Like a baby in pain. Quickly, Bryan pulled up his shade and surveyed the lawn. Nothing to worry about. Just two cats fighting. He started to turn away, but found himself rooted to the spot. Watching. Empathizing. The mangy orange had gotten the worst of it. Gashes down his side, ears split wide open. No match for the other Tom. As the larger cat sprang forward, claws tearing into soft flesh, Bryan felt a shiver run down his spine. All at once, he was screaming uncontrollably.

"Run, Orange. Run! You're free, you dummy! Get away!"

"Bryan!" The raised voice sounded annoyed. "Be quiet! I'm talking to someone on the phone . . . Yes, Ms. Wickert," he heard his father say, "Bryan's adjusting very well."

"TUG OF WAR OVER A CHILD'S CUSTODY," I read Kay Wickert's by-line the following Wednesday. Capped by a large picture of Rita, "organizer for PWP . . . marshalling the forces," the facts had been skillfully weighted to present a judicial see-saw in which both sides were equally (un)balanced:

> An eleven-year-old, freckle-faced boy, the perfect model for a corn-flakes commercial, has been spirited away.

Nancy Simmons, a 33-year-old divorcee (sic), knows where her son is and who took him, but local authorities have chosen to look the other way. The man who took Bryan is the boy's father, Paul Simmons, now remarried and living in Oklahoma.

Mrs. Simmons says the Massachusetts and California courts have granted her custody of her only child . . . Paul Simmons says the Oklahoma courts have given him the right to his child. Both have papers to prove their points . . . and that's only the barest framework of this very broken home...

I searched through the article for my "points of law" but, it seemed, the parents' viewpoints were "clouded" with "emotional overlay."

In California and other states, the law distinguishes between kidnapping and child-stealing. The latter, perpetuated by a parent, is generally not regarded as a serious offense. Police and prosecutors are loathe to be involved as it is often difficult to tell right from wrong.

Child-stealing (the story concluded) indicates unresolved hostility between two parents. Both are very much in pain and both are obviously reacting from rejection or anger over something. To label one good, one bad would be insane.

My father phoned the next morning with the name of a Tulsa lawyer. "Sterling R-a-p-h-a-e-l."
"Is he any good?"
"Who can be sure?" he answered. "All I know is that my friends, the Crowells, recommended him so it's better than a shot in the dark.
"And, Nance," he added, as I thanked him, "I also took the liberty of contacting a syndicated columnist."
"Oh? Did he suggest therapy to see why I'm angry at Paul?"
"I understand your being upset by yesterday's article," my father continued, "but Kent Shepard is not some sanctimonious muckraker. He's a highly respected newsman and I've just been reading some of his articles on juvenile justice. In fact, after our phone conversation, I feel more positive about him than the lawyer."
In spite of Kay Wickert, my curiosity was piqued. "What did he have to say?"

"His feelings were that in no area but domestic law does motivation annihilate the act. Mr. Shepard assured me that he'd give no more credence to understanding a child-snatcher's psyche than in letting a bank robber go unapprehended because he had an unnatural love for money. It's your decision, dear, but I'd like you to at least talk to the man."

"All right." I agreed. "But no commitments."

"No commitments. However, if you do decide to trust him, he's promised to keep your real name confidential and, more important, is willing to cover the hearing in Tulsa . . . that's why I called him. I have an idea that our case won't suffer any if the judge knows his behavior is subject to nation-wide scrutiny."

"Kidnapping is kidnapping no matter how you slice it," the news columnist was telling me an hour later. "Sure, you can call it a 'custody dispute' but it's still a crime against the person of a child." He continued in a manner that seemed to justify my father's confidence. "Mrs. Simmons, I've heard so many rationalizations for this kind of thing, it's pathetic. Love. Frustration. Uncontrollable anger. Or, in the particular case of fathers, 'the only option available to custody procedures which favor the mother.' What I'd like to know is: who's concerned about the child?"

He paused for a moment. Then answered his own question. "I think the whole situation boils down to the fact that children are still viewed as parental property."

"And possession nine-tenths of the law," I added.

"Of course. And until we elevate their status, these kidnappings will continue. Even equalizing custody is a separate issue from child-stealing. Hell, the only effect that would have on this crime is to produce as many mothers who snatch their kids as fathers."

"Mr. Shepard," I made a quick decision, "how would you like to write about it from Tulsa?"

It was a misty evening as I parked the car in front of JoAnne's white stucco cottage. The tree-lined driveway, already filled with an assortment of wet vehicles, testified to a large turnout inside. From behind my windshield, I watched while some latecomers scurried up the flagstone path and disappeared through a narrow, carved door. Trying to ignore the knot in my stomach, I wrestled with the idea of joining them.

PWP was an organization where single parents could meet each other and adjust to the changes in their lives. It had been a godsend after my divorce and, again, upon moving to San Francisco. Now, though, with other interests vying for my time, I'd limited participation in the club to a mere handful of activities—an occasional get-together, a few children's events, and the annual campout. Having lost contact with much of the membership, I felt unusually self-conscious about tonight's ordeal and, at the moment, was suppressing an impulse to jam my foot on the accelerator and retreat from the scene entirely.

"Hey!" A friendly rap on the window broke into my thoughts. "Going in?"

It was Len Greenberg, a quiet man in his early forties. Grateful for a familiar face, I nodded and quickly fell into step.

The party was in full swing when we hung up our coats and, through a din of talk and laughter, I could hear strains of Simon and Garfunkle on the stereo.

"If noise is any indication of a good time," Len commented, "it's pretty obvious that JoAnne can count on another success. C'mon." He grabbed my hand. "Let's see what the natives are doing."

I allowed myself to be pulled into the kitchen where a group of people were paying homage to the hors d'oeuvres. Their smiles were welcoming and, while Bob Tanner mixed me a drink, Norma Gardner, a slim blond with a Florida tan, insisted that we try the pickled mushrooms. In the congenial atmosphere, I soon relaxed and forgot my apprehensions. Then, at 10:30, our hostess brought a pot of coffee into the living room and announced that the meeting had officially begun.

After an initial explanation, Dianna read her letters to local politicians, and Graham Mallory, the chapter president, pointed out a basket earmarked for donations.

"It's just the beginning." He repeated JoAnne's words. "Once we have Bryan back, we intend to fund whatever causes are relevant to us as single parents. I also think we ought to form study groups so that our club will be in a better position to lobby for legislative change."

"Have there been any answers to your correspondence?" A balding man with a round face directed his question to Dianna.

"Just two," my friend replied glumly. "And both wound up referring Bryan's case back to the District Attorney."

Suddenly, the crowd began to resemble a Greek chorus:

"Jesus Christ! Our orders must be on a par with Confederate money!"

"What about those of us holding joint custody?"

"My ex has always wanted to get back at me."

"I'm just separated and, so far, there's been no formal provisions on where the kids should live."

"Hey! Everybody!" Graham was waving his hands for silence. "Let's try to keep this somewhat orderly. We can't get anything accomplished if we're all going to shout at the same time."

Half an hour later, while Mary Ann Clarke, the only lawyer in the room, was being bombarded with questions, the phone rang.

"Graham, it's for you."

He returned after a brief interlude and knelt by my chair. "Nan, can I see you a minute?"

"I'm afraid we've just received some bad news," he explained as we walked into the kitchen, where JoAnne sat slumped at the table.

"Bryan?" I panicked. "Is is about Bryan?"

"Oh, no. Nothing like that. The call was from Herb," Graham assured me, referring to PWP's District Supervisor. "He says that, since our organization is charitable, educational, and has a tax-exempt status, there are some vague IRS rules which—um—put us in a peculiar position."

"What Graham is trying to say," JoAnne's eyes were blazing, "is that we've found out government regulations prevent us from raising money for individuals or lobbying in their behalf. Ironic, isn't it? With 200,000 members all we can do is fund their activities and, when disaster strikes, weep for them."

Ten

"Dear Governor Brown,
   I cannot sleep tonight and must get this off my chest to you..."
   Three typewritten pages later, I sealed the envelope and collapsed on the bed. Sleep was elusive, though, and visions of Paul behind a monopoly board, sneering "I've won again!" kept me tossing and moaning. Finally, at 2 a.m., wishing I had a man around to comfort me, I turned the lights back on and took refuge in a book.
   Laurel had sent the slim volume of poetry for my birthday and, somehow, I'd never gotten around to reading it all. Now, propping my head against the pillows, I turned at random to something called "I Like to Think of Harriet Tubman," by Susan Griffin.

> I like to think of Harriet Tubman
> Harriet Tubman who carried a revolver,
> and had a scar on her forehead from a rock thrown
> by a slave-master (because she
> talked back), and who
> had a ransom on her head
> of thousands of dollars and who
> was never caught, and who
> had no use for law
> when the law was wrong,

who defied the law. I like
to think of her.
I like to think of her especially
when I think of the problem of
feeding children.

The legal answer
to the problem of feeding children
is ten free lunches every month,
being equal, in the child's real life,
to eating lunch every other day.
Monday but not Tuesday.
I like to think of the President
eating lunch Monday, but not
Tuesday.
And when I think of the President
and the law, and the problem of
feeding children, I like to
think of Harriet Tubman
and her revolver.

And then sometimes
I think of the President
and other men,
men who practice the law,
who revere the law,
who make the law,
who enforce the law
who live behind
and operate through
and feed themselves
at the expense of
starving children
because of the law,
men who sit in paneled offices
and think about vacations
and tell women
whose care it is
to feed children
not to be hysterical
not to be hysterical as in the word
hysterikos, the greek
for womb suffering
not to suffer in their
wombs,
not to care,
not to bother men
because they want to think
of other things

and do not want
to take the women seriously.
I want them to think about Harriet Tubman,
and remember,
remember she was beat by a white man
and she lived
and she lived to redress her grievances,
and she lived in swamps
and wore the clothes of a man
bringing hundreds of fugitives from
slavery, and was never caught,
and led an army,
and won a battle,
and defied the laws
because the laws were wrong, I want men
to take us seriously.
I am tired, wanting them to think
about right and wrong.
I want them to fear.
I want them to feel fear now
as I have felt suffering in the womb, and
I want them
to know
that there is always a time
there is always a time to make right
what is wrong,
there is always a time
for retribution
and that time
is beginning.

Had nothing changed in over a hundred years? Closing the soft covers I inwardly said "Thank you" to Harriet Tubman. The friend I'd needed tonight. My sister in pain.

Suddenly, I was a bundle of energy. Sleep? Just a five letter word. Harriet Tubman had to fight in the swamps, but things were better now. I'd be able to do battle on the city's concrete and keep my clothes clean.

Once again I pulled out the typewriter, and my fingers flew as the petition to recall Julian Garth seemed to draft itself:

We, the undersigned, residents of the City and County of San Francisco, hereby declare Julian Garth to be unfit to discharge the duties of the Office of the District Attorney.

Human beings of all ages deserve equal protection under the law. We consider children human beings.

Abduction of one human being by another, regardless of age, sex, creed or relationship, is a criminal act and, therefore, must be prosecuted by the Office of the District Attorney!

Mr. Garth has just recently been elected and already is sidestepping his responsibilities to protect the welfare of the children of this city.

Impeach Julian Garth unless he reconsiders his position and provides legal protection from abduction to ALL residents of San Francisco.

"Not bad for an amateur," I re-read the statement. With his job on the line, Garth would have to come up with a good answer for his position or, hopefully, reverse it. How many signatures would it take to make an impact? Two hundred? One thousand? Why hadn't I been more active in politics? Then I would know this sort of thing.

"Are you two holding a sit-in?" The familiar words broke into my thoughts. "A demonstration!" I said out loud. "That should draw public sympathy for Bryan." But how to do it? And where? A shopping center? Garth's house? Quickly, I pulled out the phone book to check his address and found two J. Garths. Great. It would be nice to choose the wrong one and find yourself picketing some insurance agent or a man who ran a pizza parlor. Well, I could always get that information tomorrow. I skipped to the next topic. It would have to be planned carefully or nobody'd listen . . . a quiet approach would probably be best to avoid creating animosity . . . now, what should the signs say? *Free Bryan Simmons? Bring Bryan home again?* The demonstration should be child-oriented. But how? Cartoons? Little League emblems? Nursery rhymes? Maybe that's it. ". . . dragged Bry to another state. D.A. said, 'Well, that's his fate.'" At least there's room for creativity there.

On and on I pondered and planned until I saw the first signs of light appear behind the kitchen curtains. Bursting with excitement, I waited for a decent hour and then called Dianna.

"I can't believe you're turning into a radical." Her voice rose three octaves. "But, anyhow, count me in. If we get busted, at least I'll have a day off from work."

That afternoon I had the petitions printed up and handed them out to several friends and neighbors. They were all receptive and eager to exchange ideas on the best way to stage a protest. Anne Wardlowe, who worked for the city, told me she'd inquire about permits; Rita had a few pointers from her experience with the civil rights movement; and everyone agreed to relay the event by word-of-mouth. Coming home, I realized that a time had not yet been decided, but at least we were taking a step in the right direction.

"I read your story in the newspaper." A woman, introducing herself as Lynn Edwards, called that evening. Her voice was husky and she cleared it often. "I've become a chain smoker." She apologized, relating that her own daughter had been stolen three years before.

"It was then that I learned there were organizations available to victimized parents," she continued as I listened intently. "I belong to one and that's why I've called you. I think it's important that people caught in our kind of trap know that they're not alone.

"I wish I could say that we've hit upon some magic formula to stop this crime . . . but, at the moment, there are none. You might benefit from some of our research, though, and I'd be glad to share it with you."

"Thank you, Lynn." We made an appointment to meet for coffee on Monday afternoon. "I'd be very grateful for any help, but I'm a little confused about something. Are you talking about groups that deal strictly with child-stealing?"

"Yes."

"I wasn't aware that there were enough kidnappings to warrant *one* organization, let alone more than that."

"I'm afraid you're in for a shock then," she said softly. "Nancy, there are nearly 100,000 children a year who suffer the same fate as Bryan."

"Oh, my God!" I gasped. "And your little girl? Is she all right now?"

"I have no way of knowing." Lynn choked up. "You see, at least 80% are never returned . . . and, unfortunately, Kimberly is one of them."

Eleven

"Happy birthday to you . . . happy birthday to you . . . happy birthday, dear Tiffany . . ."

Voices, weak and far away, surrounded Bryan as he sat stiffly among a group of neighborhood toddlers, a blue party hat jammed on his head.

"I can't believe she's two-years-old." A proud SuEllen smiled down at her daughter. "Why it seems like only yesterday."

Only yesterday, Bryan's thoughts faded back to last year...his own birthday party. . . .

"Strike!" Jonathan had called out loudly as the bowling ball smashed into the pins.

"Oh, no! Not again!" the rest of Bryan's friends groaned in unison.

"Yep. 132, Mrs. Simmons. Looks like I'm the high-scorer of the day."

As everyone crowded around, Bryan watched his mother present Jonathan with a game of Clue.

"It's a good game," Bryan informed him. "I've got one at home."

Returning to the apartment, Bryan cut the cake and helped his mom dish out the ice cream. What a mess! He laughed as Rusty spilled a glass of Coke on the tablecloth, but nobody seemed to mind.

"Hey, everybody!" The highlight of his eleventh birthday was now reached. "It's time for me to open my presents."

Ribbons and wrappers flew as he exclaimed joyfully, "Oh, boy! An electric football set. Thanks, Mom . . . Stratego! I played that at my Aunt Laurel's house. Thank you, Larry . . . Kevin, look! This puppet is just like yours. Now, we can put on a puppet show together. . . ."

Strange sensation of eyes on his back. Whispers behind him.

"Kid's weird, Marion. Never talks. Never smiles. Doesn't seem to know how to have fun."

"Shh! SuEllen will hear you."

"Well, I know, if he were my son, I'd sure be worried. I hate to say this but, frankly, I think the boy needs to see a psychiatrist."

"It takes time to get used to a new family, Donna. Bryan'll adjust. Kids always do."

Face flushed with excitement, I walked into the Union Street delicatessen where I was to meet Lynn Edwards. I'd spent the weekend canvassing for signatures and, to my surprise, the petitions were now half-filled.

"I told people that I was helping out a friend," I confided to the pretty brunette as we sat down at a table. "It was the only way I could approach them without quaking in my boots."

"I admire your spunk," Lynn said warmly. "It's a good asset to have."

"And the petitions?"

She quickly reached for the ashtray and fumbled with a cigarette lighter.

"Nancy, it's not easy to be the bearer of bad news," she hesitated, "but, even if Garth changes his mind, it's almost a sure bet you'll still have to go to Tulsa."

"But why? I thought—"

"Criminal warrants for child-stealing just aren't honored across state lines," she said bitterly. "I've had one out on Kimberley's father for over two years."

My mind recoiled. It was the restraining order all over again!

As I tried to digest this new information, she reached into her purse and pulled out a copy of the Congressional Record.

"The House Subcommittee on Crime held hearings on child-stealing a couple of years ago, and I think this is a pretty good example of what you can expect locally." She pointed to a paragraph on page 74. "It's a letter received from the Los Angeles District Attorney by a Victoria Ann Starkey four months after her children were stolen."

I read, "This office is prepared to extradite and prosecute Daniel Riley Starkey when he is apprehended. Service of the warrant upon Daniel Riley Starkey is beyond control of this office."

"The only people who, by law, can cross state lines to locate and retrieve our children are the F.B.I.," she continued softly, while I stared dazedly at the book, "and they refuse to get involved."

"How can we fight a situation if we're not given an accurate appraisal?" I exploded. "If this is true, it would be more humane for state officials to just admit they're in a double-bind. At least, then, we'd know where we stand."

"Nancy, you're an idealist."

"I certainly hope so, Lynn. I've found that acceptance of injustice is no great sign of wisdom."

"Are you ladies ready to order?" We broke off our conversation to study the menu. After the waiter had gone, Lynn explained that the crux of the legal problem lay in the Federal Kidnapping Statute, specifically, Section 1201, more popularly known as the "Lindbergh Law."

" 'Whoever knowingly transports in interstate or foreign commerce," she repeated from memory, " 'Any person who has been unlawfully seized, confined, inveigled, decoyed, kidnapped, abducted, or carried away and held for ransom or otherwise, *except in the case of a minor by a parent thereof. . .*' is guilty of the federal offense of kidnapping. Translated literally," she added, while the blood drained from my face, "it not only excuses the F.B.I. from offering assistance, but allows any of those things to be done to a child . . . just so long as the kidnapper's name appears on the victim's birth certificate!"

"Lynn," I said after a moment's thought, "the whole thing sounds unconstitutional to me."

"Why?"

"Because, obviously, our children are being denied equal protection under the law."

"You're probably right." She shrugged hopelessly. "But go tell it to a judge. As for me, after reading the 'Hearings', I've decided that I'm the only one who cares in the slightest about Kim's welfare. Do you realize," her eyes grew moist, "that even if my daughter were dead, the police would have no reason to be searching for her body."

As soon as I returned home, I pulled Bryan's *World Book* from the shelf. Turning to page 8372, I read:

ARTICLE 14. THE CONSTITUTION OF THE UNITED STATES.
All persons born or naturalized in the United States, and subject to the jurisdiction thereof, are citizens of the United States and of the State wherein they reside. No State shall make or enforce any law which shall abridge the privileges or immunities of citizens of the United States; nor shall any State deprive any person of life, liberty, or property, without due process of law; nor deny to any person within its jurisdiction the equal protection of the laws.

"Except in the case of a minor by a parent thereof" I added grimly, replacing the encyclopedia. Apparently the highest law of the land was superseded by an even stronger social doctrine: There shall be no outside interference with the institution of the family—even if it's no longer intact.

Dubiously, I opened the booklet Lynn had given me and prepared for some serious reading.

AMENDMENTS TO THE FEDERAL KIDNAPPING STATUTE

HEARINGS
Before the

SUBCOMMITTEE ON CRIME
COMMITTEE ON THE JUDICIARY
HOUSE OF REPRESENTATIVES

Ninety-Third Congress
Second Session
On
H.R. 4191 and H.R. 8722

February 27 and April 10, 1974

Testimony of the Hon. Charles E. Bennett, a Representative in Congress from the State of Florida.

Mr. Bennett: . . . I deeply appreciate the opportunity to testify in support of my bill H.R. 4191 which I introduced on February 8, 1973 . . .

My bill would strike existing language in the Federal kidnapping law which excludes a parent from prosecution. It would provide that a parent who has abducted his child from the person who has legal custody would be prosecutable under the Federal kidnapping law. A very important result would be that the FBI could assist the person who is seeking the return of the child to legal custody. . .

Mr. Conyers (Hon. John Conyers, Jr. of Michigan. Chairman of the Subcommittee.): "I appreciate your opening statement Mr. Bennett. I would like to raise a couple of questions and invite members of the subcommittee to join the interrogation.

First, is there any indication that these kinds of cases are increasing numerically; second, what are the views of the bar regarding parental kidnapping? . . . I am apprehensive about this legislation and I must state it candidly.

As you know, when a parent takes his child to anyplace in violation of a decree of the court or a divorce decree, they are subject to contempt of court. Is this not a more reasonable approach than to create a Federal violation, especially in view of the fact that the kidnapping statute really turns on questions involving the possibility of violence to the individual?"

Mr. Bennett: . . . The closest I ever came to finding an answer along the lines that you indicate is a case which I presently have, where the children were stolen from Jacksonville, Fla., taken to Ohio, and now they are attempting—and here is where it rests—we are attempting to see if the Governor of Ohio will accede to the request of the Governor of Florida that this particular person be made amenable to the laws of Florida.

Now, this has been underway for about two years. The Governor of Ohio has not directly answered my mail . . . what normal person in the city of Jacksonville can expect the Governor of Florida and the Governor of another State to be involved in this problem? . . . If the Governor of Ohio acceded to the request of the Governor of Florida, yes then, in fact, the contempt proceedings in the State of Florida could in fact apply to the man in Ohio, if he were extradited.

But absent that, the only thing the parent can do is start a new legal proceeding in the area where the man lives with the family that he has captured from another State, contrary to court decision. And there you have all kinds of new problems involved. There is a *prima facie* thing of a local people, local judge, that the family seems to be getting along pretty good as far as anybody knows. The *prima facie* starts off against the person who has legal custody. And certainly from the standpoint of finances, the mother, or whoever wants to get the child, has to spend thousands of dollars, if she has it. If she does not have it, I do not know what she does. I guess in those cases she does not do anything. And I have cases like that where it is absolutely impossible for the mother to leave the place where she is living already in Jacksonville and go to California or some other place, spend weeks to litigate, find a good lawyer, handle the matter. It is practically impossible.

So the suggestion you make would be good if we had 50 Governors for every State who had more time in the hands of Governors than we now have to handle it directly from the extradition way. One Governor from one State to another. But it is just not practical to do it. It never happened in the 26 years I have been here. . .

Mr. Conyers: What about the judge's responsibility when a court order is in effect violated by irrational and illegal removal on the part of one of the parents?

Mr. Bennett: If he can get custody of the man. If he lives in Jacksonville, or wherever the child lives, and flies out that night, there is no court order that goes beyond the border of the State of Florida. That is true of all States. So there is no way of doing it. A new suit has to be established wherever that State is, if you can determine where the State is. You have to first find out where the man flew to."

Mr. Conyers: This is a vexing problem, no question about it. Have any of the bar associations spoken out about this?

Mr. Bennett: They have. There are committee studies on this. They are not really very definitive. The bar association has attempted to encourage States to have a uniform custody law and, of course, if we had a uniform custody law of the type the American Bar Association favors, this problem would not be very much of a problem. But my guess is, having looked at uniform laws of this nature, I would say that it would be 10 to 50 years down the road before we had it in every State; and then probably not. . . .

Because the State legislatures have other things to do, they have pressing, immediate problems. They have to build a State university in their baliwick; take care of building highways. . . .

On the raw edge of panic, I flipped through the pages hoping to find a shred of encouragement. It was not, however, to be found in the stand taken by the U.S. Department of Justice:

Testimony of John C. Keeney, Deputy Assistant Attorney General, Criminal Division, Department of Justice

Mr. Keeney: . . . The clear public policy for over 40 years has been to exempt the parent-minor child situation from the coverage of the Kidnapping Act. We believe that exemption to be sound public policy and recommend that it be continued.

Now . . . I should like to state the policy which the Department of Justice follows in connection with a parent's abduction of a child.

If the abduction constitutes a violation and there is a filing in the local jurisdiction of a felony charge against the parent, and if the circumstances indicate that either the physical or moral welfare of the child will be impaired, the Criminal Division has a policy under the Fugitive Felon Act of asking the FBI to investigate, arrest the parent and, in particular, to free the child from what is believed in that situation to be unwholesome custody by one of his parents.

Mr. Conyers: Are you saying then, sir, the FBI does operate in questions of parental abduction?

Mr. Keeney: In very limited situations, Chairman Conyers. The situation requires that there be a felony charge filed locally, and, second, that there be evidence indicating that either the physical or moral well-being of the child is in jeopardy.

Mr. Conyers: Thank you.

Mr. Keeney: In summary I would like to offer the following comments . . . Traditionally, the individual States have borne the primary responsibility for providing for the health, welfare, and domestic affairs of their citizens and dealing with local criminal matters. In addition, the upgrading of the efficiency and effectiveness of local and State law enforcement agencies has been a prime objective of Congress, particularly in the past decade, as evidenced by the vast amounts of Federal money that have been dispensed through LEAA to the States for training and equipping local police forces. There is every indication that the desired improvement in State and local enforcement is being achieved. Thus, particularly today, there is no indication that State and local authorities are unable to adequately deal with unexplained disappearances. With the close liaison provided by the FBI, the use of its Laboratory and Identification Divisions, and its availability to check out-of-state leads upon request, we see little necessity for the FBI to become further involved in local law enforcement.

The provisions of H.R. 4191 . . . would with little reason or justification cause the Federal Government generally, and the FBI particularly, to become involved in countless marital controversies, child custody . . . situations that are of primary concern to the States involved. Accordingly, the Department is opposed to the enactment of . . . proposed . . . legislation.

Sound public policy? I stared at the words in disbelief. Tell that to Lynn Edwards! Or her little girl!

Eleven pages later, I found a scathing, statement-by-statement rebuttal by Mrs. Beth Kurrus, the grandmother of stolen children. Obviously, she, too, was unimpressed by Mr. Keeney's testimony.

The Prepared Statement (in part) of Mrs. Beth Kurrus of Newhall, California, Coordinator of the Citizens' Committee to Amend Title 18, Section 1201a, of the U.S. Code.

Mr. Chairman and Gentlemen of the Subcommittee:

Please accept our grateful appreciation for this occasion to express our views on the subject of the kidnapping of children across state lines in violation of custody orders. . .

Our appeal to you is made on two points. First . . . that states cannot or will not do the necessary investigatory work needed in such custody kidnappings, and, second . . . that when children are taken across state lines, a suitable federal vehicle is necessary—and is available—to apprehend them...

It is with deep dismay that we hear the Department state that it will not enter because it cannot get involved in cases which are civil in nature. But what of the criminal warrants that are issued for kidnapping parents? To say that a state must assume the responsibility of such cases, is, indeed, misrepresenting the issue. By the nature of the state laws, local and state jurisdiction ends at the state borders. The state of California has statutes to cover kidnapping and child-stealing. They are sections #278 and #279 of the penal code, but they cannot be effectively applied when children are taken out of California . . .

The Department of Justice has stated that it has an insufficient number of agents and that there just aren't enough to lend their investigatory powers to the problem of children taken across state lines. However, we wonder at the unusual and important use of these agents . . . stolen children must compete in the legal arena with such "things" as cars, cattle, airplanes, switchblade knives, phonograph records, lottery tickets, pinball machines, military uniforms, and most incredible of all, with Smokey the Bear and Johnny Horizen emblems! Title 18, Section 711, states, "that using the Smokey the Bear character or name as a trademark or trade name, except in public use for promotion of fire protection, after consultation with the U.S. Forest Service, Secretary of Agriculture, and advertising agencies, will bring a fine of $250.00 or a term in jail of up to six months or both." But the important thing is that it will also bring an FBI agent! This section of the code was added on May 23, 1952, 18 years after the kidnapping amendment was introduced which excluded FBI assistance to custodial parents and their stolen children . . .

What sentiment can prompt a publicly-financed department that should be cognizant of the needs of honest citizens as well as dishonest ones to state, (italics supplied when Mrs. Kurrus quotes Mr. Keeney's previous testimony) *"Traditionally, the individual states have borne the primary responsibility for providing for the health, welfare and domestic affairs of their citizens and dealing with local criminal matters."* (Local criminal matters . . . not matters that change when jurisdictions change).

"There is every indication that the desired improvement in state and local enforcement is being achieved. Thus, particularly today, there is no indication that state and local authorities are unable to adequately deal with unexplained disappearances." Unexplained disappearances. Surely, custodial parents can all too clearly explain the disappearance of their children taken in violation of custody orders. *"With the close liaison provided by the FBI, the use of its Laboratory and Identification Divisions, and its availability to check out-of-state leads upon request, we see little necessity for the FBI to become further involved in local law enforcement."* The close liaison provided by the FBI. Liaison between the custodial parent and the child? The FBI and the kidnapping parent? The FBI and the custodial parent? There appears to be little liaison with the FBI when at every turn states and individuals are told that child-stealing is a state matter and the FBI cannot become in-

volved. One wonders to what use the Laboratory and Identification Divisions is put when a kidnapping parent does not fall under the jurisdiction of the FBI and, often, cannot even be found. And surely, custodial parents need no assistance in identifying an ex-spouse. And one wonders at the availability of the FBI to check out-of-state leads upon request, when being told the nature of the cases.

If amending Title 18, Section 1201a, "*Would with little reason or justification cause the Federal Government generally, and the FBI particularly, to become involved in countless marital controversies, child-custody . . . situations that are of primary concern to the states involved,*" we again wonder at the cold bureaucratic indifference to the fact that, once children are taken across state borders, the states from which they are taken are no longer in a position to apprehend them, and the states to which they may be taken, often do nothing . . .

With the wealth of investigatory powers at its disposal, surely the FBI should be allowed to use them to help find stolen children. Why should an organization so capable in other areas . . . be loath to find small, innocent citizens who need its protective powers.

Can we not as a nation, put emphasis not only on laws, but on justice. Families become emotionally, spiritually, physically, and financially depleted by the constant tension-producing efforts to find their children . . . The 24 hour assumption of kidnapping surely could be instituted for children taken in violation of custody orders. Or, at least, the FBI should be allowed to enter such cases at any time, if it is established that children have indeed been taken interstate.

Surely such Department indifference is inimicable to all that our Government stands for in its humanitarian aspects. As important as fighting crime, pursuing Communists, and apprehending stolen slot machines is, we affirm, that children are more important than cattle and cars, and that as they are the future of their country, they deserve the highest protection that their government can provide.

Twelve

"Bastards! Sonofabitches! El Creepos!" *Lying on the bed, his eyes hot and gravelly from crying, Bryan took refuge in the forbidden words.* "Dumpheads, punks, ratfinks!" *He tried to remember other nasty epithets but his whispered soliloquy was brought to a halt by a sudden rap on the door.*

As SuEllen entered, he quickly clamped his mouth shut and drew a deep, shuddering breath.

"Coming down for dinner?" she asked with forced enthusiasm.
"I'm not hungry."
"Your father says I make the best biscuits in Oklahoma."
"I'm still not hungry."
Her voice became shrill. "Look here, young man. I spent an hour cooking this dinner and you're going to eat it. You can play the martyr role with your father, but I'm sick of it. I'm your mother now and—"
"You are not!"
"—and, if you don't stop this bratty behavior, you'll be very sorry."
He watched her slam out the door.
"Bastards! Sonofabitches . . ."

I awoke the next morning exhausted, my bruised-and-battered faith shrouded in a cloak of despair. Michael, I thought wearily, the blade of enlightenment cuts deep. It exposes not only the sought-after truth, but those ideologies cancerous with deceit.

How, I wondered, am I to believe in your system of justice when, at every turn, it proclaims unabashed apathy.

With non-committal interest, I opened March 30th's mail. On top was a copy of Michael's letter to the Oklahoma attorney.

"Sterling Raphael, Esq." the letter began.

Pursuant to our earlier conversation, and my chronology of events, I have made airline reservations for Mrs. Simmons and I to arrive in Tulsa, Oklahoma, on Sunday evening, April 4, 1976. We would like to initiate a habeas corpus action the following day, returnable within 48 hours, in order that we may get this matter resolved. At the time that the Habeas Corpus action would be brought, I am of the opinion that we should also move to set aside the custody order for various reasons. First, on the basis of improper (non) service. Secondly, on the basis of lack of jurisdiction. Thirdly, on the basis that there was no showing, nor can there be a showing, that there was any unfitness on the part of the custodial parent that would necessitate a change of custody.

I leave this alternative up to you; however, I would point out that Mrs. Simmons is heartbroken and distraught at this time. She has been without her child for almost one (1) month as it stands now.

As I indicated to you, Mrs. Simmons desires that I be present in Oklahoma and I ask to serve as your co-counsel in this matter. I am not familiar with Oklahoma rules, but in California an out-of-state attorney can make an appearance on Motion in a particular case.

I would also envision that, at the time of filing the writ of habeas corpus, that we file other motions as follows:

A Motion for visitation . . . immediately

A Motion for a physical and mental examination to verify the condition of the child

I have a feeling that, if any of this is revealed ahead of time to Mr. Morrell, the defendant may attempt to further secrete the child. Therefore, I believe that it would be in the best interests of the child that this matter be kept as secretive as possible until we have effectuated service on the defendant and/or his present wife (and that a process server or sheriff be made available for the afternoon of April 5th).

And, finally, that a Motion to disqualify Judge Martin Bernhardt for cause, as he was the judge who signed the order for change of custody.

Enclosed you will find Mrs. Simmons' check in the amount of $500.00. Hoping we may have an answer as soon as possible I remain

Very truly yours,
Michael T. Callan

"Why can't we just invoke the Fourteenth Amendment and skip all this crap?" I phoned the attorney on impulse.

Astonished, he asked, "Which section are you referring to? It has several parts."

" 'No state shall . . . deny to any person within its jurisdiction the equal protection of the laws,' " I read. "Surely, my son isn't receiving the same attention as a child kidnapped by a stranger."

"I'm afraid it's just not applicable," he answered gently. "You see, the word 'person', as interpreted by the Constitution, refers only to a male of twenty-one years or older!"

When things go wrong, it's said that they come in sets of three. I don't know about the accuracy of that statement but, in the next twenty-four hours, I witnessed a triad of events which gave credence to the maxim "We plan while God laughs."

First, Kent Sheppard's wife called to say that the columnist had suffered a gall bladder attack and would be unable to meet us in Tulsa. Then, I lost my job.

"I'm so sorry," Syd Wade, my district manager, apologized, "but word came down from headquarters that the territory has to be covered. Maybe if this were the first time . . . but, God knows how often the son-of-a-bitch intends to steal your son."

God knows, I agreed.

"I, personally, feel very badly about this. You've been doing a good job and I'm aware that it wasn't easy to pull up roots and move out here. I did manage to talk them into giving you a month's severance pay," he added quickly, "and, of course, you'll receive a high recommendation."

Poor Syd. It wasn't easy to be the hatchet man, and I could visualize him nervously chewing on a cigar.

"What will you do now?" he asked at length.

I didn't know. It seemed too remote to contemplate.

"The important thing is getting Bryan back," I told him. "As for the rest . . . I guess, like Scarlett O'Hara, I'll have to think about it tomorrow."

The next day, however, a more immediate problem took precedence.

CITY WORKERS ON STRIKE
Picketing Spreads

Six top leaders of striking city crafts workers tried to call on the San Francisco Board of Supervisors last night, and became outraged when they were told to see the City Negotiator . . .

Their anger grew into harsh warnings that a general strike is on the horizon unless the Board starts face-to-face negotiations with them . . .

About 100 airport workers, electricians, carpenters, plumbers, laborers and stationary engineers failed to report to work . . . but their absence caused no major disruption of service today.

Striking employees set up pickets at the maintenance facility and various service entrances to the airport . . . (but) barring unforeseen breakdowns in plumbing or electrical equipment, or a stepped up strike . . . San Francisco International should be able to weather the crisis . . .

(However), George Evankovitch of the Laborer's Union said that either the Supervisors talk directly with the Unions or "We escalate the strike." He did not get much more specific than that, other than to add "We will escalate it day by day."

Once again, I was panic-stricken. "Michael, what if the airport shuts down?"

"When you pick up the tickets, why not check into alternate reservations," he suggested. "Oakland. Maybe San Jose. It doesn't matter. Just so long as we leave on Sunday. But, Nan," he added firmly, "It's got to be for Sunday. I've a hearing in Sacramento next Thursday, and I don't know when else I'll have three consecutive days to spare."

"I'm sorry. No dual bookings," a clerk named Pat Ames informed me. "If and when the San Francisco airport closes, we'll attempt to reschedule our passengers. Meanwhile, you're confirmed for Monday, April 5th—"

"You mean Sunday, April 4th."

"Why, no. The computer says Monday. There's nothing open this weekend."

I tried to argue, but it was pointless. I had to find another airline.

Frantically, I raced from one counter to another trying to locate space available. If I could just solve that problem, I knew I could get around the dual bookings policy.

"Sorry."

"We're all filled up."

"We can put you on standby, though."

And then, a breakthrough.

"Your names?" asked the agent at American.
"Mr. and Mrs. Michael Callan," I lied.
"There." She smiled, handing me the tickets. "You're all set now."

Not quite, I thought.

Ducking into the nearest phone booth, I again contacted American, thankful for a new agent who didn't recognize my voice. "I'd like to make reservations for Mr. and Mrs. N. Simmons for Tulsa on April 4th . . . Yes, that's right. We'll be flying out of San Jose."

"Do you believe in omens?" Dianna asked on the eve of my departure. We were seated, along with Rita and JoAnne, in an upstairs gazebo at the Cliff House restaurant. "I hope you do because, on my way over, I spotted a license plate which said *To Life* on it . . . and, now, I'd like to propose a toast." She raised her wine glass. "To life, Nan. Yours and Bryan's."

"To life." The others joined in.

"*L'Chaim. L'Chaim.*"

"To life."

"How can I ever thank you," I said, deeply touched. "I mean for all the love and support you've given me these past weeks."

"We'll send you a bill." Rita grinned.

Conversation was kept light during dinner and, through a large window, I could see the sun peacefully setting on the Pacific. For the moment, at least, I experienced a feeling of well-being.

". . . and aside from the heavy breather," I was telling my friends over dessert, "other maniacs must be reading their newspapers also. Someone called me up last night and asked if I wanted Paul knocked off."

"Are you serious?" JoAnne's mouth fell open.

I nodded, yes. Omitted from my story, however, was the aftermath. Long, shaky hours of terror where I sat watching television with a butcher knife clutched in my hand, wondering if he'd later called Paul and posed the same question.

"Probably just some crank," I guessed now. "You know, the kind who reads the obits and plagues young widows . . . anyhow, I hung up on him."

Before we left, Rita surprised me with a going away gift. "It's another letter of reference." She looked amused. "I'll read it out loud:

> To the Honorable Judge of the Tulsa Inferior Court: It has come to my attention that you wish to investigate the character of Ms. Nancy Simmons, and I hereby submit my questionable opinion as to her unquestionable status as a character.
>
> Be it noted, Your Honor, that she has never been busted, booked nor bothered with such charges as intemperance, indecent exposure, nor inciting a riot. I feel that this certainly must mean she can provide a healthy, athletic atmosphere for her son since she can obviously run like hell!
>
> As for her participation in social affairs, Ms. Simmons is very social and wholeheartedly believes in affairs. Another positive aspect of her character is that she endorses her beliefs with affirmative action.
>
> In the literary realm, Ms. Simmons excels. On her bookshelves can be found such classics as *The Joys of Sex*, the *I hate to do Housework* manual, and a well-thumbed edition of *The T.V. Dinner Gourmet*. Surely, Your Honor will concede the benefits of a well-rounded education.
>
> As I am among her personal acquaintances, I can vouch for the high standards she uses in selecting her associates. Our children have fought each other, hit each other with pillows, suffocated each other with their equally unwashed feet, called each other names, and all the other things that provide for a healthy, happy boy-to-boy relationship. You see, Your Honor, they love each other very much.
>
> In closing, I respectfully suggest that, when you consider Ms. Simmons' lifestyle, you will undoubtedly realize that hers is the only home for her son . . . she needs him to provide her with the wisdom, guidance, stability and parental concern necessary to keep her out of trouble!"

We were all laughing as Rita put down her "testimonial." Suddenly, JoAnne raised her glass for one last toast. "To humor," she saluted. "May it always accompany our sense of outrage."

Thirteen

The glittering contours of the western coastline faded into a vast array of squares and plains. We were almost there, I realized, my heart pounding in expectation. Despite the cityworkers' strike, San Francisco's airport had remained open and now, as we circled Tulsa, I gave thanks for an uneventful trip.

"Ladies and gentlemen, we'll be descending shortly," the pilot's voice came over the loudspeaker. "Thank you for flying American, and have a pleasant stay."

Abandoned! The torturous word slowly seeped into his consciousness, pounding at his senses, demanding uninvited entry. Gnashing his teeth, slashing at his diminishing faith, Bryan tried to ward off the invasion. Salty tears streamed down his cheeks.

"I'll be good, Mommy." He reverted to the childish name. "I promise . . . I promise . . . please, don't leave me here."

"Young man!" Paul's voice boomed from the hallway. "Stop your snivelling and get out here!"

Listlessly, Brian obeyed.

Fingers, wrapped around an aerosol can, were suddenly thrust in his face. "Do you know what this is?" Paul demanded.

The child nodded.

"Well, SuEllen and I have decided to keep some around the house, but you're not to touch it. Understand?"

"No. Why do you need it?"

"Mace? Oh, you know." A thin smile crossed Paul's lips. "It keeps out intruders."

An hour later, locked in my motel room, I slipped into the shower and gratefully allowed the hot water, like piercing needles, to wash away the day's tension. It was hard to believe we were finally in Oklahoma; lulled by the thought of Bryan's nearness, I managed to sleep more peacefully than I had in weeks.

By 9 a.m., the following morning, we were seated in the plush offices of Raphael, Warren, Stevens and Graves while Ceila Livingston, an executive secretary, served us coffee from a wicker tray. "It's a pleasure to meet you." A stout gentleman in an expertly tailored suit appeared in the doorway. "I'm Sterling Raphael."

The consultant attorney, about 60, was brown-eyed, a bit shorter than Michael, and a flowing gray mustache dramatized his full head of white hair. "Gee, Mom," I could almost hear Bryan say, "he looks just like Colonel Sanders!"

The two lawyers spent the next few hours getting acquainted, comparing state procedures, and discussing points of law. I sat there, a useless appendage, trying to discern their legalese. Finally, after an extended luncheon at Mr. Raphael's club, we drove down to the county courthouse.

In spite of our careful preparation, I felt a swift stab of terror as we entered the judge's chambers. What if this were merely another exercise in futility? One more door slammed in my face?

Judge Alana Dennison, a tall brunette woman in her mid-forties, quickly put me at ease. "Won't you sit down?" she asked pleasantly, as Mr. Raphael introduced us. "I understand you've come all the way from San Francisco."

As Michael outlined what had happened, her dark eyes flashed with anger. "Do you mean to tell me that the mother has not seen nor heard from her child in nearly a month?"

"That is correct, Your Honor."

Without further preliminaries, she signed a writ of habeas corpus which set the hearing date for Wednesday, April 7, at 10 a.m.

"No, Mr. Callan." She looked up from her desk. "That is not correct. That is outrageous!"

Please, telephone, ring! I was sprawled across the bed, trying to distract myself with a book, when my prayers were answered. Only it was the wrong caller.

"Laurel? Is that you? How are you?"

"The question is, 'How are you?'"

"Fine, but nervous. You see, the judge signed a writ about four hours ago, and I'm waiting for Paul to receive the subpoena. Mr. Raphael should be phoning any min—" My sentence was cut off by a sharp knock at the door.

Michael walked in smiling. "It's good news, Nan. Although Mr. Simmons is out-of-town, we were able to serve his charming wife without any trouble."

"Oh, Michael!" On impulse, I held up the receiver. "Mr. Callan, would you please repeat that . . . loudly."

"Why, sure." He lifted his voice. "I said that we have met the enemy, and they are ours."

The following morning, Michael and I left a copy of the papers with Vincent Morrell's secretary, then retraced our steps to the county courthouse.

"My God," he exploded, as we examined case file 3878962J—Simmons vs. Simmons. "The damn thing's full of discrepancies."

I was shocked, but not surprised.

"On that March 9th custody hearing, for instance, there's no documentation, no transcript, and not a shred of evidence that anyone even *tried* to notify you in advance. Furthermore," he flipped through the pages, "remember the modifications Jerome Pollock made in your divorce decree?"

"How could I forget?"

"Well, the court quashed them, Nan. They weren't even legal."

Tactfully, I remained silent as my mind wandered back to Michael's fervent words: "The law is my life's work. I have to believe in it!"

As the day wore on, I returned to the hotel while Michael made use of Mr. Raphael's law library. Sleep was impossible, but I'd managed to wade through two more chapters of my novel when the telephone rang.

"Just calling to say hi," Rita greeted me, as Dianna said hello on the extension. "How's everything going?"

I repeated the details, while confiding my fears that Paul might have Bryan with him. "Mainly, though," I confessed, "I'm just trying to keep from thinking."

Suddenly Dianna burst into tears. "Nan . . . I really blew it. I'm so sorry."

Before I could ask what she had done, she sobbed, "I-I found a letter . . . from the D.A. . . . in your mailbox yesterday morning and thought it might be important . . . so . . . I rushed to the post office and forwarded it . . . Airmail Special Delivery . . . then, when I got home from work, I saw that there was also one waiting for me . . . "

"And me," Rita added, "and Greg, and Graham Mallory . . . and God knows who else. It seems that our illustrious District Attorney is mailing out copies of Paul's so-called custody order, along with a self-righteous letter, to everyone who sent him a telegram."

"Or, apparently," Dianna said sourly. "to those of us who are registered voters in San Francisco."

Despite their urgings to rip up the letter, I simply could not remain that detached. A few hours later, when the envelope was slipped under my door, I opened it immediately. To my surprise, Mr. Garth's correspondence was addressed to Dianna:

"Dear Ms. Foster," my carbon copy began.

> A complaint was not issued by this office charging Mr. Simmons with a criminal offense because a review of this case indicated the requisite for criminal intent could not be established. Mr. Simmons was merely maintaining custody of his son.
>
> Mr. Simmons took his son from San Francisco at a time when an Oklahoma court had concluded he was entitled to unilateral custody of the child. The court order, enclosed herein, was issued on March 9, 1976, and it is clear he was acting under the color of that order.
>
> Both Inspector Erma Halsey and Mr. Anton Cattano of this office have been in conversation with Mr. Michael Callan, attorney for Mrs. Nancy Simmons. In a conversation he had with Mr. Cattano, Mr. Callan indicated that he

sought not to hassle our office. We realize that, by proceeding criminally, our office could save Mrs. Simmons a great deal of money. She could save the expense to her of transporting her son back to California. This begs the issue of whether or not she is now legally entitled to custody of the child.

This matter does not involve the law of kidnapping. The term may have emotional appeal but it legally does not apply to these facts. What is involved here is a complex custody dispute belonging to the civil courts and not susceptible to an easy answer. To use the office of the District Attorney of San Francisco as a force to determine the custodial outcome of this proceeding would be obviously improper.
Sincerely,

Julian Garth
District Attorney of San Francisco

They were quarreling. Harsh voices raised to an angry pitch, hurling insults. Bryan drifted in and out of slumber until, at last, their fighting forced him into an uneasy awakening. Propping himself up on one elbow, he listened dazedly to the shrill sounds.

"Well what do you think he'll say if they put him on the stand?" SuEllen was screaming. "He hasn't made the slightest effort to adjust."

"And whose fault is that? If you weren't spending so much time with Tiffany—"

"She's a baby. What in the hell am I supposed to do with her. Drown her?"

"Don't you ever talk like that again! Some mother you turned—"

"Some mother? Some husband!" The sound of breaking glass drowned out the next few words. ". . . left me in my eighth month to traipse off to California. And for what? A kid from your first marriage! One you don't even know! How do you think that makes me feel?"

Bryan pulled the blanket over his head, but their noisy argument penetrated its flimsy shelter.

". . . and I don't give a damn what you want, what she wants, or what the courts want," Paul yelled defiantly. "If I have to pay for him, I'm going to keep him."

"Well, Mr. Bigshot, maybe the judge won't agree with that."

"He'd better . . . because I don't intend to lose this time. If the courts take him away," Paul hissed, "I'll simply pick him up again."

"It's always what you want, isn't it?" SuEllen spat out, slamming their bedroom door. "Well, personally," she lowered her voice, "I hope they ship the little bastard back."

As her footsteps lumbered past his room, Bryan's lips began moving. "Please ship me back." He whispered. "If you're listening, God, please ship me back."

The night twisted into spidery shadows, dancing in the darkness, stinging at my sensibilities, floating through the hidden recesses of my soul. I tossed. I turned. I fought with phantoms. Eventually, I awoke as the first streaks of light dawned in the eastern skies.

"Now," I shuddered violently. "The real battle begins."

The courtroom was empty when we arrived. Two long tables faced each other, under the auspices of an American flag, while a wooden platform peered down upon the barren scene below.

"Don't worry," Michael read my mind. "It's only nine-thirty."

"I can't help but worry. What if they don't show up?" A tense pause followed, broken by Mr. Raphael's appearance in the doorway.

"Good morning," he said heartily. "I see that we've all arrived."

"Everybody?" My heart pounded.

"Yes. The boy's upstairs, and the Simmonses are down the hall with their counsel. Vincent Morrell is 'out-of-town' but his partner, Earl Gruber, will be handling the case."

A feeling of general relief swept over me. However, it was short-lived. "You said that Bryan was upstairs. Does that mean he won't be able to testify?"

"That's right, my dear. The courts try to spare children from as much trauma as possible."

"But—"

Just then Paul walked into the room, his arm around an uncomfortable-looking SuEllen. As they sat down, kissing lightly, Michael whispered. "Ah! The loving couple."

I squelched an equally sarcastic reply, and forced myself to concentrate on the clock. The hands seemed almost immobile while, in armed camps, we waited for court to convene. At exactly 10 a.m., Judge Dennison banged down the gavel.

"Your Honor." Mr. Raphael approached the bench. "I respectfully request that the attorney from San Francisco be allowed to speak. He's better acquainted with the circumstances than I am."

"Motion granted, Counselor."

Michael stood up and, in a clear voice, began citing case file discrepancies and jurisdictional precedents. Pacing back and forth, his hands clasped behind, he quoted excerpts from Chapman vs. Walker, Lynn vs. Lynn, and Ex-Parte Miller. Finally, in a dramatic gesture, he halted before the podium and raised his arms.

"Your Honor," he pleaded, "you can see that the file of the District Court of Tulsa County is completely devoid of notice to the petitioner of a March 9th hearing . . . and *no* authority need be cited to uphold the proposition that the American concept of Due Process *requires* that such notice be given."

"Thank you, Mr. Callan."

Earl Gruber, a slight, sharp-featured man with thinning hair, also rattled off precedents. Ignoring Michael's points, he gave an interesting interpretation of the Doctrine of Full Faith and Credit and reasoned forcefully that Oklahoma was the state of jurisdiction. At the conclusion of his speech, he reached for a newspaper clipping and, waving it in the air, strode towards the judge. "Besides," his voice rose in pitch, "the mother's a psychopathic publicity seeker. What kind of home—"

"That's not true!" I cried out as Michael jumped to his feet. Pounding the table, he shouted, "I will not have my client defamed in such a manner!"

"Oh, no? Well, I'm going to prove—"

"You'll prove nothing, Mr. Gruber. You're clouding the issue and—"

"Gentlemen! Gentlemen!" Judge Dennison intervened. "Such outbursts will not be tolerated. This is a court of law!" Handing back the article, she added, "I see no relevance. Objection sustained."

Grim-faced, the attorneys reclaimed their seats, the instant passing in which Kay Wickert might have joined the annals of Oklahoma jurisprudence.

And now, once again, the waiting began.

As the magistrate studied case documents, I found my mind drifting . . . imagining a future without Bryan. It was too painful to bear and I quickly forced my way back to the present: Paul, his face darkened with anger, drumming nervously on the table top; SuEllen fidgeting with the bow of her smock; lawyers Gruber and Callan glowering at each other from across the room. It was a scene from a childhood game in which someone had called "freeze," and a moment I would never forget.

"I have reached a decision." Judge Dennison's voice broke the silence. All eyes riveted on her.

"The files in case 3878962J are absolutely devoid of any showing that notice was given to the plaintiff, Nancy Simmons, of the March 9th proceedings which took her child away and placed custody elsewhere.

"In speaking to Judge Martin Bernhardt, he informed me that when he made the order he did not have the appearance docket before him and was not cognizant of other matters which, if known, should have put his court on notice that something was wrong in this case.

"Thus, for the reason that Judge Bernhardt made the order of March 9, 1976, with no notice to plaintiff, and contrary to any procedure which we might call 'Due Process' *this court is shocked,* and, on its own motion, vacates said order at this time."

As tears of happiness rolled down my cheeks, Earl Gruber was on his feet in a flash. "Your Honor," he seemed to be threatening, "are you aware that your declarations have discredited another judge?"

Appraising him coldly, she replied, "If you would like that I ask Judge Bernhardt to come up here, Mr. Gruber, I shall be more than happy to have my clerk call him."

The lawyer's body sagged visibly. "That won't be necessary, your Honor. However, I'm putting the court on notice that we intend to appeal this decision."

"That is your prerogative, Counselor."

To my dismay, instead of sitting down, he began a new line of argument. "And, since there will be an appeal pending, we all have an immediate problem to consider. What happens to the child? Certainly, he deserves better than to be shuttled back and forth between parents. He needs a stable environment. So, for the sake of the child, I am asking the court to allow him to remain where he is while the outcome of this case is being determined."

"That kind of reasoning is perverse and illogical." Michael was livid. "In the first place, we'd all be hard pressed to consider the child's present circumstances, and how he arrived at them, a stable environment. In the second, since Your Honor has already vacated the March 9th custody order, what Mr. Gruber proposes would result in permitting custody to remain illegally changed pending the appeal of a totally void order."

Judge Dennison's gavel came crashing down.

"This case is closed! Return the child to his mother!"

Epilogue

And so we came home. Our trials were not over, however, with Judge Dennison's decision. In some ways, they were just beginning. Prior to the kidnap, Bryan had been a happy-go-lucky youngster, an A student, and president of his class. Now, he required psychiatric treatment. Afraid to venture outside the apartment, he refused to attend school and hid under the bed whenever the doorbell rang. During the day, he carried a safety pin around "for protection" and, at night, could fall asleep only with the lights on and my presence in the room. Once, his terror became so acute I had to rush him to a local crisis clinic: he was convinced that Paul was breaking through locked windows to get him.

"How shall I deal with it?" I asked his therapist.

"What do you want me to say?" was the reply. "His fears are basically realistic."

Nearly five years have passed. Years which have witnessed Bryan's recovery, yet been filled with physical and emotional upheaval. Soon after Bryan's homecoming, we moved to another city. Six weeks later, Paul tracked us down and we were forced to move again . . . and again. Pursued like prey, we have mastered the art of living like fugitives: changed identities, unlisted phone numbers, post office boxes miles from home, and the ever-present knowledge that, at any moment, Bryan could once again be seized and taken.

Paul lost his appeal. However, that is not germane to our existence. For Paul Simmons and most other child snatchers know that legal custody is not binding; and a slap on the wrist, minimal fine, or useless "contempt of court" citation will not deter them from their purpose.

So, we wait. We wait for the day when child-stealing becomes a federal crime, or Bryan reaches majority. Whichever comes first. And, until that time—when we dare to emerge as normal citizens—my son and I live in hiding.

Part Two

Introduction

"Please remember we are not simply statistics. We are living, breathing human beings who are enduring an unbelievable hell on earth."

                        Sybil Crone, mother of stolen children.[1]

"They can't do anything to me for taking Danny. It's just a misdemeanor—like spitting on the sidewalk."

                        "Alan Grant"—a lawyer who is also a child snatcher.[2]

Brooklyn, New York.

A divorced mother waved goodbye to her children, aged 3 and 5, as her ex-husband picked them up for their usual visitation. That is the last time she ever saw them.

Distraught, she has spent $7,000 in private investigator fees in addition to contacting the FBI, the New York Police Department, Legal Aid and the Bureau of Missing Persons. "So far not even a small lead has been uncovered," she states. "I still sit with all my memories around me. I see empty beds at night, toys not played with and my heart cries out. Perhaps, by some ill-will, they are dead."[3]

Pacific Palisades, California.
Susan Downer sent her three children—11, 7 and 4—for a two month visit with her ex-husband, Seth Gerchberg. In lieu of returning them, he liquidated his assets, remarried, obtained passports and fled the country. She and her present husband, Rick, spent over $30,000 while trying to locate them.

The Downers managed to obtain three New York felony warrants against Gerchberg, a contempt of court citation, and a psychiatrist's written opinion that the children were in physical as well as psychological danger. Despite this, the FBI refused them assistance.

"How can we go around spouting human rights to other nations and violate them here, blatantly and openly?" Mrs. Downer demanded to know.[4]

Richmond, Virginia. A letter to the Subcommittee on Crime, House of Representatives, 93rd Congress:

To Whom It May Concern:
Last August 18th my former wife, Helen Andrews Duggan, called for my two children. Dennis John Wilburn and Merry Melissa Wilburn were in my permanent custody (per court order). Mrs. Duggan had limited visitation rights. The day before, August 17th, Edward John Duggan, Jr., called for the children born of his previous marriage, they numbering five. Sometime after five p.m. on the 18th of August all nine persons vanished. To date we have had little police action in this "Domestic Situation." How kind of everyone to call this domestic; however, if they, the Duggans, had stolen a car, a cow or horse, etc., they would have been hunted down. It is time the parent who has fought and been found to be in charge of the child or children of a broken marriage be given equal protection under the law. Does no one in this country find it in their hearts to help?

Look in on your children tonight . . . picture us. We look on an empty bed, we see toys not played with and classmates come to call wanting to know if we know anything yet.

Our children are able to call or write, yet nothing for over eight months . . . Are they alive? Are they being cared for? Are they being mistreated? For months now this has gone on in the mind of my family here at home. We have cried, prayed, begged and written letters. Please help the children torn away from their homes. Thank you for any help that you can give. I might add here that my ex-wife (2 years ago) told my then 8-year-old daughter on one of her visits to give her baby step-sister something to choke on when no one was looking. This woman has seven children who the authorities want to call a "domestic situation."

It is time the American public called out and demanded the right thing be done. . . .

Sincerely,

Dennis J. Wilburn[5]

Why The Problem?

Like Nancy Simmons, perhaps you or someone you know has had a child stolen. Suddenly, in mentioning it to your doctor, co-worker or next door neighbor, you learn that a cousin of one or a friend of the other also shares your problem. It doesn't seem possible! If child-stealing is not uncommon, you ask yourself, why haven't we established procedures to stop it? Or at least a way to help its victims? All you seem to be getting from anyone is the run-around.

Typically, you've reported it to the police, who told you there was nothing they could do. It was a "domestic matter." The district attorney may (or may not) have issued a felony warrant, depending on what state you live in and his or her inclination, but it doesn't seem to be doing much good. No one but you is searching for your ex-spouse. "We can't decide who has custody," "The child is no longer in the state," "This belongs in the civil courts," and "We can't help in your particular case because (fill in the blank)" are all phrases you're probably used to hearing at this point. No one, it seems, cares about your child, knows what to do or is willing to do much of anything. Why?

When the Federal Kidnapping Statute, or "Lindbergh Law," was amended in 1932 to make not only kidnapping for ransom or reward but for any other unlawful purpose a federal crime, it specifically exempted parental abductors. A kidnapper was defined as:

"Whoever knowingly transports in interstate or foreign commerce any person who has been unlawfully seized, confined, inveigled, decoyed, kidnaped, abducted, or carried away and held for ransom or reward or otherwise *except in the case of a minor by a parent thereof* (author's italics)...."
Sec. 1201, U.S. Criminal Code

The eleven word exclusion was inserted because, according to Representative L.C. Dyer, who proposed it, "There is not anybody who would want to send a parent to the penitentiary for taking possession of his or her own child, even though the order of the court was violated and it was a technical kidnapping."[6]

Since child-stealing is considered by many to be a particularly devastating form of child abuse, we question that statement. However, the people who drew up the law did not. It was in accord with thousands of years of historical precedence: *Parents may do what they wish with their own children.*

Though this is a harsh concept for us to accept, ideologies which express concern for the welfare of children are relatively new. As Elin McCoy, in her article "Childhood Through the Ages," points out: "In medieval times, infants were regarded as unformed animals, and in the sixteenth century, as 'exasperating parasites' ... Throughout history, parents' treatment of infants and small children has been characterized by psychological coldness and physical brutality ... Considered possessions with no individual rights, they were used to further adult aims, and they ended up as security for debts, as ways of increasing property holdings through arranged marriages, as political hostages, and even as slaves sold for profit."[7] In short, children were their parents' property.

Our own vocabulary provides further proof of that assumption. If we look at the legal terms for releasing a child from parental authority, we see that they are the same as those used for granting freedom to slaves: "emancipation" and "manumission." In fact, the origin of the word family itself, *familia*, refers to the number of slaves belonging to one man.[8]

At the beginning of the century, a young girl named Lulu Roller, who had been raped by her father, challenged the idea of parental carte blanche by bringing suit against the man. She lost. In dismissing her action, the Washington State Supreme Court stated: "The rule of law prohibiting suits between parent and child is based on the interest that society has in preserving *harmony* in the home."[9] (Italics ours.)

"Harmony in the home" or "domestic issue." How far have we come?

In theory, perhaps, a long way. Certainly, the practices of the fifteenth century are no longer acceptable to us, and most parents express a desire to nurture their offspring, not exploit them. To this end, we have begun to speak of "the best interests of the child" in making decisions and have enacted laws to protect children from harm — no matter what its origin. Yet, something is still wrong. There appears to be a subliminal hangover from the past which puts us at cross-purposes with ourselves. The laws are often on the books, but they're vague and unworkable. Child death through parental mistreatment, the number one killer of youngsters five years and under, has less severe penalties in some states than the selling of marijuana. And, although research shows us that children need a stable environment, their traumatic abduction from the security of their homes is often met with a laissez faire attitude.

Judge Lois G. Forer, who has served on the Lawyers Committee for Civil Rights and acted as a consultant to the U.S. Commission on Civil Disorders, states: "The view that violence perpetrated on a member of the family . . . is really not a crime permeates the entire criminal justice system. Unless death occurs, police are loathe to make arrests and prosecutors are reluctant to press charges."[10]

We are now well into the 1980s. But how far have we really come?

CHILD-STEALING AND OUR LAW ENFORCEMENT AGENCIES
(Or Where Does the Buck Stop?)

The effectiveness of our laws and law enforcement agencies cannot be divorced from the attitudes of those who propose them or carry them out. This is simply human nature. It has also resulted in what appears to be a hierarchy in the types of crimes which receive the most attention. Excluding homicides, crimes involving property or the illegal attainment of property (economic crimes) seem to be at the top end of the spectrum, or what we'll call Category #1. Not-so-enthusiastically pursued are those crimes in Category #2: crimes against women. Here, the victim is more apt to be faced with providing evidence that she did not seduce the rapist, provoke the wife beater or, in some way, "deserve" her attack. And, at the bottom of the totem, in Category #3, we find crimes against children.

This last classification is strangely divided. If an outsider kidnaps, molests or in any manner harms a child, the general feeling is that he or she should be locked up and the key thrown away. However, a parent performing the same acts—child abuse, incest, child-stealing—is often excused as being well-meaning but confused, in need of counselling or "part" of a bad situation which should not be made "worse" through prosecution. We think a closer look at this dichotomy would reveal a throwback to the traditional view of children as property. Thus, parents may exercise rights of ownership with, perhaps, a slap on the wrist for misbehavior, but the violation of children by strangers constitutes a crime against the "property" of another adult—back to Category #1!

Child-stealing appears to fall into the last two categories and, while we believe its inclusion in crimes against children is self-explanatory, we'd like to add a word or two about the concept of child-stealing as a crime against women.*

True, fathers have their children stolen. True, too, they do not receive preferential treatment from the authorities. However, anyone who has studied this crime cannot help but observe that most parental victims are women. Also, policy in dealing with child-stealing was formulated years ago when chances of a man receiving custody of his children were slim. Thus, the victims—women and now men who are seen procedurally as "women"—are faced with the attitude toward all crimes in this category. What have *you* done to cause your own victimization? Did you seduce the rapist? Provoke the wife beater? Disallow visitation to the child snatcher? Why should we help?

*If you're interested in a more comprehensive look at the way women and children are treated within the context of the legal system, there are many fine books devoted to just that, and we think they are valuable for an overall understanding of the problem. So, while we concentrate on the specific crime of child-stealing, we've provided a list of reference material for you in the Appendix.

"Alan Grant," an admitted child snatcher, told a reporter from the *Novato Advance*, "If the police really wanted to find me, they could." Grant, who maintains a post office box less than 100 miles from his ex-wife's home, is convinced that "(They) are not too interested in apprehending me."[11]

Just as revealing is a statement made by Janet Sachs, a psychiatric social worker who is researching the effects of child-stealing on returned children. "Unfortunately," she remarked, weeks into the project, "I can't seem to find more than one or two people who have gotten their children back!"

Surely, in an age of sophisticated computer equipment and tracking methods, child snatchers should have more trouble disappearing than they do. Why the problem?

We've already seen the historical attitude toward intra-familial crimes. Now let's translate it into modern terms. Here is what some of our law enforcement agencies have to say about their willingness or ability to assist in child-stealing cases.

The Federal Parent Locator

"The Administration is supportive of measures to deter parental kidnapping and to locate children already kidnapped by a parent, which would help to prevent psychological and physical harm to both the children and the aggrieved parent. However, we do object to making the FPLS (Federal Parent Locator Service) available to locate children who have been taken in violation of a custody decree."
> Louis B. Hays, Deputy Director, Office of Child Support Enforcement, Dept. of Health and Human Services in a June 24, 1980, statement to Congress.[12]

State Attorneys General (a sampling)[13]

Alaska
"District Attorneys in Alaska currently do not prosecute for child-stealing. . . ."

Delaware
"In practice, prosecution . . . is rare (estimate three cases yearly)."

Iowa
"The occurrence of the problem in this state is widespread . . . the only solution I can foresee as being efficacious would be federal legislation so as to involve investigatory personnel at the national level . . . The majority of these cases involve the crossing of state lines and, therefore, state legislation in the field is meaningless."

Kentucky
"Kentucky . . . does not keep statistics. . . ."

Nevada
"In 1975, the Nevada legislature added a new section . . . which provides: 'Every person . . . who . . . detains, conceals or removes a child from a parent . . . is guilty of a misdemeanor.' To my knowledge, no one has ever been prosecuted under this provision since its enactment."

New Hampshire
". . . (A) proceeding for contempt is the only method in New Hampshire by which to resolve this problem and that, as I am sure you, are aware does not customarily allow extradition."

New Mexico
" . . . at present time New Mexico does not have a statute which addresses the problem."

The Civil Courts

"If a parent snatches a child after there's been a court order granting only visitation rights, then he's breaking the law. But the only way I can enforce it is with a contempt of court order, and you can't serve a contempt of court order across state lines. So, if a parent crosses the state line, it's out of my hands."
Superior Court Judge John Hardin.[14]

The Police

"It is neither the duty nor within the legal jurisdiction of peace officers to enforce the provisions of a restraining order."
California Police Chief William Kinney[15]

"These complaints come over the phone every day. We don't bother to take them."
A Detroit police officer.[16]

"It's a domestic thing. Police don't like to get involved in it."
An Orlando police officer.[17]

The F.B.I.

". . . The clear public policy for over 40 years has been to exempt the parent-minor child situation from coverage of the Kidnapping Act. We believe that exemption to be sound public policy and recommend that it be continued . . . there is no indication that State and local authorities are unable to adequately deal with unexplained disappearances. . . ."
Deputy Assistant Attorney General
John C. Keeney, Dept. of Justice,
1974 Congressional hearings.[18]

"The denomination of this conduct as criminal represents an entirely new, and in our view, wholly inappropriate, involvement of the federal criminal justice system. . . . (also) Investigations and prosecutions would necessarily divert precious resources from other areas."
Deputy Assistant General Mark M. Richards,
Dept. of Justice, 1980 Congressional hearings.[19]

"The FBI is not going to get into the child collection business."
Richard L. Thornburgh, a former
spokesperson for the Justice Dept.[20]

To make matters worse, until December 28, 1980, there were no federal laws requiring states to honor each other's custody orders. This resulted in a host of decrees being issued to child snatchers once they entered new states.

With so many legal loopholes, it's a wonder that *any* stolen children have been returned! For some parents, though, the outlook may be less bleak than in the past. After the 1980 Congressional hearings on child-stealing, Federal Public Law 96-611 was enacted. While its effectiveness cannot be determined yet—and is almost entirely based on the willingness of officials to adhere to its intent—it does offer a few new options to victimized parents.

The measure, which went into effect July 1, 1981, provides that 1) full faith and credit be given another state's custody determination; 2) the Federal Parent Locator Service is authorized to assist in the location of stolen children; and 3) FBI services will be made available in cases where the parental kidnapper has fled the state, a UFAP (Unlawful Flight to Avoid Prosecution) Warrant has been issued, and the state requesting aid has felony provisions for the crime.

What it will not do is address the problem of children taken before the issuance of custody, rarely considered a crime; prescribe penalties; grant FBI assistance to states where child-stealing is a misdemeanor or no crime at all; make the FPLS available to states which do not have an agreement with that agency; or automatically bring in the FBI or FPLS even in authorized states when local officials do not make a request.* Certainly, P.L. 96-611 is a step in the right direction. But it's just a step.

For child-stealing to be effectively controlled, we need more comprehensive measures. California's Alameda County Deputy District Attorney Robert Hutchins, a leader in this field of law enforcement, offers a few thoughts on the matter which we think deserve critical attention. (While we, personally, would like to see the crime taken completely out of the realm of "misdemeanor," his focus on D.A. discretion in determining charges is more likely to make the package appealing to legislators.)

*Another problem appears to be in activating the new law. The states have been slow in adopting procedures for use of the FPLS, and the Justice Department's unwillingness to comply with the intent of P.L. 96-611 has made Congressional Hearings on the matter necessary. See Appendix C.

Recommendations

1) Laws addressing this act could be more easily enforced if they were worded to make the crime one of "taking, detaining or concealing a child with the intent to deprive the other parent of access to that child." This would eliminate the many complications and nuances of interpreting the word "custody."

2) In dealing with this crime, we need to keep in mind that there are two distinct victims. Child-stealing refers to the parent as victim; however, if force were used the child could be considered a victim of kidnapping. False imprisonment is another charge which recognizes the harm done to the child.

3) A Uniform Child-Stealing Act should be enacted with appropriate penalties to deter the would-be abductor. It should be directed not only at the parental kidnapper, but at *any* person found taking, detaining or concealing a child with the intent to deprive a parent of access. Also, if he or she refuses to disclose the whereabouts of the child, the penalties would escalate.

4) The act of child-stealing should be a continuing one for each day the child is missing. This would prevent the risk of a parent being so successful in hiding the child that the statute of limitations runs out.

5) Child-stealing is best classified as a "felony-misdemeanor." This means that charges could be reduced to a misdemeanor but the assistance offered in felony cases would be available. Extradition, for example, is unrealistic on simple misdemeanor charges. Also, in order for the police to make an arrest on a misdemeanor, they must have personally witnessed the crime.

Another point in opting for this classification is that it would reduce our dependence on the FBI. Agents could relay their information to the local police, who would then be free to arrest and hold the suspect until the agents arrived for extradition.

5) We need to make state and federal records available in cases of child-stealing. This would not necessitate revealing information on earnings or anything else not pertinent to the crime. However, we should have access to documents stating an abducting parent's whereabouts.

6) In any criminal action, including child-stealing, the police should follow the same procedures.

"The key to locating a stolen child," Hutchins concludes, "is in finding the child as soon as possible, and that means getting the national police network, including the FBI, into motion. You could intercept abductors at airports. If they thought there was no chance of making it anywhere with the children, this whole thing would dry up."[21]

TAKING THE REINS IN YOUR OWN HANDS

Now that we've looked at some of the problems inherent in child-stealing, let's explore a few avenues of self-help. Unfortunately, there are no proven methods which, when used, will guarantee the return of your child. However, you can do several things to expedite the search, and these may run the gamut from keeping careful records to chaining yourself to the district attorney's desk until, tired of tripping over you, he decides to look for your son or daughter.

If you've been keeping a family file including birth dates, social security numbers and a list of mutual friends with whom you exchange Christmas cards, you're already a step ahead. You will then have the information on hand to fill out a data sheet on your ex-spouse and child which you, a district attorney or private investigator can use in tracking down the missing parent. We have drawn a sample data sheet based on the one suggested by Eileen Baris Luboff and Constance L. Posner in *How to Collect Your Child Support and Alimony*.[22] The procedures for skip tracing either for collecting debts or for locating a stolen child are quite similar. In your case, however, you'll want to add all pertinent information about your offspring because the child snatcher might send for school records, pediatric history, etc.

You might even want to fill out the form although your child has not been stolen. The information could prove useful for other purposes, and in the unfortunate event that you do become a victim, you'll have saved precious time which could be put to better use elsewhere.

By the same token, it is wise to keep abreast of changes in your ex-spouse's life. Has he or she recently moved, remarried or quit a job? Changed patterns in visitation or amount of interest shown in your children? Or have *you* moved, instigated a law suit, or remarried? These are all situations which should be monitored since they frequently precede a child snatch. We would also advise obtaining an immediate temporary custody order if you are planning a legal separation, and considering having the other parent post a bond if visitation occurs out-of-state. While these measures won't prevent a child from being stolen, they may act as deterrents.

DATA SHEET

Abductor's Name _____
                  First   Middle   Last   (Maiden)   (Known Alias)

Address _____ Phone _____
                        Last Known

Date of Birth _____ Place of Birth _____ Age _____

Physical Description _____ Height _____ Weight _____

Hair Color _____ Eye Color _____ Other _____

1st Child's Name _____
                   First   Middle   Last

Date of Birth _____ Place of Birth _____ Age now _____

Physical Description _____ Height _____ Weight _____

Hair Color _____ Eye Color _____ Other _____

1st Child's School _____ Name _____ Address _____ Phone _____

Principal's Name _____ Teacher's Name _____

Child's Friends _____ Name _____ Address _____ Phone _____

_____

_____

2nd Child's Name _____ First _____ Middle _____ Last

Date of Birth _____ Place of Birth _____ Age now _____

Physical Description _____ Height _____ Weight _____

Hair Color _____ Eye Color _____ Other _____

124 The Child Snatchers

2nd Child's School _____ Name _____ Address _____ Phone

Principal's Name _____ Teacher's Name _____

Child's Friends _____ Name _____ Address _____ Phone

_____

_____

Pediatrician or other Doctors

Name _____ Address _____ Phone

Special conditions requiring medicine, special devices or attention _____

Witnesses to Abduction:

Name _____ Address _____ Phone

Name _____ Address _____ Phone

Name _____ Address _____ Phone

The Child Snatchers   125

School Guard or Yard Attendant _____ (if applicable)

Time of Abduction _____ Date _____ Place _____

Car Used _____
Year _____ Make _____ Model _____ Color _____ License Plate _____

Physical Description of Accomplice _____
Height _____ Weight _____

Hair Color _____ Eye Color _____ Other _____

Abduction Reported to: _____
_____
_____

Were you referred to the Parent Locator? _____

Results? _____

List of Legal Papers: _____ Custody Decree _____ Visitation Rights

Restraining Order _____ Felony Warrant _____ Other

126   The Child Snatchers

Does Child Snatcher have a prior police record? _____

Where? _____ For What? _____

Name of Probation Officer _____

Abductor's Social Security Number _____ Driver's License _____

List of Vehicles owned by Abductor:

Car _____ Year _____ Make _____ Model _____ Color _____ Plate _____

Boat _____ Year _____ Make _____ Model _____ Color _____ Plate _____

Other (Recreational Vehicle, Plane, Motorcycle) _____

_____ Year _____ Make _____ Model _____ Color _____ Plate _____

Abductor's Lawyer Name _____ Address _____ Phone _____

List of Abductor's Relatives:

Name _____ Address _____ Phone _____ Relationship _____

List of Abductor's Friends:

Name _____ Address _____ Phone _____

_____

_____

_____

_____

Abductor's Last Employer _____

Name _____ Address _____ Phone _____

Past Employers _____

What Schools has He/She Attended?:
College

Name _____ Address _____ Phone _____

Name _____ Address _____ Phone _____

Employable Skills _____

_____

Does most recent employer have company branch offices? _____

Where? _____

Is Abductor collecting Unemployment Insurance? _____ Welfare? _____

State Disability? _____ Social Security? _____ Other? _____

Does He/She belong to a Labor Union? _____

Which? _____ Where? _____ Local Number _____

Does He/She belong to a Professional Association? _____

Graduate School _____ Name _____ Address

Special Training _____ Name _____ Address

Has He/She filed a lawsuit against anyone in the last year? _____

Where? _____ Against Whom? _____

Has He/She become entitled to an inheritance through the death of a relative? _____

Who? _____ When? _____

Where? _____ State _____ County

Does He/She own Real Estate? _____ What State? _____

Address _____ Street _____ Town _____ County

Does He/She belong to a Credit Union? _____ Have an account with them? _____

Where? _____ Account Number _____

Does the Abductor have a Checking Account? _____ Bank _____

Branch _____ Account Number _____

A Savings Account? _____ Bank _____

Branch _____ Account Number _____

Insurance Policies? _____ What kind? _____

Insurance Company _____ Agent _____

His/Her Religious Affiliation _____

Was the Abductor ever in the Armed Forces? _____ Which Branch? _____

What Rank? _____ Served How Long? _____ Regular Military? _____

Retired? _____ Disabled? _____

What are His/Her Hobbies? _____

_____

Magazine Subscriptions _____

What are the Clubs and Organizations to which He/She belongs? _____

Credit Card Information:

Card _____ Number _____ Date of Expiration _____

_____

_____

Do you still have duplicate cards? _____

Does He/She have friends in or connections with any Foreign Country? _____ Which _____

Speak any Foreign Languages? _____

List pertinent information about his/her present spouse or person with whom he or she may be living (Physical description, job, car, children, receiving any government assistance, etc.)

_____

_____

_____

Who are your Government Representatives?

Local ____Name_____ Address_____

State ____Name_____ Address_____

U.S. Senate ____Name_____ Address_____

U.S. House ____Name_____ Address_____

Miscellaneous Information _____

_____

_____

_____

HOW TO USE YOUR DATA SHEET

The information you've just jotted down on your data sheet can be the key to finding a stolen child. For instance, for a small fee, you can obtain a "Request for Driver Record Information" from the Driver's License Section of the Department of Motor Vehicles. When you fill in the appropriate data, they will inform you of your ex-spouse's last reported address and driving record. If he or she has committed any vehicle code violations, the location of those violations may give you a clue to his or her present whereabouts. It should be noted, however, that the D.M.V. notifies licensees about inquiries made on their files, so decide whether, in your particular case, this inquiry would be a wise move or not. Perhaps it would be disasterous to let your ex-spouse know that you're on the right track. Why not see if your insurance agent will do you a favor? Insurance companies check driving records all the time.

Perhaps your ex-spouse always complained because you weren't enough like his or her momma or poppa. It was infuriating then, but could turn out to be a blessing now. If this was the case, chances are that "Momma's boy" or "Daddy's little girl" is still calling "home" and reversing the charges. If you've filled in the section on relatives, it is now possible in many states to get the district attorney to issue a warrant for the phone bills of those most likely to have the child snatcher's number on them. We warn you. It probably won't be easy, but here's where chaining yourself to the desk comes into play. If it is legally possible for the D.A. to obtain such information, insist on it.

Is the child snatcher a trucker, teacher or real estate agent? People in these and many other fields have to be licensed by the state or members of unions in order to work. By writing the appropriate agency in each state, you may obtain a lead on your ex-spouse's present address or at least the state of residence. The same goes for hobbies. If the child-snatcher fancied him or herself a budding Dashiell Hammett or Agatha Christie and once belonged to the Mystery Writers of America, Inc., it is possible the membership is still in effect. Or maybe sailing into the wild blue yonder was your ex's particular thrill. In that case, don't neglect checking with the Federal Aviation Administration in Oklahoma City, Oklahoma, to see what they have on file.

At this point, it seems impossible to imagine child-snatchers as having good reputations anywhere. But particular pains might have been taken to guard a credit rating and they may not be willing to risk changing names and starting out all over again. Of course, unless you still have joint credit, you won't be allowed access to the records. However, a close friend or neighbor who works at a bank or department store, for instance, might be willing to do some research for you.

Past employers (who might have been contacted for a reference), ex-landlords still holding deposits, colleges sending out the alumni bulletin and, of course, the Parent Locator (which will be discussed later) are all valuable sources of possible information. And if you need the address or phone number of a professional association, trade organization, fraternal society, esoteric periodical to which he or she may be subscribing (or even a geographic listing for various types of schools), your public library can probably provide it. There are over 5,000 directories containing this type of information and a friendly librarian or publication such as Gale Research Company's *Directory of Directories* can guide you through the maze.

ORGANIZATIONS AND SUPPORT GROUPS

A sense of isolation is an almost universal feeling among parents of stolen children. Most people can sympathize with you, but it's difficult for them to empathize. Their inability is understandable. They haven't been through the experience; nor have they faced the same set of complex emotions. This is poignantly illustrated in many cases of remarriage. A husband or wife tries to understand the mood swings, periods of withdrawal, seeming obsession with the missing child, feelings of guilt or anger, but often winds up frustrated or exasperated. Perhaps, the answer is a support group. Your spouse, if you have one, might also benefit from talking to others experiencing a similar situation.

"I felt better before I even called you," Nina Gorey of San Francisco told a member of "Take Action Against Child-Stealing," a Bay Area support group for parents of stolen children. "Just reading that you existed and were nearby made me feel less alone."

The Bay Area group started from a small ad in a local newspaper. In just a few months, its membership grew from six people to over sixty. "I can finally talk about what happened without someone implying that I must have done something wrong or deserved it," said one member. "I was beginning to think I must be crazy."

At monthly meetings, cases are discussed, the names of lawyers or private investigators exchanged, laws explained or debated, guest speakers invited to share their area of expertise and, sometimes, homecomings celebrated.

"Nearly every victimized parent we've talked with considers the value of talking to someone who has been 'through it' greater than the value of their lawyer," observes Arnold Miller, President of Children's Rights, Inc.[23] C.R.I (pronounced cry) was a nationwide, nonprofit, volunteer organization which, until a recent break from activities, put out a quarterly newsletter, dispensed technical information to local and federal agencies, brought media attention to the problem and provided a "Lend-An-Ear" program where volunteers throughout the country manned hotlines. "Since our inception in 1975, we have counselled (nonlegal) over 5,000 parents victimized by child-snatching, as well as tens of thousands of other parents with restraint or custody-related problems. We receive a daily average of 22 pieces of mail, as well as 16 telephone requests per day for information . . . (The work) has been exhausting, but it has been well worth the effort, because we have helped."[24]

The number of parent groups concerned with child-stealing has more than tripled over the past few years and seems likely to continue its acceleration. The following is a list of some of the current organizations. You might want to contact one of them or, if there's nothing available in your area, consider starting your own. We do not think it's mere coincidence that California had several active coalitions prior to the state's enactment of some of the most comprehensive legislation in the country.

Please note that our listing of a group does not constitute an endorsement. We strongly urge you to investigate a prospective organization you're interested in and see if their philosophy and manner of dealing with the problem are in line with your own.

List of Groups and Organizations

Bay-Area Center for Victims of Child-Stealing

1165 Meridian
San Jose, California 95148
A nonprofit corporation which provides information and

education on the subject of child-stealing through individual counselling, media promotion and interaction with other agencies. Operating primarily in the Bay Area, the center sponsors T.A.A.C.S. (Take Action Against Child Stealing), a parent support group with chapters in San Francisco and San Jose.

Child Find, Inc.

P.O. Box 277
New Paltz, New York 12561
A not-for-profit corporation whose objective is to establish a central registration point for parents and children to find each other. The major goal of Child Find is to communicate to children that: 1) there is an address and phone number for their use in making contact with lost parents; 2) there are other children who face the same problem; 3) parents do care and are searching for them; and 4) it's okay to make contact with a lost parent.

Children's Rights of New York, Inc.

19 Maple Avenue
Stony Brook, NY 11790
A nonprofit agency, affiliated with the American Society for the Prevention of Cruelty to Children, composed of parents and lay people working against child-stealing. They have referral lists of attorneys, private investigators and lay persons who may assist in locating a child. Operating primarily in the Northeast, their main purpose is to educate the public and conduct research in the field of child abuse along with providing support and advice to parents of stolen children.

ChildSearch

6 Beacon Street, Suite 600
Boston, Massachusetts 02108
ChildSearch publishes the pictures of stolen children and sends the tabloid to approximately 98,500 public schools with a phone number to call in case a child is recognized. The fee for one insertion is $275.

Parents-Against Legal Kidnapping

1887 Wright Road
Buda, Texas 78610
A parent support group which counsels victims of child snatching, promotes public awareness of the problem, urges

legislation to prevent child stealing and works for the enforcement of present laws.

Parents Alone

c/o Mary Anne Havey
Department of Psychology
Wichita State University
Wichita, Kansas
A mutual support group which assists parents in coping with a child-stealing situation. They will also educate parents as to what the laws can and cannot do for them, with an emphasis placed upon not taking the law into one's own hands.

Parents Helping Parents

Route 1
Box 406 D
Myakka City, Florida 33551
A parent support group which provides information on child-stealing, promotes public awareness through the media and seeks to protect children through neighborhood involvement programs.

People Against Parental Kidnapping

298 Hurley Street
Cambridge, Massachusetts 02141
This newly formed group was created to serve child snatching victims in Massachusetts. Their main focus is on support work for those in need during the crisis of the child snatching incident.

Sacramento Stolen Children Action Network

5125 47th Avenue
Apt. 56
Sacramento, CA 95824
S.S.C.A.N. is a nonprofit community resource organization which assists parents of stolen children. They provide education to the general public about the seriousness of child abduction, referrals to proper agencies, and assistance in finding ways to deal with the emotional problems which accompany child-stealing.

Stolen Children Information Exchange

Box 465
Anaheim, California 92805

Phone: (714) 847-2676
This organization operates a 24-hour hotline for parental victims of child snatching. In addition, they maintain a parent support group named "KIDS."

United Parents Against Child Stealing, Inc.

P.O. Box 35428
Tucson, Arizona 85740
A nonprofit group formed by parents to comfort and assist victims of child-stealing. The organization operates primarily in Tucson, Arizona.

How to Start a Parent Support Group

It's really not difficult. All you need are people and a place to meet. Your home will do for the second requisite, but how do you find other parents of stolen children?

For one thing, you can put an ad in your local newspaper under the "personal" column. It need not be long. Something like "Support group forming for parents of stolen children. Call (your phone number)" will do. Also, some newspapers offer free space for announcements of public service meetings and, after you've gained a few members, you might want to take advantage of this resource.

Your district attorney's office provides another vehicle for finding potential members. See if you can post a referral notice where it is likely to be seen by staff members answering the telephones.

A word of caution here. Although you want to continuously keep the name of your group and contact information in the public eye, it's wisest not to put an address on anything which will be seen by the general public, unless it's a P.O. box number. What you don't need at this point are crank visits!

Other useful sources for locating membership are social service agencies, children's rights groups, legal aid, offices of the Parent Locator, private investigators, and the Victim Witness Assistance Program.

We think you'll find most agencies helpful in referring people or giving you other numbers to call, so by all means, tell them what you are doing.

Once a few parents have expressed their interest in meeting, set a date. It's probably best to poll your members on what time and day of the week are most convenient and then stick to a regular schedule. For instance, the first Tuesday of every month at 7:30 p.m. On the other hand, you might want to try rotating the place of assembly so that everyone becomes involved in hosting the meetings.

The agenda will depend on your particular group. Why have most people come to the meeting? What do they expect to gain? Do they have any ideas for group projects? What resources do you have among you? Although most self-help groups form from a sense of powerlessness, it's amazing how many hidden assets you'll find once you start asking. Perhaps one member has access to a copying machine. Another might have a neighbor who went to school with a local news reporter. Or someone's Aunt Minnie won a contest for her homemade pecan pie. Not relevant, you say? It could be if you decide to sell Aunt Minnie's pies and use the money to take a lobbying trip to the state capital. Just by joining forces, you've multiplied your strength. Now find out how to use it.

As a stepping off point, here are some things which other groups are doing or have done in the past: Citizens Committee to Amend Title 18 studied the inequities involved in the FBI's treatment of child-stealing cases versus their policies towards other inter-state crimes. Parents Against Child-Stealing brought media attention to the problem. Children's Rights of New York, Inc. and Children's Rights, Inc. were influential in educating public officials about the need for stronger state and federal laws respectively. Stop Parental Kidnapping, Inc. sent out flyers of stolen children to schools and pediatricians across the country. And Child Find is acting as a clearinghouse for stolen children wishing to locate their parents. Or, perhaps, you want to focus your efforts at raising consciousness on a local level. T.A.A.C.S. frequently invites Bay Area officials to sit in or speak at their meetings.

Other activities to consider are letter writing campaigns, preparing a list of recommended attorneys and private investigators—including those to avoid—holding a workshop on the problem, starting a newsletter, drawing up a list of steps to take if a child has been stolen and passing it out to new members and applicable agencies, contacting reporters and television/radio interview shows to do a story or program on the issue, or even holding a demonstration. We're sure you'll be able to think of many other things once you begin to brainstorm.

If lobbying is one of your interests, you might gain some pointers from Andy Humm's booklet *How to Organize a Self-Help Group*, which is listed in the appendix. In it, he includes this advice: 1) In making an appointment to visit your legislator, identify yourself and the organization you represent; 2) Make sure you inform the legislator that you are a registered voter in his or her district; 3) Deal in facts and leave supporting documents; 4) Get your point across in the fewest possible words and don't resort to threats or name-calling; 5) Be a good listener when he or she is expressing their point of view; 6) Don't be afraid to admit ignorance on specific points. Just say you will find out the answer and report back; 7) Leave on friendly terms since you may want to contact him or her again; 8) Give special recognition to those legislators who are on your side, and ask them for advice or help in reaching the others; 9) If lobbying as a group, try to have one member act as spokesperson.

There's no question about it, a demonstration can bring valuable attention to the problem of child-stealing. However, before you dredge up your 1960s marching boots, we urge you to plan carefully so you don't attract the wrong kind of spotlight. We recommend dressing conservatively (that means suits for men, dresses or pantsuits for women) and a low key demeanor that doesn't stereotype you as a radical fringe group. For that last statement, we apologize to radical fringe groups.

Call your local police to see if you need a permit. You can pose it as a hypothetical question so they don't try to talk you out of it. The rule of thumb, however, is that you don't need a permit if you're holding a peaceful demonstration on a public sidewalk, but you do have to keep moving so you don't block pedestrian traffic. We're assuming that you won't be using sound equipment or marching in the streets; if you do, a permit generally becomes necessary.

If you're planning to picket the arraignment or trial of an accused child snatcher—an opportune time for a demonstration—**don't**, under any circumstances, mention the case or the accused's name on your placards or in interviews. The last thing you want is to prejudice the trial and have it thrown out of court! One group, in this situation, held up signs saying "100,000 Children Each Year Are Stolen" and posters with their children's pictures including such statements as "Missing 5 Years." Other signs declared "Child Stealing is Child Abuse" or "Do You Know Where Your Children Are? I Don't!"

Since the object of a demonstration is publicity, you'll want to contact your local newspapers and television/radio stations before the event. This can be done in the form of a phone call to the newsroom or city editor's desk. If you plan on writing a press release, be sure to address it to the city editor with the heading "For Release (Date)" or "For Immediate Release" and include the name and phone number of someone to contact should further information be desired.

Now to the meetings, themselves. You'll soon develop your own style and format but, as an initial guide, T.A.A.C.S. members have offered to share the format that they've worked out. They stress, though, that it is not a rigid schedule and they often deviate from it depending on the topics under discussion and what seems important at the moment.

7:30 p.m.	People arrive and talk informally.
7:45-8:45	The meeting begins. People introduce themselves and discuss their personal cases. Information is exchanged and emotional support given. At a first or second meeting, this will probably take up most, if not the entire, evening.
8:45-9:00	Take a break. This is important because some people are not able to speak easily in groups and this will give them a chance to talk to one or two individuals of their own choosing.
9:00-10:00	Topic planned for the agenda. This may be a speaker, a project, a particular case under discussion, new information on laws or policies, or even a continuation of the earlier part of the evening.
10:00-10:30	Wrap it up and discuss plans for next meeting.

Once you get the ball rolling, you might want to register your group with The American Bar Association's Child Custody Project. The director maintains a list of parent support groups and organizations interested in child-stealing cases, and can be very helpful in keeping you posted on the latest legal developments. The address to write is:

    Director
    Child Custody Project
    American Bar Association
    1800 M Street, N.W.
    Washington, D.C. 20036

A final word about support groups: Don't be discouraged if you find that some people come to a meeting, jot down information, and never return. In all probability, useful data is all they wanted from the group and, by providing it, you have fulfilled your purpose. You have assisted them with their particular needs and, in doing so, exemplified what support groups are all about. Carry on!

REMOVAL TO ANOTHER COUNTRY

Before January 1, 1981, proof of legal custody or consent of the second parent was not required by the U.S. Passport Office when applying for a child's passport. As a result, children were able to leave the country by travelling on their parent's passport or, in some cases, to be whisked out without a passport. Happily, this has been amended. Also, if the custodial parent registers a certified copy of his or her custody order with the Passport Office and expressly denies exit from the country without permission, the office will try to cooperate. We think it is a wise preventive measure, in any case, to send your custody order along with names, dates and places of birth of both the ex-spouse and child to: U.S. Passport Office, Legal Division, 1425 K Street, N.W., Washington, D.C. 20415. Be sure to include your present address and telephone number so, if necessary, you may be contacted immediately.

A passport, once issued, can only be revoked under certain conditions, not usually applicable to child-stealing cases. However, if the correct documents are on file, the office will notify you of your child's renewal address when it expires. Further, if you know where your children are located, they will offer assistance in contacting the U.S. Embassy or Consulate of the foreign country in which they are being restrained and aid in obtaining a duplicate passport for them to travel back on. Prior to the passage of The Parental Kidnapping Act of 1980, the U.S. Passport Office was the only federal agency willing to furnish support in cases of child-stealing, and they average 30 to 40 inquiries a week regarding preventive measures.

Even though present policy dictates against the revocation of passports, Judge Samuel Conti of San Francisco, in a federal case on February 10, 1978, did order the State Department to revoke the passport of a stolen child being held in West Germany.[25] Perhaps, this decision can serve as a precedent in future cases.

What about extradition? Can a child snatcher be brought back to the United States when criminal charges are filed? Unfortunately, this is only possible if the country to which he or she fled has a treaty with the United States providing extradition for the crime and if the crime is a federal offense in the U.S. Needless-to-say, it is practically impossible to get extradition for child snatch cases and depends entirely on the cooperation of foreign government officials. In addition, some countries, notably in South America, refuse to allow a custodial mother to reclaim her children without legal permission from the father.

On a more optimistic note, work has begun on a proposed international treaty regarding this crime. Outlined at the Hague Conference on private international law in October 1980, it would provide for extradition of stolen children between the United States and Argentina, Australia, Austria, Belgium, Canada, Czechoslovakia, Denmark, Egypt, Finland, France, Germany, Great Britain, Greece, Ireland, Israel, Italy, Japan, Luxemburg, the Netherlands, Norway, Portugal, Spain, Surinam, Sweden, Switzerland, Turkey, Venezuela and Yugoslavia. Before it takes effect, however, it still needs to be ratified by the nations involved.

PARENT LOCATOR SERVICES

The First Annual Report to the Congress on the Child Support Enforcement Program by the Department of Health, Education and Welfare (now Health and Human Resources) states: "With the enactment of Public Law 93-647, the Secretary of HEW was given the responsibility under title IV-D of the Social Security Act to establish a Federal/State Child Support Enforcement program designed to locate absent parents and obtain support payments from them...

"The Federal Parent Locator Service attempts to obtain *the last known address and most recent place of employment* (our italics) of absent parents on behalf of State child support agencies. Although courts of competent jurisdiction and parents, attorneys, guardians, or agents of children who are not recipients of public assistance are also permitted to receive address information through the Federal PLS, they must make their request to the State child support agency. All requests to the Federal PLS must be made through the State PLS in the State child support enforcement agency, and the State must make a reasonable and diligent effort to locate the absent parent before making the request."[26]

Now, with the enactment of the Parental Kidnaping Prevention Act of 1980, Public Law 96-611, you too are entitled to the service of the Federal Parent Locator *if your state enters into an agreement to do so with the Parent Locator!* (Read section nine of the new law for the exact wording.) In order to get specific information on how your state intends to handle requests for PLS assistance in locating abducting parents, you should write or call your local state office. Remember, you're probably going to have to do a lot of the groundwork yourself if you want action taken, so learn the rules; if your district attorney doesn't think to take advantage of this resource, remind him. You might also see if it can be requested that your case be made a priority. There's usually a waiting list for the PLS but, when a child's life is in question, it should take precedence over repayment of funds to state agencies.

Alabama
>Division of Child Support Activities
>Bureau of Public Assistance
>State Department of Pensions and Security
>64 North Union Street
>Montgomery, Alabama 36130
>Telephone: (205) 832-6561

Alaska
>Child Support Enforcement Agency
>Department of Revenue
>201 E. 9th Avenue, #202
>Mail Stop 01
>Anchorage, Alaska 99501
>Telephone: (907) 276-3441, Ext. 65

Arizona
>Child Support Enforcement Unit
>Department of Economic Security
>Post Office Box 6123
>Phoenix, Arizona 85005
>Telephone: (602) 255-4759

Arkansas
>Office of Child Support Enforcement
>Arkansas Social Services
>Post Office Box 3358
>Little Rock, Arkansas 72203
>Telephone: (501) 371-1614

California
>State Parent Locator
>1800 I Street
>P.O. Box 13300
>Sacramento, California 95813
>Telephone: (916) 445-6215

Colorado
Division of Child Support
Enforcement
Department of Social Services
1575 Sherman Street
Denver, Colorado 80203
Telephone: (303) 839-2422

Connecticut
Child Support Unit
Connecticut State Department
of Citizens
Social Services
110 Bartholomew Ave.
Hartford, Connecticut 06105
Telephone: (203) 566-3053

Delaware
State Parent Locator Service
Bureau of Child Support Enforcement
Department of Health & Social Services
920 Church Street
Wilmington, Delaware 19801
Telephone: (302) 571-3620

District of Columbia
Office of Paternity and Child
  Support Enforcement
Department of Human Resources
601 Indiana Avenue, NW, Room 1000
Washington, D.C. 20001
(202) 724-8811

Florida
Child Support Enforcement
Department of Health & Rehabilitation Services
1317 Winewood Boulevard
Tallahassee, Florida 32301
Telephone: (904) 488-9900

Georgia
Child Support Recovery Unit
State Department of Human Resources
618 Ponce De Leon Avenue, N.E.
Atlanta, Georgia 30308
Telephone: (404) 894-4118

Hawaii
Program Development Office
Department of Social Services and Housing
Post Office Box 339

Honolulu, Hawaii 96809
Telephone: (808) 548-5779

Idaho
Child Support Section
Department of Health and Welfare
Statehouse Mail
Boise, Idaho 83720
Telephone: (208) 384-2480

Illinois
Bureau of Resources and Support
Support Enforcement Section
Department of Public Aid
316 South 2nd Street
Springfield, Illinois 62762
Telephone: (217) 782-1383

Indiana
Child Support Division
Department of Public Welfare
141 S. Meridian St., 4th Floor
Indianapolis, Indiana 46225
Telephone: (317) 633-6906

Iowa
Child Support Recovery Unit
Iowa Department of Social Services
Hoover Building, 1st Floor
Des Moines, Iowa 50319
Telephone: (515) 281-5767

Kansas
Department of Social & Rehabilitation Services
Biddle Building, 2nd Floor
700 West 6th
Topeka, Kansas 66606
Telephone: (913) 296-4180

Kentucky
Child Support Branch
Department for Human Resources
Bureau for Social Insurance
275 E. Main St., 6th Fl. East
Frankfort, Kentucky
Telephone: (502) 564-2285

Louisiana
Office of Family Security
Health & Human Resource Admin.

P.O. Box 44065
Baton Rouge, Louisiana 70804
Attn: John Landry
Telephone: (504) 342-4780

Maine
Central Location Section
Support Enforcement Program
Department of Human Services
State House
Augusta, Maine 04333
Telephone: (207) 289-2886

Maryland
Bureau of Support Enforcement
Social Services Administration
11 South Street
Baltimore, Maryland 21202
Telephone: (301) 383-3284

Massachusetts
Child Support Enforcement Unit
Department of Public Welfare
600 Washington
Boston, Massachusetts 02111
Telephone: (617) 727-7820

Michigan
Office of Child Support
Michigan Department of Social Services
300 South Capitol Avenue, Box 30037
Lansing, Michigan 48909
Telephone: (517) 373-7570

Minnesota
Office of Child Support
Minnesota Department of Public Welfare
Centennial Office Building
St. Paul, Minnesota 55155
Telephone: (612) 296-2542

Mississippi
Child Support Enforcement Unit
Department of Public Welfare
P.O. Box 352
Jackson, Mississippi 39205
Telephone: (601) 354-0341

Missouri
Child Support Enforcement Unit
Department of Social Services

Broadway State Office Building
Jefferson City, Missouri 65101
Telephone: (314) 751-3274

Montana
Department of Revenue
Child Support Enforcement Bureau
323 Sam Mitchell Building
Helena, Montana 49601
Telephone: (406) 449-2846

Nebraska
Parent Location Specialists
Child Support Enforcement Office
301 Centennial Mall South, 5th Floor
Box 95026
Lincoln, Nebraska 68509
Telephone: (402) 471-3121 Ex. 132 & 133

Nevada
Child Support Unit
Nevada State Welfare Division
Department of Human Resources
251 Jeanell Drive
Carson City, Nevada 89710
Telephone: (702) 885-4744

New Hampshire
Central Locate Unit
Child Support Enforcement Service
Health & Welfare Bldg., Hazen Drive
Concord, New Hampshire 03301
Telephone: (603) 271-4428

New Jersey
Bureau of Child Support & Paternity Programs
Division of Public Welfare
3525 Quakerbridge Road
Trenton, New Jersey 08625
Telephone: (609) 890-9500

New Mexico
Child Support Enforcement Division
Department of Health and Social Services
Post Office Box 2348–Crown Building
Santa Fe, New Mexico 87503
Telephone: (505) 827-5591

New York
    Parent Locator Service
    Department of Social Services
    40 North Pearl Street
    Albany, New York 12243
    Telephone: (518) 474-9091

North Carolina
    Child Support Enforcement
    Division of Social Services
    Department of Human Resources
    325 North Salisbury Street
    Raleigh, North Carolina 27611
    Telephone: (919) 733-4120

North Dakota
    Child Support Enforcement Agency
    Social Service Board of N.D.
    Russel Building—Highway 83 North
    Bismarck, North Dakota 58505
    Telephone: (701) 224-3582

Ohio
    Bureau of Child Support and Fraud
    Department of Public Welfare
    State Office Tower
    30 East Broad Street
    Columbus, Ohio 43215
    Telephone: (614) 466-3234

Oklahoma
    Child Support Enforcement Unit
    Social and Rehabilitative Services
    Post Office Box 25352
    Oklahoma City, Oklahoma 73125
    Telephone: (405) 521-3641

Oregon
    Support Enforcement Division
    Department of Justice
    325 NE 13 Street, Suite 603
    Salem, Oregon 97310
    Telephone: (503) 378-5596

Pennsylvania
    Child Support Programs
    Office of Income Maintenance

Department of Public Welfare
Post Office Box 2675
Harrisburg, Pennsylvania 17120
Telephone: (717) 787-3660

Rhode Island
Family Support and Domestic Relations
Social and Rehabilitative Services
77 Dorrance Street
Providence, Rhode Island 02903
Telephone: (401) 277-2847

South Carolina
Public Assistance Division
Department of Social Services
Post Office Box 1520
Columbia, South Carolina 29202
Telephone: (803) 758-8860

South Dakota
Office of Child Support Enforcement
Richard F. Kneip Building
Illinois Street
Pierre, South Dakota 57501
Telephone: (605) 773-3641

Tennessee
Department of Human Services
111-19 7th Avenue, North
Nashville, Tennessee 37203
Telephone: (615) 741-3289

Texas
Parent Locator Service
Child Support Enforcement Branch
Department of Human Resources
John H. Reagan Building
Austin, Texas 78701
Telephone: (512) 475-7071

Utah
Parent Locator Unit
2250 S. Redwood Road
Salt Lake City, Utah 84111
Telephone: (801) 533-7695

Vermont
Support Enforcement Unit
Department of Social Welfare,

Agency of Human Services
State Office Building
Montpelier, Vermont 05602
Telephone: (802) 241-2860

Virginia
Bureau of Child Support Enforcement
Department of Welfare
8004 Franklin Farms Drive., Box K-199
Richmond, Virginia 23288
Telephone: (804) 281-9154

Washington
Locate Section
Office of Support Enforcement
Department of Social & Health Services
P.O. Box 9162-MS FU-11
Olympia, Washington 98504
Telephone: (206) 753-1429

West Virginia
Absent Parent Unit
State of West Virginia
Department of Welfare
1900 Washington Street East
Charleston, West Virginia 25305
Telephone: (304) 348-3780

Wisconsin
Bureau of Child Support
Division of Economic Assistance
18 S. Thornton Avenue, P.O. Box 8913
Madison, Wisconsin 53708
Telephone: (608) 266-0252

Wyoming
Child Support Enforcement Section
Department of Health and Social Services
State Department of Public Health and Social Services
Hathaway Building
Cheyenne, Wyoming 82001
Telephone: (307) 777-7561

The military also maintains files on their personnel; if your former spouse is in the armed forces, it's probably worth your while to contact his or her particular branch of service. In requesting information, try to include full name, social security number, rank and last known place of assignment.

For Army Personnel

For information on officers, either active or retired, contact:

Personnel Records, Division (TAGO)
Department of the Army
Washington, D.C. 20310

For information on active duty enlisted personnel, write:

U.S. Army Personnel Service Support Center
Fort Benjamin Harrison, Indiana 46249

You can also call Army World Wide Personnel Information at (512) 221-2948 or (512) 221-3315

For Navy Personnel

Requests for information on active duty personnel should be directed to:

Chief, Navy Personnel
Department of the Navy
Washington, D.C. 20370
(202) 694-2768

To locate Naval reserve personnel, write:

Commanding Officer
Naval Reserve Personnel Center
New Orleans, Louisiana 70149

For Air Force Personnel

The Air Force maintains a world wide locator at (512) 652-5774.

For Marine Personnel

Active duty Marines can be located by writing to:

Commandant of the Marine Corps (CODE MSRP-22)
Headquarters, Marine Corps
Washington, D.C. 20380

Records on retired Marine personnel can be found by writing:

Marine Corps Retired Branch, (CODE MMSR-2)
Headquarters, Marine Corps
Washington, D.C. 20380

For Coast Guard Personnel

Requests for information on active duty personnel should be directed to:

Commandant
U.S. Coast Guards (PE)
2100 2nd Street, S.W.
Washington, D.C. 20593
(202) 426-8898

To locate Coast Guard reserve personnel, write:

Commandant
U.S. Coast Guards (G-RA-2)
2100 2nd Street, S.W.
Washington, D.C. 20593

PRIVATE DETECTIVES

If you seem to be receiving little help from any of the agencies designated to assist you in finding your child, chances are you've thought about hiring a private detective. This could result in the quickest way of locating your youngster or total disaster, so be selective. Detectives run the gamut from highly reputable to those whose motives and techniques are questionable. We've heard many stories of private investigators who took the money and ran, would as soon help a child snatcher as the parent with legitimate custody, or asked for fees which were out of line with the work accomplished. Unfortunately, many people are waiting to prey upon those caught in a desperate situation.

Most detectives charge an hourly (or set) fee plus expenses, and an out-of-town search may well run into thousands of dollars. "If you've got $500, you're risking it," commented John Barker, an agent with the John T. Lynch Detective Agency. "You might spend $500 just explaining the details to a detective."[27] One Chicago father, who was reunited with his son after an exhaustive four year search covering four continents and ten trips to England, found that his expenses approximated $30,000 . . . and that was in 1976. More recently, a San Jose couple estimated the cost of tracing her daughter to Mexico at $75,000 and a San Francisco couple report an outlay of $68,000 in trying to find and regain a child abducted to Belgium. Does this mean that you can't enlist the aid of an investigator unless you've just struck oil? No, not really. A competent, ethical detective should be willing to tell you how much he or she can do for the sum you are able to spend. If it is possible to raise more money later, further work can be accomplished then. Be wary of anyone quoting a lump sum figure without agreed upon guarantees in the contract. At the outset, they cannot know how much work your case will entail.

Once the child is located, you have another decision to make: whether to take a chance on legal proceedings or to retrieve the child yourself. It is a difficult choice either way. Legal procedures might involve delay, the possibility of the child snatcher disappearing, perhaps a civil case in which the other side has a more convincing lawyer, and often fees for one or more attorneys. Reclaiming the child with professional assistance means detective fees, the possibility of breaking the law yourself, a potential for danger and, in most cases, an emotionally distressing experience for the child. If you do select this option, be forewarned. Many children cry when they see their parents even if they are happy to be back with them a few days later. Keep in mind that you don't know what your child has been told about you. Several children in this situation had thought that their mother or father was dead.

Not-so-surprisingly, some authorities recommend the latter approach. "Why go into another court if you don't have to?" asked one member of the Maryland Bar's family law section. "I don't see any point in looking for litigation in another state."[28]

While there are parents who are justifiably adverse to this type of suggestion, its pragmatism cannot be denied. Also, the trauma of a hasty retrieval must be weighed against the emotional toll taken by your child's present living conditions with the kidnapper. The decision can only be yours, for only you know the situation and people involved. Think hard, but not too long, about what would be best for you and your child. Then, if you do elect to hire a detective, interview him or her thoroughly and don't forget to trust your instincts. As a further note, if your children are found to be in a foreign country and you hire a detective to accompany you in retrieving them, make sure the investigator has researched the laws and customs of that country. You don't want to be faced with any sudden stumbling blocks that could have been avoided.

Under the category of detectives (but not necessarily one), we would like to mention another phenomenon: the professional "vigilante." Eugene Austin, originally of Foley, Missouri, claims he's no longer in the business of resnatching children, yet his former activities were among the most flamboyant of this group. "Mean Gene," as he likes to call himself, is something of a folk hero in certain circles and, limiting his services to divorced fathers for many years, boasts of 500 "recoveries." Aided and abetted by a loosely-knit underground of "Safe-Houses," Austin even carried out four of his abductions while out on bail. "His methods," recalls David I. Gilbert, the Miami prosecutor in the only case with which Austin was successfully charged (for throwing mace in a mother's face), "were more than inappropriate. They were unconstitutional, criminal and downright violent."[29] Yet, for the most part, Austin's "reconnoitering" of children went largely ignored by the legal establishment—which, incidentally, can't seem to match his location record either, despite vast government resources and budgets certainly amounting to more than $350 plus expenses. It's something to think about, isn't it?

Also included under the concept of "vigilantes" is an even more frightening aspect. A small number of fathers' groups have managed to retreat from the law entirely and, instead of seeking legal redress in the courts, are advocating the stealing of children as a solution to their problems. We are not talking about "recovery" now, but actual child-stealing. In his book, *Stolen Children*, John Gill interviews Hiram Belforte of Texas who speaks of "a highly militant organization" which "is into child stealing as well as hiding guys. It may have killed four people (while taking kids), but I don't know about them directly."[30]

As an augmentation or viable alternative to the hiring of private investigators, several groups are experimenting with sending out newsletters to schools and pediatricians across the country. Packets contain children's photographs, brief descriptions, information regarding possible whereabouts, and an address or phone number to contact in case a child is located. Thus far, there have been both successes and problems with this approach. However, if funding can be acquired, it offers real hope.

THE PHYSICAL AND EMOTIONAL ASPECTS OF CHILD-STEALING

In 1974, Congress passed the Child Abuse Prevention and Treatment Act, Public Law 93-247. It defines child abuse and neglect as the following:

> The physical or mental injury, sexual abuse, negligent treatment, or maltreatment of a child under the age of eighteen by a person who is responsible for the child's welfare under circumstances which indicate that the child's health or welfare is harmed or threatened thereby.

We consider child-stealing a form of child abuse. Not only are the children uprooted from their stable environment under traumatic conditions, but they are frequently moved from state to state, told the other parent is dead or doesn't want them, and, in the tragic case of more than one child, killed during an abduction. An eight-year-old, when asked how he viewed the situation, replied, "How would you like to be a ping-pong ball?"

Arnold Miller, who estimates that 90% of all returned children eventually require psychiatric treatment, states, "Many people think that because the child is with the parent he's safe and o.k.

That is a myth. We have too many stories of children who were taken at gun point, children who were wrapped in blankets to muffle their screams (or) thrown into trunks of cars until they were safely across the state line."[31]

For example, Jerome Yanoff sent his reluctant 12-year-old to visit with his mother who had joined the Hare Krishna sect. When he flew to California to bring the boy home, he found him with shaved head, sarong and mantra pouch. The father and son clung to each other before ten group members threw Yanoff to the ground and disappeared with his son. Although Jerome Yanoff has custody, he is unable to locate his son—and, somewhere, David Yanoff is the unwilling captive of a cult.

Another child, taken from San Francisco to Florida, was told that her mother had been killed by drug dealers and, if she didn't flee with her father, they would kill her too. At 4-years-old, she wasn't in a position to question the statement and, when she was reunited with her mother six months later, she was a very paranoid little girl.

"The harm done to children by their experience can hardly be overestimated," according to the Commissioners on Uniform State Laws. "(A child) . . . may well be crippled for life, to his own lasting detriment and the detriment of society."[32]

In March 1977, newly-elected Los Angeles County District Attorney John Van de Kamp held a public hearing on child-stealing. John Gill stated, "Parents who had recovered their children gave the most interesting testimony. They spoke of how their children were afraid to be alone now, locked themselves into rooms, clung to relatives. Some needed therapy and had trouble in the classroom. They were tormented by anger or they withdrew from other people. They feared the darkness, ran from strangers, felt unwanted and became edgy at the sound of doorbells and telephones . . . All the parents, as well as child psychologists, agreed that snatching was a form of child abuse."[33]

Dr. Philip Weeks of Pasadena, a psychologist at Children's Hospital, voiced the opinion that child-stealing is "one of the most subtle and brutal forms of child abuse. The child is made to feel helpless, he has no choice in what is happening to him. Stealing a child is making the child a pawn of adult problems, acting out through the children."[34]

One of the most chilling cases presented at the hearing was that of Alfred Meyers. At the time of testimony, his son and daughter had been gone nearly five years.

Mr. Meyer's daughter, Lisa, was born on February 14, 1964. Shortly thereafter, his wife Socorro died in a bus crash and, in 1969, he married Kathleen Shipman. Their son, William, was born in May of 1971.

The following year, upon learning that Meyers had filed for divorce, Mrs. Meyers abducted *both* children and ran off with a man who had recently been committed to a state hospital for child molesting.

After a four year search, Alfred Meyers located his children in Tacoma, Washington, only to learn that his daughter had had an abortion by the age of ten. To top it off, the couple, now married, were filing for adoption of Lisa. Washington officials told Meyers that the pending adoption was their only matter of legal concern!

Surely, if appropriate action is to be taken in real life situations, the assumption that "biological parent" is the same as "nurturing parent" must be dispensed with once and for all. In fact, we are amazed to hear this type of equation so often used by officials of government agencies who, at the very least, should be cognizant of statistics put out by the government. According to the Department of Health and Human Resources, more young children die of parental maltreatment and neglect than from any other cause.[35] Further, a booklet written by the California Attorney General's office called *Child Abuse: The Problem of The Abused and Neglected Child*, contains a direct challenge to the traditional policy of laissez-faire in family matters. It states: "Child-rearing has traditionally been a private family matter. However, times have changed and a growing awareness of the incidence and degree of child mistreatment is altering the public's attitude. There is increasing concern that children must be protected from harm regardless of the origin of the harm. The right of the child to enjoy a healthy, satisfying life should be granted equal status with parental rights."[36] The fact that this is a trailblazing booklet, yet still places parental "rights" on an equal basis with a child's welfare, demonstrates the deep-rootedness of the child as property concept. And what can you do with your own property? Why just about anything. In his testimony to Congress at the 1980 hearings on child-stealing, Arnold Miller stressed that using a gun in an abduction, throwing children into speeding cars or having violent confrontations in public places such as shopping centers are not the acts of mature, loving parents concerned with the welfare of their children. To illustrate his point, he cited the case of Stacey Duncan and Christine Sutherland.

On May 8, 1979, 7-year-old Stacey Duncan was snatched by her father. It took sixteen days to obtain a California felony warrant, and three months before her mother was notified that a little girl fitting Stacey's description had been located—in a Mississippi hospital. "Nineteen hours later, I was crying and praying for my daughter who was in an intensive care unit," her mother states. "She had been severely beaten and burned about her tiny body. She had to have a portion of her brain removed to save her life. The doctors still had no hope that she'd live. She had been in a coma but started coming out of it when I arrived. After a second brain surgery and tracheotomy, Stacey is now off the critical list and in a hospital at home in California...." A subsequent newspaper article reported that "Blows to Stacey caused extensive brain damage, requiring surgery that doctors believe will severely impair her intellect, sight and muscular control for the rest of her life."[37]

In the case of Christine Sutherland, the *Casper Star-Tribune*, December 3, 1979, reported: "The body of Christine Sutherland was found floating in the North Platte River near Glenrock early Sunday morning. The 9-year-old girl was abducted from her Casper home early September 16th. Several duck hunters spotted the clothed body floating in the river just below the Dave Johnson power plant. When Christine disappeared, a child-stealing warrant was issued."[38]

Although the primary victims of this crime are the children, the heartbreak and anguish of their helpless parents cannot be ignored. "It's like death, only worse," says Karen Yoder of Fort Wayne, Indiana. "When a child dies, you can deal with it and it's over. This way it leaves you with a void there's no way to fill. There are so many questions you have no answers for."[39]

"The loss is too terrifying for most people to comprehend," adds Jack Gorey, whose stepson was taken to Europe. "... (I feel that) my family has been raped."[40]

Although many legal agencies profess to believe that a parent kidnaps his or her child out of love, other professionals who have delved into the problem generally take a different stance. "The abducting parent is using the child to provoke, agitate and attack the opposing parent," states Peg Edwards, a Santa Ana social worker.[41] A 17-year-old former victim agrees. "Stealing a child is not love," he stresses, "and don't think kids, even young ones, don't know when someone loves them."

Francis Muller, a California father with custody of his daughter, Allison, and son, Andrew, can also testify to the hostility behind the act. When his ex-wife absconded with the children to Scotland, he received a phone call telling him that now he could suffer for the rest of his life.

Other parental kidnappers have displayed little interest in the children prior to abduction, have used them as hostages to try and force reconciliation with an unwilling spouse, or have abandoned them once they were snatched. Five-year-old Monica Rios is a good case in point. Her father stole when she was 13 months old, and reportedly took her to a festival where she became "lost" in the crowd. Four years later, her mother traced the youngster to a small Mexican suburb where she was living with Rios' relatives. Meanwhile, he continued to reside in Northern California, not far from his ex-wife's home but over a thousand miles from where his daughter had been dropped off. Obviously, Monica was not the issue.

At an emotional meeting of victimized Long Island parents, gruesome stories of spiteful child snatching were exchanged. One woman related that her husband stole their son and later sent black carnations for Mother's Day. Another received letters from her children saying they no longer cared for her. And Valerie Edwards of East Meadow, whose son was returned three months later, told the group, "My husband actually had some woman write me a Christmas card that said, 'thanks for the greatest Christmas present in my life. Your son.' "[42]

The trauma of a child snatch can be more than legal and emotional for many parents—it often has physical manifestations as well. In the Bay Area support group alone, one parent developed bleeding ulcers, another has been on physical disability since his children were taken, a third has been in and out of hospitals for stomach problems, and a young woman with a past history of heart disease suddenly found her condition worsened after the abduction and had to undergo open heart surgery. Is there any correlation? We think so. Stress can be the causative factor or contributing agent to a host of illnesses, and can anything be more stressful than not knowing where your children are?

The sad case of a Marin mother inevitably comes to mind when we correlate child-stealing and physical deterioration. After she discovered that her eight-year-old daughter had been taken by her ex-husband and niece, she found herself unable to swallow food. An attractive woman but pathetically frail now, she has been hospitalized several times for intravenous feedings and is becoming progressively more susceptible to a variety of minor and serious diseases. "How can I eat," she asks tearfully, "when every time I go to take a bite, I wonder if my daughter is going hungry?"

If parental victims are prime candidates for stress-related illnesses, they are also prone toward outward behavior which, under the circumstances, can only be termed "normal" desperation.

"What advice can you give me?" asked a custodial mother whose ex-husband has made several thwarted attempts to take the children. "I sit in front of my son's school two and a half hours a day, four days a week to protect him a little. But now my younger son will be starting nursery school in the fall and I don't know how I can physically be in two different places at the same time."

Or there's the case of Regina Samuels. With no clue as to where her child might have been taken, she and her present husband, Norman, consulted an occultist. Following the advice given, they left California to go on a wild goose chase through uncharted areas of Northern Arizona. "We went through places where the roads had no names and even where there were no roads," Mr. Samuels recalls.[43]

Francis Muller, another example, turned a blind eye toward danger in order to see his two children. With the aid of a detective, he located his youngsters in Glascow and decided to visit. In retrospect, it appears that the presence of the detective kept things on an even keel because his ex-wife's relatives looked "ready to pounce." Despite the evident risk, Muller was so anxious to talk with his children again that he returned to the apartment alone. This time, he states, his ex-wife's brothers held him prisoner for five hours.

"I was deathly tired and fearing for my life," says the San Anselmo father. "When I found a chance to escape, I bolted out the door . . . and I never felt safe until I got to Heathrow Airport in London."[44]

The obvious humane question is: why should this type of desperation be necessary? Why should the Samuels be driving through the backwoods, Francis Muller risking his life, and a Marin mother wasting away? Part of the answer lies in the examples of Stacey Duncan and Christine Sutherland. For unless our law enforcement agencies start making a concerted effort to find these children and bring them home again, it is conservatively estimated that 80% of their parents will never know where their children are, how they are living or, in fact, if they are even alive. Isn't it time we gave a damn?

Appendix A
THE PARENTAL KIDNAPPING PREVENTION ACT OF 1980
PUBLIC LAW 96-611

Elsewhere in the book, we have referred to the new federal child-stealing law. Now, what does it mean to you? Basically, three things. We've included the entire relevant text, however, so that you will have easy access to it in case your lawyer, district attorney or other authorized persons wish to see it or you find it necessary to show it to them.

The three principal parts to the law are:

(1) It establishes "full faith and credit" between states regarding custody orders. One state will be required to honor another state's previous custody determination, which should cut down on the practice of parental kidnappers taking youngsters to new states and being granted custody there.

However, it must be noted that this section of P.L. 96-611, based on the Uniform Child Custody Jurisdiction Act, does contain some significant loopholes. For instance, a court may refuse to honor a previous custody decision if (a) the child snatcher and child have resided in the new state for six consecutive months or more; (b) the child and at least one contestant have a "significant connection" with the new state; (c) there is a question of child abuse involved; or (d) the court believes it is "in the best interests of the child" that the new state assume jurisdiction.

Needless-to-say, while the intent of the Full Faith and Credit

Clause will influence many judicial decisions, a great amount of discretion is still left to the individual judge.

(2) The new law allows use of the Federal Parent Locator, per agreement with your state, in finding the most recent address and place of employment of the missing parent. Until now, this type of service was restricted to the location of absent parents owing child support.

(3) In states where child-stealing is a felony, Unlawful Flight to Avoid Prosecution (UFAP) Warrants can be issued on child snatchers who have fled the state. These warrants are important because, theoretically at least, they may lead to FBI assistance. The Parental Kidnapping Prevention Act also includes a "watchdog" measure on FBI compliance. The Attorney General of the United States is to submit a report to Congress 120 days after its enactment, and every six months thereafter for the first three years, describing the activities of the Justice Department in conforming to their duties in cases of child-stealing. Unfortunately, in order to benefit from this new area opened to victimized parents and their children, you must be living in a state which has felony provisions for child-stealing, the child snatcher must have fled the state and the district attorney's office must request assistance and be willing to extradite. More important (see October 21, 1981 *Congressional Record* reprint in Appendix C) the Justice Department must be made to honor the intent of the new law!

While the Parental Kidnapping Prevention Act reflects progress in recognition of the problem, it is not enough. If we are serious about wishing to put an end to child-stealing, we need serious laws.

On March 16, 1982, fifteen months after the enactment of P.L. 96-611, one of the authors received two phone calls from parents whose children had been snatched prior to divorce proceedings (no custody order; no assistance) and the other author found the following article in her morning newspaper.

Mineola, N.Y.
Arthur Liebling, who abducted his 8-year-old daughter and lived with her in Costa Rica for two years, was per-

mitted to plead guilty yesterday to a reduced charge of disorderly conduct.

Nassau County Court Judge Paul Lawrence then freed Leibling on the condition that he stay out of trouble with the law for one year.[45]

We rest our case.

Text of the Parental Kidnaping Prevention Act of 1980
Public Law 96-611
(Relevant Text: Sections 7-10)

FINDINGS AND PURPOSES

Sec. 7.(a) The Congress finds that—

(1) there is a large and growing number of cases annually involving disputes between persons claiming rights of custody and visitation of children under the laws, and in the courts, of different States, the District of Columbia, the Commonwealth of Puerto Rico, and the territories and possessions of the United States;

(2) the laws and practices by which the courts of those jurisdictions determine their jurisdiction to decide such disputes, and the effect to be given the decisions of such disputes by the courts of other jurisdictions, are often inconsistent and conflicting;

(3) those characteristics of the law and practice in such cases, along with the limits imposed by a Federal system on the authority of each such jurisdiction to conduct investigations and take other actions outside its own boundaries, contribute to a tendency of parties involved in such disputes to frequently resort to the seizure, restraint, concealment, and interstate transportation of children, the disregard of court orders, excessive relitigation of cases, obtaining of conflicting orders by the courts of various jurisdictions, and interstate travel and communication that is so expensive and time consuming as to disrupt their occupations and commercial activities; and

(4) among the results of those conditions and activities are the failure of the courts of such jurisdictions to give full faith and credit to the judicial proceedings of the other jurisdictions, the deprivation of rights of liberty and property without due process of law, burdens on commerce among such jurisdictions and with foreign nations, and harm to the welfare of children and their parents and other custodians.

(b) For those reasons it is necessary to establish a national system for locating parents and children who travel from one such jurisdiction to another and are concealed in connection with such disputes, and to establish national standards under which the courts of such jurisdictions will determine their jurisdiction to decide such disputes and the effect to be given by each such jurisdiction to such decisions by the courts of other such jurisdictions.

(c) The general purposes of sections 6 to 10 of this Act are to—

(1) promote cooperation between State courts to the end that a

determination of custody and visitation is rendered in the State which can best decide the case in the interest of the child;

(2) promote and expand the exchange of information and other forms of mutual assistance between States which are concerned with the same child;

(3) facilitate the enforcement of custody and visitation decrees of sister States;

(4) discourage continuing interstate controversies over child custody in the interest of greater stability of home environment and of secure family relationships for the child;

(5) avoid jurisdictional competition and conflict between State courts in matters of child custody and visitation which have in the past resulted in the shifting of children from State to State with harmful effects on their well-being; and

(6) deter interstate abductions and other unilateral removals of children undertaken to obtain custody and visitation awards.

FULL FAITH AND CREDIT GIVEN TO CHILD CUSTODY DETERMINATIONS

Sec. 8. (a) Chapter 115 of title 28, United States Code, is amended by adding immediately after section 1738 the following new section:

"§1738A. Full faith and credit given to child custody determinations

"(a) The appropriate authorities of every State shall enforce according to its terms, and shall not modify except as provided in subsection (f) of this section, any child custody determination made consistently with the provisions of this section by a court of another State.

"(b) As used in this section, the term—

"(1) 'child' means a person under the age of eighteen;

"(2) 'contestant' means a person, including a parent, who claims a right to custody or visitation of a child;

"(3) 'custody determination' means a judgment, decree, or other order of a court providing for the custody or visitation of a child, and includes permanent and temporary orders, and initial orders and modifications;

"(4) 'home State' means the State in which, immediately preceding the time involved, the child lived with his parents, a parent, or a person acting as parent, for at least six consecutive months, and in the case of a child less than six months old, the State in which the child lived from birth with any of such persons. Periods of temporary absence of any of such persons are counted as part of the six-month or other period;

"(5) 'modification' and 'modify' refer to a custody determination which modifies, replaces, supersedes, or otherwise is made subsequent to, a prior custody determination concerning the same child, whether made by the same court or not;

"(6) 'person acting as a parent' means a person, other than a parent, who has physical custody of a child and who has either been awarded custody by a court or claims a right to custody;

"(7) 'physical custody' means actual possession and control of a child; and

"(8) 'State' means a State of the United States, the District of Columbia, the Commonwealth of Puerto Rico, or a territory or possession of the United States.

"(c) A child custody determination made by a court of a State is consistent with the provisions of this section only if—
　"(1) such court has jurisdiction under the law of such State; and
　"(2) one of the following conditions is met:
　　"(A) such State (i) is the home State of the child on the date of the commencement of the proceeding, or (ii) had been the child's home State within six months before the date of the commencement of the proceeding and the child is absent from such State because of his removal or retention by a contestant or for other reasons, and a contestant continues to live in such State;
　　"(B)(i) it appears that no other State would have jurisdiction under subparagraph (A), and (ii) it is in the best interest of the child that a court of such State assume jurisdiction because (I) the child and his parents, or the child and at least one contestant, have a significant connection with such State other than mere physical presence in such State, and (II) there is available in such State substantial evidence concerning the child's present or future care, protection, training, and personal relationships;
　　"(C) the child is physically present in such State and (i) the child has been abandoned, or (ii) it is necessary in an emergency to protect the child because he has been subjected to or threatened with mistreatment or abuse;
　　"(D)(i) it appears that no other State would have jurisdiction under subparagraph (A), (B), (C), or (E), or another State has declined to exercise jurisdiction on the ground that the State whose jurisdiction is in issue is the more appropriate forum to determine the custody of the child, and (ii) it is in the best interest of the child that such court assume jurisdiction; or
　　"(E) the court has continuing jurisdiction pursuant to subsection (d) of this section.
"(d) The jurisdiction of a court of a State which has made a child custody determination consistently with the provisions of this section continues as long as the requirement of subsection (c)(1) of this section continues to be met and such State remains the residence of the child or of any contestant.
"(e) Before a child custody determination is made, reasonable notice and opportunity to be heard shall be given to the contestants, any parent whose parental rights have not been previously terminated and any person who has physical custody of a child.
"(f) A court of a State may modify a determination of the custody of the same child made by a court of another State, if—
　"(1) it has jurisdiction to make such a child custody determination; and
　"(2) the court of the other State no longer has jurisdiction, or it has declined to exercise such jurisdiction to modify such determination.
"(g) A court of a State shall not exercise jurisdiction in any proceeding for a custody determination commenced during the pendency of a proceeding in a court of another State where such court of that other State is exercising jurisdiction consistently with the provisions of this section to make a custody determination."
(b) The table of sections at the beginning of chapter 115 of title 28, United States Code, is amended by inserting after the item relating to section 1738 the following new item:

"1738A. Full faith and credit given to child custody determinations.".

(c) In furtherance of the purposes of section 1738A of title 28, United States Code, as added by subsection (a) of this section, State courts are encouraged to—
    (1) afford priority to proceedings for custody determinations; and
    (2) award to the person entitled to custody or visitation pursuant to a custody determination which is consistent with the provisions of such section 1738A, necessary travel expenses, attorneys' fees, costs of private investigations, witness fees or expenses, and other expenses incurred in connection with such custody determination in any case in which—
        (A) a contestant has, without the consent of the person entitled to custody or visitation pursuant to a custody determination which is consistent with the provisions of such section 1738A, (i) wrongfully removed the child from the physical custody of such person, or (ii) wrongfully retained the child after a visit or other temporary relinquishment of physical custody; or
        (B) the court determines it is appropriate.

USE OF FEDERAL PARENT LOCATOR SERVICE IN CONNECTION WITH THE ENFORCEMENT OR DETERMINATION OF CHILD CUSTODY AND IN CASES OF PARENTAL KIDNAPING OF A CHILD

Sec. 9. (a) Section 454 of the Social Security Act is amended—
    (1) by striking out "and" at the end of paragraph (15);
    (2) by striking out the period at the end of paragraph (16) and inserting in lieu thereof "; and"; and
    (3) by inserting after paragraph (16) the following new paragraph:
"(17) in the case of a State which has in effect an agreement with the Secretary entered into pursuant to section 463 for the use of the Parent Locator Service established under section 453, to accept and transmit to the Secretary requests for information authorized under the provisions of the agreement to be furnished by such Service to authorized persons, and to impose and collect (in accordance with regulations of the Secretary) a fee sufficient to cover the costs to the State and to the Secretary incurred by reason of such requests, to transmit to the Secretary from time to time (in accordance with such regulations) so much of the fees collected as are attributable to such costs to the Secretary so incurred, and during the period that such agreement is in effect, otherwise to comply with such agreement and regulations of the Secretary with respect thereto."

(b) Part D of title IV of the Social Security Act is amended by adding at the end thereof the following new section:

"USE OF FEDERAL PARENT LOCATOR SERVICE IN CONNECTION WITH THE ENFORCEMENT OR DETERMINATION OF CHILD CUSTODY AND IN CASES OF PARENTAL KIDNAPING OF A CHILD

"Sec. 463. (a) The Secretary shall enter into an agreement with any State which is able and willing to do so, under which the services of the Parent Locator Service established under section 453 shall be made available to such State for the purpose of determining the whereabouts of any absent parent or child when such information is to be used to locate such parent or child for the purpose of—

"(1) enforcing any State or Federal law with respect to the unlawful taking or restraint of a child; or

"(2) making or enforcing a child custody determination.

"(b) An agreement entered into under this section shall provide that the State agency described in section 454 will, under procedures prescribed by the Secretary in regulations, receive and transmit to the Secretary requests from authorized persons for information as to (or useful in determining) the whereabouts of any absent parent or child when such information is to be used to locate such parent or child for the purpose of—

"(1) enforcing any State or Federal law with respect to the unlawful taking or restraint of a child; or

"(2) making or enforcing a child custody determination.

"(c) Information authorized to be provided by the Secretary under this section shall be subject to the same conditions with respect to disclosure as information authorized to be provided under section 453, and a request for information by the Secretary under this section shall be considered to be a request for information under section 453 which is authorized to be provided under such section. Only information as to the most recent address and place of employment of any absent parent or child shall be provided under this section.

"(d) For purposes of this section—

"(1) the term of 'custody determination' means a judgment, decree, or other order of a court providing for custody or visitation of a child, and includes permanent and temporary orders, and initial orders and modification;

"(2) the term 'authorized person' means—

"(A) any agent or attorney of any State having an agreement under this section, who has the duty or authority under the law of such State to enforce a child custody determination;

"(B) any court having jurisdiction to make or enforce such a child custody determination, or any agent of such court; and

"(C) any agent or attorney of the United States, or of a State having an agreement under this section, who has the duty or authority to investigate, enforce, or bring a prosecution with respect to the unlawful taking or restraint of a child."

(c) Section 455(a) of such Act is amended by adding after paragraph (3) the following: "except that no amount shall be paid to any State on account of amounts expended to carry out an agreement which it has entered into pursuant to section 463."

(d) No agreement entered into under section 463 of the Social Security Act shall become effective before the date on which section 1738A of title 28, United States Code (as added by this title) becomes effective.

PARENTAL KIDNAPING

Sec. 10. (a) In view of the findings of the Congress and the purposes of sections 6 to 10 of this Act set forth in section 302, the Congress hereby expressly declares its intent that section 1073 of title 18, United States Code, apply to cases involving parental kidnaping and interstate or international flight to avoid prosecution under applicable State felony statutes.

(b) The Attorney General of the United States, not later than 120 days after the date of the enactment of this section (and once every 6 months during the 3-year period following such 120-day period), shall submit a report to the Congress with respect to steps taken to comply with the intent of the Congress set forth in subsection (a). Each such report shall include—

    (1) data relating to the number of applications for complaints under section 1073 of title 18, United States Code, in cases involving parental kidnaping;

    (2) data relating to the number of complaints issued in such cases; and

    (3) such other information as may assist in describing the activities of the Department of Justice in conformance with such intent.

The Fugitive Felon Act

§1073. **Flight to avoid prosecution or giving testimony.**

Whoever moves or travels in interstate or foreign commerce with intent either (1) to avoid prosecution, or custody or confinement after conviction, under the laws of the place from which he flees, for a crime, or an attempt to commit a crime, punishable by death or which is a felony under the laws of the place from which the fugitive flees, or which, in the case of New Jersey, is a high misdemeanor under the laws of said State, or (2) to avoid giving testimony in any criminal proceedings in such place in which the commission of an offense punishable by death or which is a felony under the laws of such place, or which in the case of New Jersey, is a high misdemeanor under the laws of said State is charged, or (3) to avoid service of, or contempt proceedings for alleged disobedience of, lawful process requiring attendance and the giving of testimony or the production of documentary evidence before an agency of a State empowered by the law of such State to conduct investigations of alleged criminal activities, shall be fined not more than $5,000 or imprisoned not more than five years, or both.

Violations of this section may be prosecuted only in the Federal judicial district in which the original crime was alleged to have been committed, or in which the person was held in custody or confinement, or in which an avoidance of service of process or a contempt referred to in clause (3) of the first paragraph of this section is alleged to have been committed, and only upon formal approval in writing by the Attorney General or an Assistant Attorney General of the United States, which function of approving prosecutions may not be delegated.

June 25, 1948, c. 645, 62 Stat. 755; Apr. 6, 1956, c. 177, § 1, 70 Stat. 100; Oct. 4, 1961, Pub. L. 87-368, 75 Stat. 795; Oct. 15, 1970, Pub. L. 91-452, Title III § 302, 84 Stat. 932.

Appendix B
Current Child Stealing Laws
A State by State Listing

Criminal laws addressing the problem of child-stealing, generally termed "Interference with Custody," vary from state to state. Some treat the act as a felony, others a misdemeanor, and several make the distinction between removing the child from the state (a felony) or remaining within its borders (a misdemeanor). A few states have no specific custodial interference laws but a child snatcher may be charged under related statutes; and, at present, the District of Columbia, New Hampshire, West Virginia and the Virgin Islands do not address the problem at all. Even in states which consider the matter felonious, there is usually the presumption of a custody order which has been violated—thus making parental kidnapping legal in more instances than not.

For your convenience, we've included a state-by-state survey of current child-stealing laws and would like to thank Patricia Hoff, Director of the American Bar Association's Child Custody Project, for making the information available to us. Please note that other statutes directed at kidnapping are listed; however, only those which may apply to parental kidnapping are included in full.

ALABAMA

Applicable Laws (effective May 17, 1978):
§ 13A-6-41   Unlawful imprisonment in the first degree; misdemeanor.
§ 13A-6-42   Kidnapping in the first degree; felony.
§ 13A-6-45   Interference with custody; Class A misdemeanor

§ 13A-6-45.   Interference with custody.
(a) A person commits the crime of interference with custody if he knowingly takes or entices:
(1) Any child under the age of 18 from the lawful custody of its parent, guardian or other lawful custodian, or
(2) Any committed person from the lawful custody of its parent, guardian or other lawful custodian. "Committed person" means, in addition to anyone committed under judicial warrant, any neglected, dependent or delinquent child, mentally defective or insane person or any other incompetent person entrusted to another's custody by authority of law.
(b) A person does not commit a crime under this section if:
(1) The actor is a relative of the child, and
(2) The actor's sole purpose is to assume lawful control of the child. The burden of injecting the issue is on the defendant, but this does not shift the burden of proof.
(c) Interference with custody is a Class A misdemeanor. (Acts 1977, No. 607, § 2215.)

§ 13A-6-40.   Definitions.
(3) RELATIVE. A parent or stepparent, ancestor, sibling, uncle or other lawful custodian, including an adoptive relative of the same degree through marriage or adoption. (Acts 1977, No. 607, § 2201.)

§ 13A-6-45   Commentary.
Section 13A-6-45 is adapted from Michigan Revised Criminal Code § 2215; New York Revised Penal Law § 135.45; and New Jersey Penal Code § 2C:13-4. Here the main interest protected is not freedom from physical danger, since that is covered elsewhere, but the **protection of parental custody against unlawful interruption. The proposal renders inapplicable the kidnapping sections to nonserious cases that involve an unlawful taking of a child under 18 years of age from his natural parent or guardian or a committed person from the custodian or institution to whom he has been entrusted**, e.g., inmate from Boys Industrial School, Alabama Hospital for Insane, Alabama Department of Pensions and Security, etc. Any resulting harm or unlawful restraint is covered by assaults and related offenses, §§ 13A-6-20 through 13A-6-25, unlawful imprisonment, §§ 13A-6-41 and 13A-6-42 or sexual offenses, Chapter 6, Article 4. Of course, an abduction would come under one of the kidnapping offenses, §§ 13A-6-43 and 13A-6-44. There may be some overlap with the provisions of Chapter 10, Article 2, on escapes, but this does not seem serious. Cf. 13A-10-45, giving criminal assistance to escapee. (Underscoring added for emphasis.)

The age of 18 is used in this section as it is the growing normal limit of parental authority in custody matters, since this is the age at which most youths become independent or seek self-support and enter higher education, the military service, marriage, etc.

Special provision is made to prevent abuse in certain custody battles between estranged parents. Under § 13A-6-45(b), the offense of custodial interference cannot be committed if the actor is a "relative," as defined in § 13A-6-40(3), and the actor's sole purpose was to assume lawful control or custody. This is the counterpart to § 13A-6-42(b), a similar exception based on custody wrangles.

ALASKA

Applicable laws (effective January 1, 1980)
§ 11.41.300 (a)(1) and (a)(2) Kidnapping; unclassified felony (Note affirmative defense to prosecution under § 11.41.300 (a)(2)(A) if dependant is relative of child under 18 and restrains the victim by secreting and holding him in a place where not likely to be found in order to assume his custody).
§ 11.41.320 Custodial Interference in the first degree. Class C Felony.
§ 11.41.330 Custodial Interference in the second degree; Class A misdemeanor.

Sec. 11.41.320. Custodial interference in the first degree. (a) A person commits the crime of custodial interference in the first degree if he violates §330 of this chapter and causes the victim to be removed from the state.
(b) Custodial interference in the first degree is a class C felony, (§ 3 ch 166 SLA 1978).
Sec. 11.41.330. Custodial interference in the second degree. (a) A person commits the crime of custodial interference in the second degree if, being a relative of a child under 18 years of age or a relative of an incompetent person and knowing that he has no legal right to do so, he takes, entices, or keeps that child or incompetent person from his lawful custodian with intent to hold him for a protracted period.
(b) Custodial interference in the second degree is a class A misdemeanor (§ 3 ch 166 SLA 1978).
Sec. 11.41.370. Definitions.
(1) "lawful custodian" means a parent, guardian, or other person responsible by authority of law for the care, custody, or control of another;
(2) "relative" means a parent, stepparent, ancestor, descendant, sibling, uncle, or aunt, including a relative of the same degree through marriage or adoption;

ARIZONA

Applicable laws (effective October 1, 1978)
§ 13-1302   Custodial Interference; class 6 Felony unless child is returned unharmed prior to arrest, in which case it is a class 1 misdemeanor.
§ 13-1303   Unlawful Imprisonment; felony; may be reduced to misdemeanor as in § 13-1302; defense that defendant was relative of person restrained and sole intent was to assume lawful

custody and restraint was accomplished without physical force.
§ 13-1304 Kidnapping; felony; may be reduced to lesser felony.

§ 13-1302 **Custodial interference; classification.**
A. A person commits custodial interference if, knowing or having reason to know that he has no legal right to do so, such person knowingly takes, entices or keeps from lawful custody any child less than eighteen years of age or incompetent, entrusted by authority of law to the custody of another person or institution.
B. Custodial interference is a class 6 felony unless the person taken from lawful custody is returned voluntarily by the defendant without physical injury prior to the arrest in which case it is a class 1 misdemeanor.
Added Laws 1977, Ch.142, § 62, eff. Oct. 1, 1978.

ARKANSAS

Applicable laws (effective January 1, 1976)
§ 41-1702 Kidnapping; felony; may be reduced to lesser felony.
§ 41-1703 False imprisonment in the first degree; felony.
§ 41-1704 False imprisonment in the second degree; misdemeanor.
§ 41-2411 Interference with custody; Class D felony if child removed from state; otherwise Class A misdemeanor.

§ 41-2411. **Interference with custody.**—(1) A person commits the offense of interference with custody if, knowing that he has no lawful right to do so, he takes, entices, or keeps any person entrusted by court decree to the custody of another person or to an institution from the lawful custody of that person or institution.
(2) Interference with custody is a class D felony if such person taken, enticed, or kept without the state of Arkansas. Otherwise, it is a class A misdemeanor. (Acts 1975, No. 280, § 2411.)

Commentary

§ 41-2411. The Commission was not completely without sympathy for those who engage in such conduct and recognized that affection for the child is often the motivating factor for the offense, not greed or hostility. However, criminal sanctions are warranted if for no other purpose than to facilitate the enforcement of child custody orders. The Commission was persuaded for two reasons that felony liability is appropriate when the child is taken out of the state. First, as in the case of nonsupport, this should enhance the chances of extraditing the offender. Secondly, the person who removes the child entrusted to the care of another from this state has, in effect, nullified a decision of an Arkansas court, since the custody question must be relitigated in the courts of the jurisdiction to which the offender flees.

§ 41-1704. Section 1704, by its terms, applies to the parent who takes a child entrusted to the custody of the other parent. The Commission intended, however, that the criminal law be used in custody disputes, if at all, only pursuant to section 2411, defining the offense of interference with custody. The possibility of prosecution under section 1704 in such a situation should not create problems. Except where the child is taken outside the state, both offenses carry the same penalty. Furthermore, section

105(1)(d) prevents conviction of both false imprisonment and interference with custody as a result of the same conduct.

CALIFORNIA

Applicable laws (Title 8, Penal Code, effective July 1, 1977).
§ 207 Kidnapping; felony.
§ 236, 237 False imprisonment; misdemeanor; if effected by violence, menace, fraud, or deceit it is a felony.
§ 278 Child abduction; by a person having no right of custody; felony or misdemeanor.
§ 278.5 Wrongful removal, retention or concealment of a child in violation of custody or visitation rights; misdemeanor.

§ 278 Definition; punishment; return; expenses.
(a) Every person not having a right of custody who maliciously takes, entices away, detains or conceals any minor child with intent to detain or conceal such child from a parent, or guardian or other person having the lawful charge of such child shall be punished by imprisonment in the state prison for two, three or four years, a fine of not more than ten thousand dollars ($10,000), or both.

(b) A child who has been detained or concealed in violation of subdivision (a) shall be returned to the person having lawful charge of the child. Any expenses incurred in returning the child shall be reimbursed as provided in Section 4605 of the Civil Code. Such costs shall be assessed against any defendant convicted of a violation of this section. Added by Stats 1976, c. 1399, § 10. Amended by Stats, 1976, c. 1399, § 10.5, operative July 1, 1977.

§ 278.5. Violation of custody decree; punishment; return; expenses.
(a) Every person who in violation of a custody decree takes, retains after the expiration of a visitation period, or conceals the child from his legal custodian, and every person who has custody of a child pursuant to an order, judgment or decree of any court which grants another person rights to custody or visitation of such child, and who detains or conceals such child with the intent to deprive the other person of such right to custody or visitation shall be punished by imprisonment in the state prison for a period of not more than one year and one day or by imprisonment in a county jail for a period of not more than one year, a fine of not more than one thousand dollars ($1,000), or both.

(b) A child who has been detained or concealed in violation of subdivision (a) shall be returned to the person having lawful charge of the child. Any expenses incurred in returning the child shall be reimbursed as provided in Section 4605 of the Civil Code. Such costs shall be assessed against any defendant convicted of a violation of this section. (Added by Stats. 1976, c. 1399, § 11.)

COLORADO

Applicable laws (1973 Colorado Revised Statutes; 1978 Replacement Volume)
§ 18-3-301 First degree kidnapping; felony.
§ 18-3-302 Second degree kidnapping; felony; not applicable to person

who takes, entices, or decoys his own child with intent to keep or conceal child from his guardian; exclusion may **not** apply to parent's agent.
§ 18-3-303 False imprisonment; misdemeanor.
§ 18-3-304 Violation of custody; class 5 felony; affirmative defense that offender believed conduct was necessary to preserve safety or child over 14 was taken away at his own instigation or without enticement.

§ 18-3-304 Violation of custody. (1) Any person, including a natural or foster parent, who, knowing that he has no privilege to do so or heedless in that regard, takes or entices any child under the age of eighteen years from the custody of his parents, guardian, or other lawful custodian commits a class 5 felony.

(2) Any parent or other person who violates an order of any district or juvenile court of this state, granting the custody of a child under the age of eighteen years to any person, agency, or institution, with the intent to deprive the lawful custodian of the custody of a child under the age of eighteen years, commits a class 5 felony.

(3) It shall be an affirmative defense either that the offender reasonably believed that his conduct was necessary to preserve the child from danger to his welfare, or that the child, being at the time more than fourteen years old, was taken away at his own instigation without enticement and without purpose to commit a criminal offense with or against the child.
Source: R & RE.L.71, p. 422. § 1: C.R.S. 1963. § 40-3-304.

CONNECTICUT

Applicable laws (effective October 1, 1971)
§ 53a-92 Kidnapping first degree; felony.
§ 53-94 Kidnapping second degree; felony.
§ 53a-95 Unlawful restraint first degree; felony.
§ 53a-96 Unlawful restraint second degree; misdemeanor.
§ 53a-97 Custodial interference, first degree, Class D felony.
§ 53a-98 Custodial interference, second degree; Class A misdemeanor.

§ 53a-97 **Custodial interference in the first degree: Class D felony**
(a) A person is guilty of custodial interference in the first degree when he commits the crime of custodial interference in the second degree as defined in section 53a-98:

(1) Under the circumstances which expose the child or person taken or enticed from lawful custody to a risk that his safety will be endangered or his health materially impaired; or

(2) if he takes or entices the child or person out of this state.

(b) Custodial interference in the first degree is a class D felony. (1969, P.A. 828, § 99, eff. Oct. 1. 1971.)

§ 53a-98. **Custodial interference in the second degree: Class A misdemeanor.**

(a) A person is guilty of custodial interference in the second degree when:

(1) Being a relative of a child who is less than sixteen years old and intending to hold such child permanently or for a protracted period and

knowing that he has no legal right to do so, he takes or entices such child from his lawful custodian; or

(2) knowing that he has no legal right to do so, he takes or entices from lawful custody any incompetent person or any person entrusted by authority of law to the custody of another person or institution.

(b) Custodial interference in the second degree is a class A misdemeanor. (1969, P.A. 828, § 100, eff. Oct. 1, 1971.)

Commission Comment—1971

The offenses labeled "custodial interference" are for the purpose of specifically dealing with situations involving intentional and knowing violations of custody of children under sixteen and incompetent persons or persons the legal custody of whom has been given to some other person or institution. The first degree offense deals with the situation where the victim's safety or health was endangered, or where the child is taken out of the state.

Notes of Decisions

Where requisitioning warrant for extradition was issued on information based upon affidavits charging abduction of child by parent, but affidavit failed to prove absence of consent, by complaining mother of allegedly abducted child, affidavits failed to establish commission of crime charged and warrant would not support extradition. People ex rel. Kuzner v. Police Dept. of City of New York (Sup. 1950) 102 N.Y.S.2d 614.

Connecticut statute defining crime of abduction of child by parent as occurring when parent shall decoy or forcibly take such child is violated only where consent is in fact lacking and possession of child was taken by decoy or by force. 1d.

DELAWARE

Applicable laws (1979 Replacement Volume Title 11, Delaware Code Annotated)
§ 784   Affirmative defense to unlawful imprisonment and kidnapping if accused was relative of victim and sole purpose was to assume custody. Liability, if any, governed by § 785.
§ 785   Interference with custody; Class A misdemeanor; Family Court Jurisdiction over such violation.

§ 784. Defense to unlawful imprisonment and kidnapping.
In any prosecution for unlawful imprisonment or kidnapping, it is an affirmative defense that the accused was a relative of the victim, and his sole purpose was to assume custody of the victim. In that case, the liability of the accused, if any, is governed by § 785 of this title, and he may be convicted under § 785 when indicted for unlawful imprisonment or kidnapping. (11 Del. C. 1953, § 784 58 Del. Laws, c.497, § 1.)

§ 785. Interference with custody; class A misdemeanor.
A person is guilty of interference with custody when:

(1) Being a relative of a child less than 16 years old, intending to hold the child permanently or for a prolonged period and knowing that he has no legal right to do so, he takes or entices the child from his lawful custodian; or

(2) Knowing that he has no legal right to do so, he takes or entices from lawful custody any incompetent person or other person entrusted by authority of law to the custody of another person or an institution. Interference with custody is a class A misdemeanor. (11 Del. C. 1953, § 785; 58 Del. Laws, c. 497, § 1.)

Cross reference. As to exclusive original criminal jurisdiction of Family Court for violation of this section, see § 922 of Title 10.

DISTRICT OF COLUMBIA

Applicable laws (D.C. Code Encyclopedia, Annotated, 1978)
§ 22-2101 Kidnapping; felony; parents expressly excluded.
No specific child abduction or restraint law.

§ 22-2101. Definition and penalty—Conspiracy
Whoever shall be guilty of, or of aiding or abetting in, seizing, confining, inveigling, enticing, decoying, kidnaping, abducting, concealing, or carrying away any individual by any means whatsoever, and holding or detaining, or with the intent to hold or detain, such individual for ransom or reward or otherwise, except **in the case of a minor by a parent thereof,** shall, upon conviction thereof, be punished by imprisonment for life or for such term as the court in its discretion may determine. This section shall be held to have been violated if either the seizing, confining, inveigling, enticing, decoying, kidnaping, abducting, concealing, carrying away, holding, or detaining occurs in the District of Columbia. If two or more individuals enter into any agreement or conspiracy to do any act or acts which would constitute a violation of the provisions of this section, and one or more of such individuals do any act to effect the object of such agreement or conspiracy, each such individual shall be deemed to have violated the provisions of this section. Mar. 3, 1901, ch. 854, § 812, 31 Stat. 1322; Feb. 18, 1933, ch. 103, 47 Stat. 858; Nov. 8, 1965, Pub. L. 89-347, § 3, 79 Stat. 1307.

Encyclopedic Commentary

Abduction or kidnaping by parent. The purpose of the amendment of this section by the Act of November 8, 1965, in, among other things making this section inapplicable to cases involving the taking of a minor child by one of the parents of such child, was to bring this section into closer conformity with the Federal statute on kidnaping, 18 U.S.C.A. §§ 1201, 1202.

FLORIDA

Applicable laws (Title 44, effective October 1, 1975)
§ 787.01 Kidnapping; felony. Includes confinement of child under 13 if without consent of his parent or legal guardian and if other elements of offense are present.
§ 787.02 False imprisonment, felony. Comment, above, also applies.
§ 787.03 Interference with custody; first degree misdemeanor; applies to children 17 and under; defense that defendant reasonably believed action was neccessary to protect child from danger or child was taken away at his own instigation without enticement.

§ 787.04 Felony in third degree to remove children from state or to conceal child contrary to court order, to remove child during pending custody proceeding of which he has notice, or to fail to produce child in the court pursuant to court order.

787.03 Interference with custody.
(1) Whoever, without lawful authority, knowingly or recklessly takes or entices any child 17 years of age or under or any incompetent person from the custody of his parent, guardian, or other lawful custodian commits the offense of interference with custody and shall be guilty of a misdemeanor of the first degree, punishable as provided in § 775.082, or § 775-083 or § 775.084.
(2) It is a defense that:
(a) The defendant reasonably believes that his action was necessary to preserve the child or the incompetent person from danger to his welfare.
(b) The child or incompetent person was taken away at his own instigation without enticement and without purpose to commit a criminal offense with or against the child (or incompetent person).
(3) Proof that a child was 17 years (of age) or under creates the presumption that the defendant knew the child's age or acted in reckless disregard thereof.

787.04 Felony to remove children from state or to conceal children contrary to court order.
(1) It is unlawful for any person, in violation of a court order, to lead, take, entice, or remove a child beyond the limits of this state, or to conceal the location of a child, with personal knowledge of the order.
(2) It is unlawful for any person, with criminal intent, to lead, take, entice, or remove a child beyond the limits of this state, or to conceal the location of a child, during the pendency of any action or proceeding affecting custody of the child, after having received notice as required by law of the pendency of the action or proceeding, without the permission of the court in which the action or proceeding is pending.
(3) It is unlawful for any person, who has carried beyond the limits of this state any child whose custody is involved in any action or proceeding pending in this state, pursuant to the order of the court in which the action or proceeding is pending, or pursuant to the permission of the court, thereafter, to fail to produce the child in the court or deliver the child to the person designated by the court.
(4) Any person convicted of a violation of this law shall be guilty of a felony of the third degree, punishable as provided in § 775.082, § 775.083, or § 775.084.
Amended by Laws 1980, c.80.102, § 1, eff. Oct. 1, 1980.

GEORGIA

Applicable laws (Effective July 1, 1978)
§ 26-1308 False imprisonment; felony.
§ 26-1311 Kidnapping; felony; applies to a person over 17 when he forcibly, maliciously, or fradulently leads, takes, or carries away, or decoys or entices away, any child under 16 against the will of the child's parents or other person having lawful custody.
§ 26-1312 Interference with custody; felony to remove from state; other-

wise misdemeanor. Crime includes bringing child into state without consent of lawful custodian.

26-1312 Interference with custody.
(a) A person commits interference with custody when he:
(1) Knowingly or recklessly takes or entices any committed person away from lawful custody when he is not privileged to do so.
(2) Knowingly brings into this State a committed person who has been committed to the custody of another person who is a resident of another state or nation, without the consent of the person with legal custody.
(3) Knowingly harbors any committed person who has absconded.
(b)(1) Except as provided in paragraph (2) of this subsection, any person violating the provisions of this section is guilty of a misdemeanor and upon conviction shall be punished as for a misdemeanor.
(2) A person convicted of interference with custody by taking a committed person beyond the limits of this State shall be punished by imprisonment for not less than one nor more than five years.
(c) As used in this section:
(1) Person includes a parent of a committed person.
(2) "Committed person" means, in addition to anyone committed or whose custody is awarded under judicial warrant or court order, any orphan, neglected, or delinquent child, mentally defective or insane person, or other dependent or incompetent person entrusted to another's custody by authority of law.
(Acts 1968, pp. 1249, 1283; 1978, p. 1420, eff. July 1, 1978.)
Note:
Acts 1978, p. 1420, entirely superseded the former section.

HAWAII

Applicable laws.
§ 707-721 Unlawful imprisonment in first degree; felony.
§ 707-722 Unlawful imprisonment in second degree; misdemeanor; affirmative defense that (a) the person restrained was less than eighteen years old, (b) the defendant was a relative of the victim, and (c) his sole purpose was to assume custody over the victim. In that case, the liability of the defendant, if any, is governed by (section 707.723) section____ and he may be convicted under (section 707-723) section____ although charged under this section.

§ 707-723 Custodial Interference; misdemeanor; (effective 1972); repealed, 1981.
§ 707-   Custodial Interference in the first degree; Class C felony; effective June 17, 1981.
§ 707-   Custodial Interference in the second degree; misdemeanor; effective June 17, 1981.

§ 707-   Custodial interference in the first degree. (1) A person commits the offense of custodial interference in the first degree if: (a) Being a relative of the person, he knowingly takes or entices a person less than eighteen years old from any other person who has a right to custody pursuant to a court order, judgment, or decree; and (b) He removes himself and the person less than eighteen years old from the State. (2) Custodial interference in the first degree is a class C felony.

§ 707- **Custodial interference in the second degree.** (1) A person commits the offense of custodial interference in the second degree if: (a) He knowingly takes or entices a person less than eighteen years old from his lawful custodian, knowing that he has no right to do so; or (b) He knowingly takes or entices from lawful custody any incompetent person, or other person entrusted by authority of law to the custody of another person or an institution. (2) Custodial interference in the second degree is a misdemeanor.

EXCERPT FROM BILL REPORT

The purpose of this bill is to create a new crime of custodial interference in the first degree which makes it a class C felony for a relative of a child to knowingly take the child away from a person who has the right to the child's custody based on a court order, and to leave the State with the child. Presently, custodial interference is a misdemeanor under Section 707-723. Further, the bill retains the present language in Section 707-723, but reclassifies the offense as custodial interference in the second degree.

Since child snatching is presently not a felony crime in Hawaii, a state fugitive felony warrant cannot be issued, and the federal criminal provisions under this Act (i.e. the Parental Kidnapping Prevention Act of 1980) would not be applicable. The change in classification of custodial interference in the first degree to a class C felony will enable the issuance of a state fugitive felony warrant, whereupon the FBI could be called on to track down the child snatching parent.

This felony provision is intended to cover a specific, limited situation in which the following three elements must be present: (1) The snatcher must be a relative; (2) The child must be taken in violation of a court order; and (3) the person and the child must leave the state. This statute would not, for example, cover the situation where a child is sent to the mainland to visit with the non-custodial parent who lives there, and the parent decides not to return the child to the parent in Hawaii. The bill is aimed at deterring, overcoming, and prosecuting the most overt and blatant type of child snatching situation.

This misdemeanor provision (custodial interference in the second degree) is intended to cover situations where a relative or non-relative of a child takes and conceals a child in violation of a court order, oftentimes not leaving the State.

IDAHO

Applicable laws.
§ 18-4501   Kidnapping; felony; applies to every person who willfully . . .
—2. Leads, takes, entices away or detains a child under the age of sixteen years, with intent to keep or conceal it from its parent, guardian or other person having lawful care or control thereof, or with intent to steal any article upon the person of the child; or,
§ 18-1502   Kidnapping, first degree; for ransom; felony.
§ 18-4503   Kidnapping, second degree; not for ransom; felony.

No specific child abduction or restraint law.

ILLINOIS

Applicable laws, Title 38.
§ 10-1 Kidnapping; felony; confinement of child under 13 considered against his will if without consent of his parent or legal guardian.
§ 10-2 Aggravated kidnapping; felony; if violates § 10-1 and . . . (2) takes as his victim a child under 13.
§ 10-3 Unlawful restraint; felony.
§ 10-5 Child Abduction; Class 4 felony; removal of child from state, or concealing child within state with intent to violate court order. Three affirmative defenses set forth. (Effective August 22, 1978).

§ 10-5 Child Abduction.
(a) Definitions. (1) "Court order," as used in this Section, means an order of an Illinois court having jurisdiction over the person of a child; (2) "Child," as used in Subsections (b)(1) and (b)(2) means a person under the age of 14 at the time of violation of this Section is alleged to have occurred.
(b) Offense. A person commits child abduction when, with intent to violate a court order awarding custody of a child to another, he or she:
(1) removes the child from Illinois without the consent of the person lawfully having custody of the child; or
(2) conceals the child within Illinois.
(c) Affirmative Defenses. It shall be an affirmative defense that:
(1) at the time the court order awarding custody of the child to another was entered, the defendant had custody of the child pursuant to a valid order of a court having jurisdiction over the person of that child; or
(2) after the court order awarding custody of the child to another was entered, the defendant obtained custody of the child pursuant to the order of a court which had jurisdiction over the person of that child, and which had been advised of the prior court order, and which court specifically found the prior court order to be invalid as a matter of law; or
(3) within 72 hours of the alleged violation of this Section, the defendant submitted the child to the jurisdiction of an Illinois court.
(d) Limitations. Nothing contained in this Section shall be construed to limit the court's civil contempt power.
(e) Penalty. Child abduction is a Class 4 felony.

Laws 1961, p. 1983, § 10-5, added by P.A. 80-1393, § 1, eff. August 22, 1978.

Section 2 of P.A. 80-1393, approved August 22, 1978, provided: "This amendatory Act takes effect upon its becoming a law."

INDIANA

Applicable laws.
§ 35-42-3-2 Kidnapping; felony.
§ 35-42-3-3 Criminal confinement; felony; includes knowing or intentional removal of a person under 18 to a place outside Indiana when the removal violates a child custody order of a court. However, return of child to custodial parent within 7 days of removal may be considered as mitigating circumstance. (Effective 1979).

35-42-3-3 Criminal confinement.
Sec. 3. (a) A person who knowingly or intentionally:
(1) confines another person without his consent;
(2) removes another person, by fraud, enticement, force, or threat of force, from one place to another, or
(3) removes another person, who is under eighteen (18) years of age, to a place outside Indiana when the removal violates a child custody order of a court:
commits criminal confinement, a Class D felony. However, the offense is a Class C felony if the child is not his child, and a Class B felony if it is committed while armed with a deadly weapon or results in serious bodily injury to another person.

(b) With respect to the violation of subdivision (a)(3) of this section, it may be considered as a mitigating circumstance if the accused person returned the other person to the custodial parent within seven (7) days of the removal. As amended by Acts 1979, P.L. 299, SEC. 1.
1979 Amendment. Acts 1979, P.L. 299, Sec. 1, rewrote the section.

IOWA

Applicable laws (Effective January 1, 1978)
§ 710-2 Kidnapping in first degree; felony.
§ 710-3 Kidnapping in second degree; felony.
§ 710-4 Kidnapping in third degree; felony.
§ 710-5 Child stealing; Class C felony.
§ 710-6 Violating custodial order; Class D felony when removed from state; serious misdemeanor in described cases.
§ 710-7 False imprisonment; serious misdemeanor.

710.5 Child stealing.
A person commits a class C felony when, knowing that he or she has no authority to do so, forcibly or fraudulently takes, decoys, or entices away any child with intent to detain or conceal such child from its parents or guardian, or other persons or institution having the lawful custody of such child, unless the person is a relative of such child, and the person's sole purpose is to assume custody of such child.
Acts 1976 (66 G.A.) ch.1245, ch. 1, § 1005, eff. Jan. 1, 1978.

710.6 Violating custodial order.
Any relative of a child who, acting in violation of any order of any court which fixes, permanently or temporarily, the custody of such child in another, takes and removes such child from the state, and conceals the child's whereabouts without the consent of the person having lawful custody, commits a class D felony.

Any parent of a child living apart from the other parent who takes and conceals that child from another within the state in violation of a custodial order and without the other parent's consent shall be guilty of a serious misdemeanor.

Any parent of a child living apart from the other parent who conceals that child in violation of a court order granting visitation rights and without the other parent's consent, shall be guilty of a serious misdemeanor.
Acts 1976 (66 G.A.) ch. 1245, ch. 1, § 1006, eff. Jan. 1, 1978. Amended by Acts 1978 (67 G.A.) ch. 1029. § 49.

KANSAS

Applicable laws (Effective July 1, 1970)
§ 21-3420   Kidnapping; felony
§ 21-3421   Aggravated kidnapping; felony.
§ 21-3422   Interference with parental custody; Class A misdemeanor.
§ 21-3422(a)   Aggravated interference with parental custody; Class E felony; (Effective July 1, 1978).
§ 21-3424   Unlawful restraint.

21-3422. Interference with parental custody.
Interference with parental custody is leading, taking, carrying away, decoying or enticing away any child under the age of fourteen (14) years, with the intent to detain or conceal such child from its parent, guardian, or other person having the lawful charge of such child.

Interference with parental custody is a class A misdemeanor. (L.1969, ch. 180, § 21-3422 July 1, 1970.)

21-2322a. Aggravated interference with parental custody.
(1) Aggravated interference with parental custody is hiring someone to commit the crime of interference with parental custody, as defined by K.S.A. 21-3422, or commiting interference with parental custody, as defined by K.S.A. 21-3422, when done with the intent to deprive of custody such child's parent, guardian, or other person having the lawful charge or custody of such child, and when:

(a) Committed by a person who has previously been convicted of interference with parental custody, as defined by K.S.A. 21-3422;

(b) committed by a person for hire;

(c) committed by a person who takes the child outside the state without the consent of either the person having custody or the court;

(d) committed by a person who, after lawfully taking the child outside the state while exercising visitation rights, refuses to return the child at the expiration of such rights; or

(e) committed by a person who, at the expiration of visitation rights outside the state, refuses to return or impedes the return of such child.

Aggravated interference with parental custody is a class E felony.

(2) This section shall be a part of and supplemental to the Kansas criminal code. History: L.1978, ch. 121, § 1; July 1.

KENTUCKY

Applicable laws (Effective 1980)
§ 509-060   Defense to any unlawful imprisonment or kidnapping charge that defendant was a relative of victim and his sole purpose was to assume custody of victim.
§ 509-070   Custodial interference; Class D felony or Class A misdemeanor if defendant is relative of victim.

509.070. Custodial interference.
(1) A person is guilty of custodial interference when, knowing that he has no legal right to do so, he takes, entices or keeps from lawful custody any mentally disabled or other person entrusted by authority of law to the custody of another person or to an institution.

(2) It is a defense to custodial interference that the person taken from

lawful custody was returned by the defendant voluntarily and before arrest or the issuance of a warrant for arrest.

(3) Custodial interference is a Class D felony unless the person taken from lawful custody is returned voluntarily by the defendant or unless the defendant is a relative of the victim in which case it is a Class A misdemeanor. (Enact. Acts 1974, ch. 406, § 79.), amended 1980.

LOUISIANA

Applicable laws
§ 14.45   Simple kidnapping; felony. Includes parent taking child in violation of custody order without consent and with intent to defeat the jurisdiction of court that issued decree.
§ 14.46   False imprisonment; misdemeanor.

§ 14.45   Simple kidnapping.
A. Simple kidnapping is: (4) The intentional taking, enticing or decoying away and removing from the state, by any person to whom custody has been awarded by any court of competent jurisdiction of any state, without the consent of the legal custodian, with intent to defeat the jurisdiction of the said court over the custody of the child.
(5) The taking, enticing or decoying away and removing from the state, by any person, other than the parent, of a child temporarily placed in his custody by any court of competent jurisdiction in the state, with intent to defeat the jurisdiction of said court over the custody of the child.
B. Whoever commits the crime of simple kidnapping shall be fined not more than two thousand dollars or be imprisoned, with or without hard labor, for not more than five years, or both.
Amended by Acts 1962, No. 344, § 1; Acts 1966, No. 253, § 1.

s45.1   Interference with the custody of a child; misdemeanor.
Section 1. Section 45.1 of Title 14 of the Louisiana Revised Statutes of 1950 is hereby enacted to read as follows:
s45.1.   Interference with the custody of a child
A. Interference with the custody of a child is the intentional taking, enticing or decoying away of a minor child by a parent not having a right of custody, with intent to detain or conceal such child from a parent having a right of custody pursuant to a court order or from person entrusted with the care of the child by a parent having custody pursuant to a court order. It shall be an affirmative defense that the offender reasonably believed his actions were necessary to protect the welfare of the child.
B. Whoever commits the crime of interference with the custody of a child shall be fined not more than five hundred dollars or be imprisoned for not more than six months, or both. Costs of returning a child to the jurisdiction of the court shall be assessed against any defendant convicted of a violation of this Section, as court costs as provided by the Louisiana Code of Criminal Procedure.
Section 2. If any provision or item of this Act or the application thereof is held invalid, such invalidity shall not affect other provisions, items, or applications of this Act which can be given effect without the invalid provisions, items, or applications, and to this end the provisions of this Act are hereby declared severable.
Section 3. All laws or parts of laws in conflict herewith are hereby repealed.

MAINE

Applicable laws (effective 1979)
§ 17A-301   Kidnapping; Class A crime. Defense that person restrained is the child of the actor.
§ 17A-302   Criminal restraint; Class D crime. Defense that the actor is the parent of the person taken, retained, enticed or restrained.
§ 17A-303   Criminal restraint by parent; Class E crime (apparently equivalent to misdemeanor).

§ 17A-303   Criminal restraint by parent.
1. A person is guilty of criminal restraint by parent if, being the parent of a child under the age of 16, he takes, retains or entices the child from the custody of his other parent, guardian or other lawful custodian, knowing he has no legal right to do so and with the intent to remove the child from the State or to secrete the child and hold him in a place where he is not likely to be found.

2. Consent by the person taken, enticed or retained is not a defense under this section.

3. A law enforcement officer shall not be held liable for taking physical custody of a child whom he reasonably believes has been taken, retained or enticed in violation of this section and for delivering the child to a person whom he reasonably believes is the child's lawful custodian or to any other suitable person.

4. A law enforcement officer may arrest without a warrant any person who he has probable cause to believe has violated or is violating this section.

5. Criminal restraint by parent is a Class E crime.
Added by 1979, c. 512, § 26.

MARYLAND

Applicable laws (effective July 1, 1978)
Art. 27, § 337   Kidnapping; felony. Specifically exempts parents.
Art. 27, § 2A   Child Abduction; misdemeanor.

§ 2A. Child abduction.
(a) "Lawful custodian" defined. As used in this section, "lawful custodian" means a person authorized, either alone or together with another person or persons, to have custody and exercise control over a child less than 12 years of age at the time and place of an act to which any provision of this section is, or may be alleged to be, applicable. The term shall include any person so authorized:

(1) By an order of a court of competent jurisdiction of this State.

(2) By an order of a court of competent jurisdiction of another state, territory, or the District of Columbia. However, when there has been a designation of a lawful custodian by an order of a court of this State and there appears to be a conflict between that order and a custody order issued by the court of another state or jurisdiction qualifying some other person as the custodian of the child, the "lawful custodian" is the person appointed by order of a court of this State unless the order of the other state or jurisdiction:

(i) Is later in date than the order of a court of this State; and
(ii) Was issued in proceedings in which the person appointed by a custody order of a court of this State either consented to the custody order entered by the court of the other state or jurisdiction, or participated therein personally as a party.

(b) Meaning of "relative." As used in this section, "relative" means a parent, other ancestor, brother, sister, uncle, or aunt, or one who has at some prior time been a lawful custodian.

(c) Prohibited acts. A relative, who is aware that another person is a lawful custodian of a child, may not:

(1) Abduct, take, or carry away a child under 12 years of age from the lawful custodian;

(2) Detain a child under 12 years of age away from the lawful custodian for more than 48 hours after return is demanded by the lawful custodian;

(3) Harbor or secrete a child under 12 years of age knowing that the physical custody of the child has been obtained or retained in violation of this section; or

(4) Act as an accessory to any of the actions forbidden in this section.

(d) Penalty. A person convicted of violating any provision of this section is guilty of a misdemeanor; and upon conviction, shall be imprisoned for a period not exceeding 30 days, or fined a sum not exceeding $250, or both.

(e) Determination constituting defense. If the court determines that the abducting, detaining, or secreting of a child by a relative was done at a time or times when to do otherwise would have resulted in a clear and present danger to the health, safety, or welfare of the child, and if, within 96 hours of such abducting, detaining, or secreting, the relative submits a petition to a court of competent jurisdiction within this State explaining the circumstances and seeking to revise, amend, or clarify the existing custody order, then this determination shall be a complete defense to any action brought pursuant to this section. (1978, ch. 435.)

MASSACHUSETTS

Applicable laws

265 § 26   Kidnapping; felony. The provisions shall not apply to the parent of a child under eighteen years of age who takes custody of such child unless such parent acts in violation of any court order or decree relating to the adoption or custody of such child. (Effective 1971)

265 § 26A   Custodial Interference by Relatives; misdemeanor unless child exposed to danger, in which case it is a felony.

265 § 26A Custodial Interference by Relatives.

Whoever, being a relative of a child less than eighteen years old, without lawful authority, holds or intends to hold such a child permanently or for a protracted period, or takes or entices such a child from his lawful custodian, or takes or entices from lawful custody any incompetent person or other person entrusted by authority of law to the custody of another person or institution shall be punished by imprisonment in the house of correction for not more than one year or by a fine of up to one thousand dollars, or both. Whoever commits any offense described in this section under circumstances which expose the person taken or enticed from lawful custody to a risk which endangers his safety shall be punished by a fine of not more than five thousand dollars, or by imprisonment in the state prison for not more than five years, or by both such fine and imprisonment. (1979, 465, § 2, approved Aug. 9, 1979, effective 90 days thereafter.)

MICHIGAN

Applicable laws.
§ 750-349 (§ 28-581) Kidnapping; felony.
§ 750-350 (§ 28-582) Enticing away, etc., child under 14; felony.

750.350. Enticing away, etc., Child under 14 years of age
Any person who shall maliciously, forcibly or fraudulently lead, take or carry away, or decoy or entice away, any child under the age of 14 years, with intent to detain or conceal such child from its parent or guardian, or from the person or persons who have lawfully adopted said child or from any other person having the lawful charge of said child, shall be guilty of a felony, punishable by imprisonment in the state prison for life or any term of years. In case such child shall have been adopted by a person or persons other than its parents, in accordance with the statute providing for such adoption, then this section shall apply as well to such taking, carrying, decoying or enticing away of such child, by its father or mother, as by any other person.

MINNESOTA

Applicable laws.
§ 609.25   Kidnapping; felony. Commentary indicates the legislative intent is to distinguish parental from other kidnapping; seems this statute would not be applied to parents.
§ 609.26   Obtaining or retaining a child; misdemeanor; (effective May 30, 1979).

Be it enacted by the Legislature of the State of Minnesota:
  Section 1. Minnesota Statutes 1978, Section 609-26, is amended to read 609.26. Obtaining or retaining a child.
  Subdivision 1. Whoever intentionally takes, detains or fails to return his own child under the age of 18 years in violation of an existing court order which grants another person rights of custody may be sentenced as provided in subdivision 5.
  Subd. 2. Whoever detains or fails to return a child under the age of 18 years knowing that the physical custody of the child has been obtained or retained by another in violation of subdivision 1 may be sentenced as provided in subdivision 5.
  Subd. 3. A person who violates this section may be prosecuted and tried either in the county in which the child was taken, concealed or detained or in the county of lawful residence of the child.
  Subd. 4. A child who has been obtained or retained in violation of this section shall be returned to the person having lawful custody of the child. In addition to any sentence imposed, the court may assess any expense incurred in returning the child against any person convicted of violating this section.

Subd. 5. Whoever violates this section may be sentenced as follows:
(1) To imprisonment for not more than 90 days or to payment of a fine of not more than $500, or both, if he voluntarily returns the child within 14 days after he takes, detains or fails to return the child in violation of this section; or
(2) Otherwise to imprisonment for not more than one year and one day or to payment of a fine of $1,000, or both.
Sec. 2. Effective date. This act is effective on the day following final enactment and applies to all crimes committed on or after that date.
Approved May 29, 1979.

MISSISSIPPI

Applicable laws.
§ 97-3-53 Kidnapping; felony; includes forcibly seizing, inveigling, or kidnapping of child under 10 without lawful authority and secretly confining child against the will of the parents or guardian or person having lawful custody.
§ 97-5-5 Enticing child under 14 for concealment, prostitution or marriage; misdemeanor or felony.
§ 97-3-53 Kidnapping—capital punishment authorized.

Any person who shall without lawful authority forcibly seize and confine any other person or shall inveigle or kidnap any other person with intent to cause such person to be secretly confined or imprisoned against his or her will, or shall without lawful authority **forcibly seize, inveigle or kidnap any child under the age of ten (10) years and secretly confine such child against the will of the parents or guardian or person having the lawful custody of such child** shall, upon conviction, be imprisoned for life in the state penitentiary if the punishment is so fixed by the jury in its verdict. If the jury fails to agree on fixing the penalty at imprisonment for life the court shall fix the penalty at not less than one (1) year nor more than thirty (30) years in the state penitentiary.

This section shall not be held to repeal, modify or amend any other criminal statute of this state.

SOURCES: Laws, 1974, ch. 576, § 3, eff. from and after passage (approved April 23, 1974).

§ 97-5-5 **Enticing child for concealment, prostitution or marriage.**
Every person, who shall maliciously, wilfully, or fraudulently lead, take, carry away, decoy or entice away, any child under the age of fourteen years, with intent to detain or conceal such child from its parents, guardian, or other person having lawful charge of such child, or for the purpose of prostitution, concubinage, or marriage, shall, on conviction, be imprisoned in the penitentiary not exceeding ten years, or imprisoned in the county jail not more than one year, or fined not more than one thousand dollars, or both.

MISSOURI

Applicable laws (Effective January 1, 1979).
§ 565.110 Kidnapping; felony.

The Child Snatchers 199

§ 565.120 Felonious restraint.
§ 565.130 False imprisonment; in state, misdemeanor; out-of-state; felony.
§ 565.140 Defenses to false imprisonment for parents and relatives.
§ 565.150 Interference with custody; in-state—Class A misdemeanor; if child removed from state, it is a Class D felony.

565.140. Defenses to false imprisonment.
1. A person does not commit false imprisonment under section 565.130 if the person restrained is a child under the age of seventeen and
 (1) A parent, guardian or other person responsible for the general supervision of the child's welfare has consented to the restraint; or
 (2) The actor is a relative of the child; and
 (a) The actor's sole purpose is to assume control of the child; and
 (b) The child is not taken out of the state of Missouri.
2. For the purpose of this section, "relative" means a parent or stepparent, ancestor, sibling, uncle or aunt, including an adoptive relative of the same degree through marriage or adoption.
3. The defendant shall have the burden of injecting the issue of a defense under this section.
L.1977, S.B.No.60, § 1, eff. Jan. 1, 1979.

565.150. Interference with custody.
1. A person commits the crime of interference with custody if, knowing that he has no legal right to do so, he takes or entices from lawful custody any person entrusted by order of a court to the custody of another person or institution.
2. Interference with custody is a class A misdemeanor unless the person taken or enticed away from legal custody is removed from this state, in which case it is a class D felony.
L.1977, S.B.No.60, § 1, eff. Jan. 1, 1979.

MONTANA

Applicable laws. (Montana Code Annotated)
§ 45-5-301 Unlawful restraint; misdemeanor.
§ 45-5-302 Kidnapping; felony.
§ 45-5-303 Aggravated kidnapping; felony.
§ 45-5-304 Custodial interference; felony. Person who returns child within specified periods does not commit offense. Effective 1979.)

45-5-304. Custodial interference. (1) A person commits the offense of custodial interference if, knowing that he has no legal right to do so, he takes, entices, or withholds from lawful custody any child, incompetent person, or other person entrusted by authority of law to the custody of another person or institution.
(2) A person convicted of the offense of custodial interference shall be imprisoned in the state prison for any term not to exceed 10 years.
(3) A person who has not left the state does not commit an offense under this section if he voluntarily returns such person to lawful custody prior to arraignment. A person who has left the state does not commit an offense under this section if he voluntarily returns such person to lawful custody prior to arrest.

History: En. 94-5-305 by Sec. 1, Ch. 513, L.1973; R.C.M. 1947, 94-5-305; and. Sec. 1, Ch. 274, L.1979.

Commission Comment.
Violation of lawful custody, especially of children, requires special legislation notwithstanding its similarity in some respects to kidnaping. The interest protected is not freedom from physical danger or terrorization by abduction, since that is adequately covered by sections 94-5-302 and 94-5-303, but rather the maintenance of parental custody against all unlawful interruption, even when the child is a willing, undeceived participant in the attack on the parental interest. The problem is further distinguishable from kidnapping by the fact that the offender will often be a parent or other person favorably disposed toward the child. One should be especially cautious in providing penal sanctions applicable to estranged parents struggling over the custody of their children, since such situations are better regulated by custody orders enforced through contempt proceedings. Despite these distinctive aspects of childstealing and the existence of special provisions on the subject in most jurisdictions, the problem is frequently covered by kidnaping and the penalties and exceptions do not adequately reflect the special circumstances.

NEBRASKA

Applicable laws.
§ 28-313 Kidnapping; felony.
§ 28-314 False imprisonment, first degree; felony.
§ 28-315 False imprisonment, second degree; misdemeanor.
§ 28-316 Violation of custody; Class II misdemeanor unless violation contravenes court award of custody in which case it is a Class IV felony. (Effective January 1, 1979.)

28-316. Violation of custody; penalty. (1) Any person, including a natural or foster parent, who, knowing that he has no legal right to do so or, heedless in that regard, takes or entices any child under the age of eighteen years from the custody of its parent having legal custody, guardian, or other lawful custodian commits the offense of violation of custody.

(2) Except as provided in subsection (3) of this section, violation of custody is a Class II misdemeanor.

(3) Violation of custody in contravention of an order of any district or juvenile court of this state granting the custody of a child under the age of eighteen years to any person, agency, or institution, with the intent to deprive the lawful custodian of the custody of such child, is a Class IV felony.
Source: Laws 1977, LB 38, § 31.
Operative date January 1, 1979.

NEVADA

Applicable laws.
§ 200.310, 320, 330 Kidnapping, felony; includes every person who leads, takes, entices, or carries away or detains any minor with the intent to keep, imprison, or confine

§ 200.340 it from its parents, guardians, or any other person having lawful custody of such minor.
§ 200.340 Penalty for aiding and abeting.
§ 200.350 Consent of person under 18 not a defense.
§ 200.359 Detention, concealment, removal of child from person having lawful custody in violation of court order a misdemeanor.

200.359. Detention, concealment, removal of child from person having lawful custody in violation of court order a misdemeanor. Every person having a limited right of custody to a child pursuant to an order, judgment or decree of any court, or any parent having no right of custody to the child, who in violation of an order, judgment or decree of any court detains, conceals or removes such child from a parent, guardian or other person having lawful custody is guilty of a misdemeanor.
(Added to NRS by 1975, 1397)

Signed by the Governor May 22, 1981, Chpt. 305 NRS
SECTION 1. NRS 200.359 is hereby amended to read as follows:
200.359. 1. Except as provided in subsection 3, every person having a limited right of custody to a child pursuant to an order, judgment or decree of any court, including a judgment or decree which grants another person rights to custody or visitation of the child, or any parent having no right of custody to the child, who in violation of an order, judgment or decree of any court willfully detains, conceals or removes the child from a parent, guardian or other person having lawful custody or a right of visitation of the child shall be punished by imprisonment in the state prison for not less than 1 year nor more than 6 years, or by a fine of not less than $1,000 nor more than $5,000, or by both fine and imprisonment.
2. Upon conviction, the court shall order the defendant to provide restitution for any expenses incurred by the parent, guardian or other person in locating or recovering the child.
3. The prosecuting attorney may recommend to the judge that the defendant be sentenced as for a misdemeanor and the judge may impose such a sentence if he finds that:
(a) The defendant has no prior conviction for this offense.
(b) The interests of justice require that the defendant be punished as for a misdemeanor.

NEW HAMPSHIRE

Applicable laws. (Effective Nov. 1, 1973).
§ 633.1 Kidnapping; felony.
§ 633.2 Criminal restraint; felony; covers confinement of child under 16 if accomplished without consent of his parent or guardian.
§ 633.3 False imprisonment; Misdemeanor applies to children in same manner as § 633.2.
No specific child abduction or restraint law.

NEW JERSEY

Applicable laws (Effective September 1, 1979).
§ 2C:13-1 Kidnapping; crime of first or second degree includes kidnap-

§ 2C:13-2 ping of child under 14 if it is accomplished without consent of a parent, guardian, or other person responsible for general supervision or welfare.
§ 2C:13-2 Criminal restraint; crime of the third degree; affirmative defense to prosecution under subsection (b) if the person held was a child less than 18 years old and the actor was a relative or legal guardian of such child and his sole purpose was to assume control of such child.
§ 2C:13-3 False imprisonment; disorderly persons offense; same affirmative defense as in criminal restraint.
§ 2C:13-4 Interference with custody; disorderly persons offense.

2C:13-4. Interference With Custody
a. Custody of children. A person commits an offense if he knowingly takes or entices any child under the age of 18 from the custody of its parent, guardian or other lawful custodian, when he has no privilege to do so, or he does so in violation of a court order. It is an affirmative defense that:
(1) The actor believed that his action was necessary to preserve the child from danger to its welfare; or
(2) The child, being at the time not less than 14 years old, was taken away at its own volition and without purpose to commit a criminal offense with or against the child.
Proof that the child was below the critical age gives rise to a presumption that the actor knew the child's age.
The offense is a crime of the fourth degree if the actor is neither a parent of or person in equivalent relation to the child and if he acted with knowledge that his conduct would cause serious alarm for the child's safety or in reckless disregard of a likelihood of causing such alarm. In all other cases it is a disorderly persons offense.

NEW MEXICO

Applicable laws. (New Mexico Statutes Annotated. 1978).
§ 30-4-1 Kidnapping; felony.
§ 30-4-3 False imprisonment; felony.
§ 30-4-3 **Custodial interference, 4th degree felony; requires removal of child from state.**

30-4-4. Custodial interference; penalty.
A. Custodial interference consists of the taking from this state or causing to be taken from this state, or enticing to leave this state or causing to be enticed to leave this state, a child who is less than sixteen years of age by a parent with the intention of holding the child permanently or for a protracted period, knowing that he has no legal right to do so.
B. Whoever commits custodial interference is guilty of a fourth degree felony.

NEW YORK

Applicable law
§ 135.15 Unlawful imprisonment.
In any prosecution for unlawful imprisonment, it is an affirmative defense that (a) the person restrained was a child less than sixteen years

The Child Snatchers

old, and (b) the defendant was a relative of such child, and (c) his sole purpose was to assume control of such child.
L.1965, c. 1030.

Practice Commentaries, by Arnold D. Hechtman

The exclusion applies only to the taking of children "less than sixteen years old." The net effect is that a relative who unlawfully takes a child from its lawful custodian solely for "control" purposes is guilty of custodial interference if the child is less than sixteen but of unlawful imprisonment if he is sixteen or older. Under no circumstances is he guilty of kidnapping (see § 135.30).

§ 135.30 Kidnapping; defense.

In any prosecution for kidnapping, it is an affirmative defense that (a) the defendant was a relative of the person abducted, and (b) his sole purpose was to assume control of such person.
L.1965, c. 1030.

Practice Commentaries, by Arnold D. Hechtman

This section renders the kidnapping statutes inapplicable to cases involving unlawful taking of a child by a parent or other "relative" from another parent or relative who is its lawful custodian, purely for purposes of assuming control over the child. Although these "custody" offenses constituted kidnapping under the former Penal Law (§ 1250), under the Revised Penal Law they are prosecutable only as "custodial interference" if the child is less than sixteen years old (§§ 135.45, 135.50), and only as "unlawful imprisonment" if the child is sixteen years of age or older (§§ 135.05, 135.10, 135.15).

The exclusion of the instant section, it should be noted, applies only where the relative's "sole purpose" was assumption of physical control over the child. A relative who, for example, abducts a child for the purpose of ransom, extortion or terrorization of its mother or other lawful custodian is guilty of kidnapping.

§ 135.45   Custodial interference in second degree; Class A misdemeanor.
§ 135.50   Custodial interference in first degree; Class E felony. (Effective July 27, 1981)

§ 135.45 Custodial interference in the second degree.

A person is guilty of custodial interference in the second degree when:
    1. Being a relative of a child less than sixteen years old, intending to hold such child permanently or for a protracted period, and knowing that he has no legal right to do so, he takes or entices such child from his lawful custodian; or
    2. Knowing that he has no legal right to do so, he takes or entices from lawful custody any incompetent person or other person entrusted by authority of law to the custody of another person or institution.

Custodial interference in the second degree is a class A misdemeanor.
L.1965, c. 1030.

§ 135.50 Custodial interference in the first degree.

A person is guilty of custodial interference in the first degree when he commits the crime of custodial interference in the second degree:
    1. With intent to permanently remove the victim from this state, he removes such person from the state; or
    2. Under circumstances which expose the victim to a risk that his safety will be endangered or his health materially impaired. It shall be an

affirmative defense to a prosecution under this section that the victim has been abandoned or that the taking was necessary in an emergency to protect the victim because he has been subjected to or threatened with mistreatment or abuse.

Custodial interference in the first degree is a class E felony.

Excerpt from memorandum in support of S.5710:
Custodial interference has occurred with alarming frequency in recent years . . . This bill extends custodial interference in the first degree to include removal of the child from New York State . . . As an E-felony, extradition will be increased . . . This legislation is necessary to implement recently enacted Federal legislation. . .

NORTH CAROLINA

Applicable laws.
§ 14-39   Kidnapping; felony.
§ 14-41   Abduction of children under 14; felony.
§ 14-42   Conspiring to abduct children; felony.
§ 14-320.1 Transporting or keeping child outside the State with intent to violate custody order. Class J felony. (Effective July 1, 1980.)

§ 14.320.1 **Transporting child outside the State with intent to violate custody order.** When any court of competent jurisdiction in this State shall have awarded custody of a child under the age of sixteen years, it shall be a felony for any person with the intent to violate the court order to take or transport, or cause to be taken or transported, any such child from any point within this State to any point outside the limits of this State or to keep any such child outside the limits of this State. Such crime shall be punishable as a Class J felony. Provided that keeping a child outside the limits of the State in violation of a court order for a period in excess of seventy-two hours shall be prima facie evidence that the person charged intended to violate the order at the time of taking. (1969, c. 81.)

(Amendment Effective July 1, 1980. Session Laws 1979, c. 760, s.5, effective July 1, 1980, will rewrite the second sentence of this section to read as follows: "Such crime shall be punishable as a Class J felony.")

(Session Laws 1979, c.760.s.6, provides: "This act shall become effective on July 1, 1980, and shall apply only to offenses committed on or after that date, unless specific language of the act indicates otherwise.")

§ 14-41. **Abduction of children.** If anyone shall abduct or by any means induce any child under the age of fourteen years, who shall reside with its father, mother, uncle, aunt, brother or elder sister, or shall reside at a school, or be an orphan and reside with a guardian, to leave such person or school, he shall be guilty of a felony, and on conviction shall be fined or imprisoned in the State's prison for a period not exceeding fifteen years. (1879, c.81; Code, s.973; Eev., s.3358; C.S., s.4223.)

§ 14.42. **Conspiring to abduct children.** If anyone shall conspire to abduct, or by any means to induce any child under the age of fourteen years, who shall reside with any of the persons designated in § 14-41, or shall reside at school, to leave such persons or the school, he shall be guilty of a felony, and on conviction shall be punished as prescribed in that section:

Provided, that no one who may be a nearer blood relation to the child than the persons named in § 14-41 shall be indicted for either of said offenses. (1879, c.81, s.2; Code, s.974; Rev., s.3359; C.S..s.4224.)

NORTH DAKOTA

Applicable laws
§ 12.1-18-01 Kidnapping; felony.
§ 12.1-18-02 Felonious restraint; includes secreting or holding person in place not likely to be found.
§ 12.1-18-03 Parents have defense to prosecution for unlawful imprisonment.
§ 14-14-22.1 Removal of child from state in violation of custody decree; Class C felony. (Effective 1979.)

14-14-22.1 Removal of child from state in violation of custody decree — Penalty. Any person who intentionally removes, causes the removal of, or detains his or her own child under the age of eighteen years outside North Dakota with the intent to deny another person's rights under an existing custody decree shall be guilty of a class C felony. Detaining the child outside North Dakota in violation of the custody decree for more than seventy-two hours shall be prima facie evidence that the person charged intended to violate the custody decree at the time of removal.
Source: S.L. 1979, ch. 198, § 1.

OHIO

Applicable laws.
§ 2905.01 Kidnapping felony; includes removing another from the place where found or restraining another of his liberty by any person by any means in case of a victim under 13.
§ 2905.02 Abduction; felony.
§ 2905.03 Unlawful restraint; misdemeanor.
§ 2905.04 Child stealing; felony if committed by person other than relative or if relative removes child under 14 from state; misdemeanor in other cases. Affirmative defense that conduct was necessary to preserve child's health or welfare.
§ 2919.23 Interference with custody; misdemeanor of third degree.

§ 2905.04 Child stealing.

(A) No person, by any means, and with purpose to withhold a child under the age of fourteen or mentally incompetent from the legal custody of his parent, guardian, or custodian, shall remove such child from the place where he is found.

(B) It is an affirmative defense to a charge under this section that the actor reasonably believed that his conduct was necessary to preserve the child's health and welfare.

(C) Whoever violates this section is guilty of child stealing, a felony of the second degree. If the offender is a natural or adoptive parent, or a stepparent of the child, but not entitled to legal custody of the child when the offense is committed, child stealing is a misdemeanor of the first degree unless the offender removes the child from this state, in which case child stealing is a felony of the fourth degree.

History: 134 v H 511. Eff. 1-1-74.

Committee Comment

Although this section retains the elements of the former offense of child stealing, it adds two significant features. First, it expressly provides an affirmative defense to the crime based on the actor's good faith belief that his action was necessary to preserve the child's health or welfare. Second, the section provides for a lesser penalty when the offender is a natural or adoptive parent or a step-parent of the child, but not entitled to custody.

The rationale for providing the affirmative defense is that the law ought not to unduly discourage persons from taking children away from those who otherwise have legal custody, when there are reasonable grounds to believe that such action is dictated by some danger to the child's health or welfare. If the actions of such persons are not unreasonable, and are done in good faith, then no harm has been done even though they may have been mistaken in seeing some hazard to the child.

The reason for providing a lesser penalty when the offender is a parent of the child is that the offense of child stealing as such is often committed by separated or divorced parents who take the child from the parent having custody, and in such cases there is little if any danger to the child. Under such circumstances, the offense cannot be considered as grave as when it is committed by a stranger having no claim whatever on the child. In order to permit extradition, however, the section makes the offense a felony of the lowest degree when committed by a parent who takes the child out of the state.

To a limited extent, interference with custody under section 2919.23 is a lesser included offense to this section.

Child stealing is a felony of the second degree. If the offender is a parent, adoptive parent, or stepparent not entitled to custody of the child, the offense is a misdemeanor of the first degree, unless the offender takes the child out of state, in which case the offense is a felony of the fourth degree.

§ 2919.23 Interference with custody.

(A) No person, knowing he is without privilege to do so or being reckless in that regard, shall entice, take, keep, or harbor any of the following persons from his parent, guardian, or custodian:

(1) A child under the age of eighteen, or a mentally or physically handicapped child under the age of twenty-one;

(2) A person committed by law to an institution for delinquent, unruly, neglected, abused, or dependent children;

(3) A person committed by law to an institution for the mentally ill or mentally deficient.

(B) It is an affirmative defense to a charge of enticing or taking under division (A)(1) of this section, that the actor reasonably believed that his conduct was necessary to preserve the child's health or safety. It is an affirmative defense to a charge of keeping or harboring under division (A) of this section, that the actor in good faith gave notice to law enforcement or judicial authorities within a reasonable time after the child or committed person came under his shelter, protection, or influence.

(C) Whoever violates this section is guilty of interference with custody, a misdemeanor of the third degree.
HISTORY: 136 v H.85. Eff 11-28-75.

OKLAHOMA

Applicable laws.
21 § 741   Kidnapping; felony; consent of victim no defense if victim 12 or younger.
21 § 891   Child stealing; felony or misdemeanor.

§ 891. Child stealing—Punishment, Chpt. 35.

Whoever maliciously, forcibly or fraudulently takes or entices away any child under the age of twelve years, with intent to detain and conceal such child from its parent, guardian or other person having the lawful charge of such child is punishable by imprisonment in the penitentiary not exceeding ten years, or by imprisonment in a county jail not exceeding one year, or by a fine not exceeding five hundred dollars, or by both such fine and imprisonment. R.L. 1910, § 2435.

Historical Note
St.1890, § 2190; St.1803, § 2180; St.1903, § 2271; Comp Laws 1909, § 2373; Comp.St.1921, § 1858. Origin: Comp. Laws Dak.1887, § 6541.

OREGON

Applicable laws. (Effective 1971.)
§ 163.225   Kidnapping in second degree; felony; defense that person taken or confined is under 16 and the defendant is a relative whose sole purpose is to assume control of that person.
§ 163.235   Kidnapping in the first degree; felony.
§ 163.245   Custodial interference in the second degree; Class A misdemeanor.
§ 163.257   Custodial interference in the first degree; Class C felony; covers removal of child from state or exposure of child to substantial risk of illness or injury.

163.245 Custodial interference in the second degree. (1) A person commits the crime of custodial interference in the second degree if, knowing or having reason to know that he has no legal right to do so, he takes, entices, or keeps a person from his lawful custodian with intent to hold him permanently or for a protracted period.

(2) Custodial interference in the second degree is a Class A misdemeanor. (1971 c.743 s.100)
163.250 (Repealed by 1971 c.743 s.432)
163.255 (1955 c530 s1; repealed by 1971 c743 s.432)

Approved by the Governor, August 21, 1981
Section 1. ORS 163.245 is amended to read:
163.245. (1) A person commits the crime of custodial interference in the second degree if, knowing or having reason to know that [he] the person has no legal right to do so, [he] the person takes, entices or keeps [a] another person permanently or for a protracted period.

(2) Expenses incurred by a lawful custodial parent in locating and regaining physical custody of the person taken, enticed or kept in violation of this section are "pecuniary damages" for the purposes of restitution under ORS 137.103 to 137.109.

[(2)](3) Custodial interference in the second degree is a Class [A misdemeanor] C felony.

163.257 Custodial interference in the first degree. (1) A person commits the crime of custodial interference in the first degree if he violates ORS 163.245 and:

(a) Causes the person taken, enticed or kept from his lawful custodian to be removed from the state; or

(b) Exposes that person to a substantial risk of illness or physical injury.

(2) Custodial interference in the first degree is a Class C felony. (1971 c.743 s.101)

163.260 (Amended by 1955 c.366 s.1; repealed by 1971 c.743 s.432)
163.270 (Amended by 1955 c.371 s.1; 1957 c.640 s.1; repealed by 1971 c.743 s.432)

Approved by the Governor, August 21, 1981
Section 2. ORS 163.257 is amended to read:

163.257. (1) A person commits the crime of custodial interference in the first degree if [he] the person violates ORS 163.245 and:

(a) Causes the person taken, enticed or kept from [his] the lawful custodian to be removed from the state; or

(b) Exposes that person to a substantial risk of illness or physical injury.

(2) Expenses incurred by a lawful custodial parent in locating and regaining physical custody of the person taken, enticed or kept in violation of this section are "pecuniary damages" for purposes of restitution under ORS 137.103 to 137.109.

[(2)](3) Custodial interference in the first degree is a Class [C]B felony.

PENNSYLVANIA

Applicable laws (Title 18; effective June 6, 1973)
§ 2901   Kidnapping; felony; covers unlawful removal or confinement of person under 14 if accomplished without the consent of a parent, guardian, or other person responsible for general supervision of his welfare.
§ 2902   Felonious restraint; misdemeanor of first degree.
§ 2903   False imprisonment; misdemeanor of second degree.
§ 2904   Interference with custody of children; misdemeanor in second degree unless actor (other than parent) knew that conduct would put child in danger in which case it is a misdemeanor in first degree. Three defenses provided.

§ 2904. Interference with custody of children.
(a) Offense defined. A person commits an offense if he knowingly or recklessly takes or entices any child under the age of 18 years from the custody of its parent, guardian or other lawful custodian, when he has no privilege to do so.

(b) Defenses. It is a defense that:
(1) the actor believed that his action was necessary to preserve the child from danger to its welfare; or
(2) the child, being at the time not less than 14 years old, was taken

away at its own instigation without enticement and without purpose to commit a criminal offense with or against the child; or

(3) the actor is the child's parent or guardian or other lawful custodian and is not acting contrary to an order entered by a court of competent jurisdiction.

(c) Grading. The offense is a misdemeanor of the second degree unless the actor, not being a parent or person in equivalent relation to the child, acted with knowledge that his conduct would cause serious alarm for the safety of the child, or in reckless disregard of a likelihood of causing such alarm, in which case the offense is a misdemeanor of the first degree.

1972, Dec. 6, P.L.---, No. 334 § 1, eff. June 6, 1973.

PUERTO RICO

Applicable laws (Title 33; effective 1974; from 1979 Supplement to Laws of Puerto Rico.)
§ 4171 Restraint of liberty; misdemeanor.
§ 4178 Kidnapping; felony.
§ 4179 Kidnapping outside Puerto Rico and bringing or sending victim into Puerto Rico; felony

No specific child abduction or restraint law.

RHODE ISLAND

Applicable laws.
§ 11-26-1 Kidnapping; felony.
§ 11-26-1.1 Childsnatching; felony, removal or detention of child under 18 outside the state with intent to violate R.I. custody decree.

11.26.1.1. Childsnatching. Any person who intentionally removes, causes the removal of, or detains any child under the age of eighteen (18) years outside of the state of Rhode Island with intent to deny another person's right of custody under an existing decree or order of Rhode Island Family Court shall be guilty of a felony, and upon conviction thereof shall be punished by imprisonment for a term not more than two (2) years.
History of Section.
As enacted by P.L. 1980, ch. 217, § 1.

SOUTH CAROLINA

Applicable laws.
§ 16-3-910 Parents expressly exempted from kidnapping statute.
§ 16-17-495 Transporting or keeping child under 16 outside State with intent to violate custody order; felony; if child returned to jurisdiction of court within 7 days of his removal from State, punishable as misdemeanor. (Effective 1976.)

§ 16-17-495. Transporting child under sixteen years of age outside State with intent to violate a custody order.
When any court of competent jurisdiction in this State shall have

awarded custody of a child under the age of sixteen years, it shall be a felony for any person with the intent to violate the court order to take or transport, or cause to be taken or transported, any such child from any point within this State to any point outside the limits of this State or to keep any such child outside the limits of this State. Such crime shall be punishable by a fine in the discretion of the court or by imprisonment in the State's prison for not more than three years, in the discretion of the court, or by both such fine and imprisonment; provided, that keeping a child outside the limits of the State in violation of a court order for a period in excess of seventy-two hours shall be prima facie evidence that the person charged intended to violate the order at the time of taking; provided, further, that if the person violating the provisions of this section returns the child to the jurisdiction of the court issuing such order within seven days after so removing the child from this State, such person shall be deemed guilty of a misdemeanor and upon conviction shall be punished as provided herein.
HISTORY: 1976 Act No. 592.

SOUTH DAKOTA

Applicable laws.
§ 22-19-1   Kidnapping; felony; Parents of unmarried minors excepted.
§ 22-19-7   Taking away or concealing child under 12; felony or misdemeanor.
§ 22-19-9   Taking away or keeping of unmarried minor in violation of custody or visitation rights specified in custody determination; Class 1 misdemeanor.
§ 22-19-10 Removal of child from state in violation of § 22-19-9; Class 6 felony.
§ 22-19-11 Failure to report offense within 90 days as complete defense to prosecution under § 22-19-9 and § 22-19-10.

22.19.7 **Taking away or concealing child under twelve—Punishment.** Every person who maliciously, forcibly, or fraudulently takes or entices away any child under the age of twelve years with intent to detain and conceal such child from its parent, guardian, or other person having the lawful charge of such child, is punishable by imprisonment in the state penitentiary not exceeding ten years, or by imprisonment in a county jail not exceeding one year, or by a fine not exceeding five hundred dollars, or by both such fine and imprisonment.
Source: PenC 1877, § 340; CL 1887, § 6541; RPenC 1903, § 345; RC 1919, § 4119; SDC 1939, § 13.2707. See Cal Pen Code, § 278.

22.19.9. **Taking, enticing away or keeping of unmarried minor child by parent.** Any parent who takes, entices away or keeps his unmarried minor child from the custody or visitation of the other parent, or any other person having lawful custody or right of visitation, in violation of a custody or visitation determination entitled to enforcement by the courts of this state, without prior consent is guilty of a Class 1 misdemeanor.
Amended SL 1980, ch. 174, § 1.

22.19.10. **Removal of child from state.** Any parent who violates § 22.19.9 and causes the unmarried minor child taken, enticed or kept from his

lawful custodian to be removed from the state is guilty of a Class 6 felony.
Enacted SL 1980, ch 174, § 2.

22.19.11. Failure to report offense as complete defense. It is a complete defense to a prosecution for a violation of §§ 22.19.9 and 22.19.10 that the person having lawful custody or right of visitation failed to report the offense to law enforcement authorities within ninety days of the offense.
Enacted SL 1980, ch 174, § 3.

TENNESSEE

Applicable laws.
§ 39-2601   Kidnapping; felony.
§ 39-2602   Kidnapping children under 16; felony.
§ 39-2603   Aggravated kidnapping—Class X felony; includes kidnapping of child under 13 but any seizure or kidnapping of a child by a parent shall not be considered a class X felony. (Effective 1979).

39-2602. Kidnapping children under sixteen. Penalty. Every person who unlawfully takes or decoys away any child under the age of sixteen (16) years, with intent to detain or conceal such child from its parents, guardian, or other person having the lawful charge of such child, shall, on conviction, be imprisoned in the penitentiary not less than one (1) year nor more than five (5) years. (Code 1858, § 4519; Shan., § 6465; mod. Code 1932, § 10793.)
   1. Father as Kidnapper.
   Conviction of father of kidnapping child from mother to whom custody had been awarded in her ex parte divorce proceedings was not sustained by evidence which failed to show that he knew of such award of custody. Hicks v. State (1928), 158 Tenn. 204, 12 S.W. (2d) 385.

TEXAS

Applicable laws.
§ 20.02   False imprisonment; misdemeanor unless victim recklessly exposed to substantial risk of bodily injury, in which case it is a felony; affirmative defense that actor was relative of child under 14 and sole intent was to assume lawful control of child.
§ 20.03   Kidnapping; felony; affirmative defense that abduction not coupled with intent to use or threaten use of force, actor was relative, and sole intent was to assume lawful control of the victim.
§ 25.04   Aggravated kidnapping; felony. No affirmative defense.
§ 2503.   Interference with Child Custody; felony of third degree. (Title 6) covers taking or retaining child out of state. Defense specified.
§ 25.04   Enticing a child; Class B misdemeanor; (Title 6).

§ 2503. Interference with Child Custody.
   (a) A person commits an offense if he takes or retains a child younger than 18 years out of this state when he:

(1) knows that his taking or retention violates a temporary or permanent judgment or order of a court disposing of the child's custody; or

(2) has not been awarded custody of the child by a court of competent jurisdiction and knows that a suit for divorce, or a civil suit or application for habeas corpus to dispose of the child's custody has been filed.

(b) It is a defense to prosecution under Subsection (a)(2) of this section that the actor returned the child to this state within seven days after the date of the commission of the offense.

(c) An offense under this section is a felony of the third degree.

PRACTICE COMMENTARY
By Seth S. Search III and James R. Patterson of the
Austin Bar

This section adds a new offense to Texas criminal jurisprudence, one designed primarily to deal with the parental kidnapper but formulated broadly enough to cover anyone knowingly interfering with a court's custodial jurisdiction over children. Section 25.03 replaces a variety of offenses in the prior law, all aimed at least in part at preventing interference with a custodial relationship, but none adequate to deal with the parental kidnapper.

Section 25.03 **prohibits both taking and retaining a child outside the state either in violation of a custody award, Subsection (a)(1), or to defeat the court's jurisdiction in a custody case, Subsection (a)(2). The custody award need not originate with a Texas court to come within the section;** if suit is filed in this state to enforce a California custody judgment, for example, the non custodial parent's taking the child out of Texas violates Subsection (a)(2) if the parent knows the suit has been filed. Age 18 is used for the offense because under Texas law parental custody rights in a child usually terminate at that age.

Subsection (b) highlights the chief objective of this offense: to encourage the child's return to the jurisdiction of the Texas court whose contempt power can then be used to enforce its custody award.

The offense is graded a felony to assist in invocation of the extradition and federal fugitive felon provisions.

§ 25.04. Enticing a Child

(a) A person commits an offense if, with the intent to interfere with the lawful custody of a child younger than 18 years, he knowingly entices, persuades, or takes the child from the custody of the parent or guardian or person standing in the stead of the parent or guardian of such child.

(b) An offense under this section is a Class B misdemeanor.

COMMENTARY on § 20.02 and § 20.03

The affirmative defense protects the so-called parental kidnapper, who is the object of a separate, felony-grade offense defined in Section 25.03 (interference with child custody). Unlike that section, which uses age 18 for definition purposes because custody rights usually terminate at that age (see Family Code §§ 11.01, 12.04), Subsection (b) uses age 14, a probable confusion with the age of consent for certain defensive purposes in the sexual offenses chapter (see Sections 21.09, 21.10). A more serious problem with the subsection is its ambiguity: the incomplete definition of "relative" (defined in Section 20.01 (3)) and the vagueness of the term "lawful control." Because it is an affirmative defense, however, ambiguity is the defendant's problem, since he must prove its application by a preponderance of the evidence.

UTAH

Applicable laws.
§ 76-5-301   Kidnapping; felony.
§ 76-5-302   Aggravated kidnapping; felony; a detention or moving is deemed to be by force, threat or deceit if victim is under 16 and is accomplished without the effective consent of the victim's custodial parent, guardian, or person acting as parent.
§ 76-5-303   Custodial interference; Class A misdemeanor unless child is removed from state in which case it is a felony.

76-5-303. Custodial interference. (1) A person, whether a parent or other, is guilty of custodial interference if, without good cause, he or she takes, entices, conceals, or detains a child under the age of sixteen from his or her parent, guardian, or other lawful custodian
  (a) Knowing he or she has no legal right to do so; and
  (b) With intent to hold the child for a period of substantially longer than the visitation or custody period previously awarded by a court of competent jurisdiction.
  (2) A person, whether a parent or other, is guilty of custodial interference if, having actual physical custody of a child under the age of sixteen pursuant to a judicial award of any court or competent jurisdiction which grants to another person visitation or custody rights, and without good cause he or she conceals or detains the child with intent to deprive the other person of his or her lawful visitation or custody rights.
  (3) A person is guilty of custodial interference if without good cause he or she takes, entices, conceals, or detains an incompetent or other person under the age of sixteen who has been committed by authority of law to the custody of another person or institution from the other person or institution, knowing he or she has no legal right to do so.
  (4) Custodial interference is a class A misdemeanor unless the child is removed and taken from one state to another, in which case it is a felony of the third degree.

History: C. 1953, 76-5-303, enacted by L. 1973, ch. 196, § 76-5-303; L. 1979, ch. 70, § 1.
Compiler's Notes. The 1979 amendment inserted "or she" and "or her" throughout subsecs. (1) to (3); and increased the penalty for custodial interference by rewriting subsec. (4) which previously read: "Custodial interference is a class B misdemeanor."

VERMONT

Applicable laws.
§ 2401   Kidnapping; felony (1971).
§ 2402   Kidnapping child under 16; felony offense committed regardless of child's consent.
§ 2451   Custodial interference; felony; defense specified.

§ 2451. Custodial interference.
  (a) A person commits custodial interference by taking, enticing or keeping a child from the child's lawful custodian, knowingly, without a legal right to do so, when the person is a relative of the child and the child is less than eighteen years old.

(b) A person who commits custodial interference shall be imprisoned not more than five years or fined not more than $5,000.00, or both.

(c) It shall be a defense to a charge of keeping a child from the child's lawful custodian that the person charged with the offense was acting in good faith to protect the child from real and imminent physical danger. Evidence of good faith shall include, but is not limited to, the filing of a non-frivolous petition documenting that danger and seeking to modify the custodial decree in a Vermont court of competent jurisdiction. This petition must be filed within 72 hours of the termination of visitation rights. This defense shall not be available if the person charged with the offense has left the state with the child. Added 1979, No. 149 (Adj. Sess.), § 1, eff. April 24, 1980.

VIRGINIA

Applicable laws.
§ 18.2-47 Abduction and kidnapping; if committed by parent and punishable as contempt in the pending proceeding Class 1 misdemeanor unless child removed from state, in which case it is a Class 6 felony.
§ 18.2-49 Threatening, attempting or assisting in such abduction; Class 5 felony.
§ 18.2-50 Disclosure of information and assistance to law enforcement officers required by members of immediate family; Class 2 misdemeanor.

§ 18.2-47. Abduction and kidnapping defined; punishment. Any person, who, by force, intimidation or deception, and without legal justification or excuse, seizes, takes, transports, detains or secrets the person of another with the intent to deprive such other person of his personal liberty or to withhold or conceal him from any person, authority or institution lawfully entitled to his charge, shall be deemed guilty of "abduction"; but the provisions of this section shall not apply to any law-enforcement officer in the performance of his duty. The terms "abduction" and "kidnapping" shall be synonymous in this Code.

Abduction for which no punishment is otherwise prescribed shall be punished as a Class 5 felony; provided, however, that such offense, if committed by the parent of the person abducted and punishable as contempt of court in any proceeding then pending, shall be a Class 1 misdemeanor in addition to being punishable as contempt of court. Provided further, however, that such offense, if committed by the parent of the person abducted and punishable as contempt of court in any proceeding then pending and the person abducted is removed from the Commonwealth by the abducting parent shall be a Class 6 felony in addition to being punishable as contempt of court. (Code 1950, §§ 18.1-36, 18.1-37; 1960, c. 358; 1975, cc. 14, 15; 1979, c.663; 1980, c.506.)

§ 18.2.50. Disclosure of information and assistance to law enforcement officers required. Whenever it is brought to the attention of the members of the immediate family of any person that such person has been abducted, or that threats or attempts have been made to abduct any such persons, such members shall make immediate report thereof to the police or other law enforcement officers of the county, city or town where such person resides, and shall render all such possible assistance to such officers in the capture and conviction of the person or persons guilty of the alleged offense. Any person violating any of the provisions of this section shall be guilty of a Class 2 misdemeanor. (Code 1950, § 18.1-40; 1960, c. 358; 1975, cc. 14, 15.)

VIRGIN ISLANDS

Applicable laws.
T.14 § 1051   False imprisonment and kidnapping; not applicable in any case when a parent abducts his own child. (1974)
No specific child abduction or restraint law.

WASHINGTON

Applicable laws.
§ 9A.40.020   Kidnapping in the first degree; felony.
§ 9A.40.030   Kidnapping in second degree (lesser offense); felony; defense that abduction did not include the use of, intent to use, or threat to use, deadly force and actor is relative of person abducted and sole intent is to assume custody of that person. Provides that nothing in this defense constitutes a defense to, nor precludes conviction of any other crime.
§ 9A.40.040   Unlawful imprisonment; felony.
§ 9A.40.050   **Custodial interference; gross misdemeanor.**

§ 9A.40.050 Custodial interference. (1) A person is guilty of custodial interference if, knowing that he has no legal right to do so, he takes or entices from lawful custody any incompetent person or other person entrusted by authority of law to the custody of another person or institution.
(2) Custodial interference is a gross misdemeanor.

LEGISLATIVE HISTORY
Enacted Law 1st Ex Sess 1975 ch 260 § 9A.40.050.

WEST VIRGINIA

Applicable laws.
§ 61-2-14   Kidnapping or concealing child; felony; mothers and fathers expressly excluded.
§ 61-2-14a   Kidnapping for extortion, etc.; felony.
No specific child abduction or restraint law.

WISCONSIN

Applicable laws (Title 45)
§ 940.31   Kidnapping; felony; 19-5 Attorney General's opinion excluded mother from purview of statute. A mother having temporary lawful custody of child by virtue of divorce de-

cree was not guilty of kidnapping when she took child out of state and refused to surrender it to custody of father who was entitled to permanent custody under the decree. 4 Op.Atty. Gen. 802 (1915)

§ 940.32 Abduction of child under 18 from his home or custody of his parent or guardian for unlawful purpose; felony.
§ 946.71 Interference with custody of child; Class E felony.
§ 946.715 Interference by parent with parental rights of other parent; Class E felony; under specified circumstances, no violation committed.

§ 946.71 Interference with custody of child.

Except as provided under ch. 48, whoever intentionally does any of the following is guilty of a Class E felony:

(1) Interferes with the custody of any child under the age of 18 who has been committed or whose legal custody or guardianship has been transferred under ch. 48 to the department of health and social services or to any person, county agency or licensed child welfare agency.

(2) Entices away or takes away any child under the age of 18 from the parent or other person having legal custody under an order of judgment in an action for divorce, legal separation, annulment, custody, paternity, guardianship or habeas corpus with intent to take the child out of the state for the purpose of depriving the parent or other person of the custody of the child without the consent of such parent or other person, unless the court which awarded custody has consented that the child be taken out of the state by the person who so takes the child. The fact that joint custody has been awarded to both parents by a court does not preclude a court from finding that one parent has committed a violation of this subsection.

(3) Entices away, takes away or withholds for more than 12 hours beyond the court approved visitation period any child under the age of 14 from a parent or other person having legal custody under an order or judgment in an action for divorce, legal separation, annulment, custody, paternity, guardianship or habeas corpus without the consent of the legal custodian; unless a court has entered an order authorizing the taking or withholding.

(4) Entices away, takes away or withholds for more than 12 hours any child under the age of 14 from the parents, or the child's mother in the case of a child born out of wedlock and not subsequently legitimated, without the consent of the parents or the mother, unless custody has been granted by court order to the person enticing, taking or withholding the child.

Source: L. 1967, c. 226, § 31, eff. Dec. 26, 1967.
L. 1971, c. 164, § 89, eff. Dec. 31, 1971.
L. 1977, c. 173, § 150, eff. June 1, 1977.
L. 1977, c. 161, §§ 1, 2, eff. Nov. 17, 1977
L. 1977, c. 418, § 928 (18)(b), eff. May 19, 1978
L. 1979, c. 196, § 47, eff. Aug. 1, 1980.

Applicability. L. 1979, c. 196, § 49, provides:
"This act applies to all actions affecting marriage and to all motions concerning actions affecting marriage which are commenced or filed on or after the effective date of this act, including motions or actions for modification or enforcement of orders entered prior to the effective date of this act." Cross References—Felony classifications, see § 939.50.

946.715 Interference by parent with parental rights of other parent.
(1) Any parent, or any person acting pursuant to directions from the parent, who does any of the following is guilty of a Class E felony:
(a) Intentially conceals a minor child from the child's other parent;
(b) After being served with process in an action affecting marriage but prior to the issuance of a temporary or final order determining custody rights to a minor child, takes or entices the child outside of this state for the purpose of depriving the other parent of physical custody as defined in s. 822.-02(9); or
(c) After issuance of a temporary or final order specifying joint custody rights, takes or entices a child under the age of 14 from the other parent in violation of the custody order.
(2) No person violates sub.(1) if the action:
(a) Is taken to protect the child from imminent physical harm;
(b) Is taken by a parent fleeing from imminent physical harm to himself or herself;
(c) Is consented to by the other parent; or
(d) Is otherwise authorized by law.
Source: L.1979, c. 196, § 48 eff. Aug. 1, 1980. Applicability. L. 1979, c. 196, § 49, provides: "This act applies to all actions affecting marriage and to all motions concerning actions affecting marriage which are commenced or filed on or after the effective date of this act, including motions or actions for modification or enforcement of orders entered prior to the effective date of this act."

WYOMING

§ 6-4-201   Kidnapping; felony.
§ 6-4-203   Involuntary transfer of physical custody of child under 14; felony.
§ 6-4-204   Concealment and harboring; felony.
§ 6-4-205   Abduction for profit; felony.

§ 6-4-203 Involuntary transfer of physical custody of child.
When any parent, living apart from the other parent who by express agreement or court order has the physical custody or control of a child under the age of fourteen (14) years, takes, leads, carries, decoys or entices away the child with the intent to cause a change in the physical custody of the child without the consent of the parent or guardian having physical custody or control of the child or without authorization to do so by a court having appropriate jurisdiction, is guilty of a felony and shall, upon conviction, be imprisoned in the state penitentiary for a period not to exceed one year, fined not more than $500 or both. (Effective May 20, 1981.)

§ 6-4-204. Same; concealment and harboring.
Whoever violates the provisions of W.S. 6-61.1 (§ 6-4-203) and knowingly and intentionally conceals and harbors any child so led, taken, carried, decoyed, or enticed away, or refuses to reveal the location of the child to the parent or guardian formerly having physical custody, upon conviction thereof, may be imprisoned in the state penitentiary for a period of not exceeding two (2) years and fined not more than one thousand dollars ($1,000.00). (Laws 1977, ch. 92, effective May 28, 1977.)

§ 6-4-205. Same; abduction for profit.
Whoever for payment or promise of payment enters into an agreement, confederation or conspiracy to violate the provisions of W.S. 6-61.1 (§ 6-4-203) or 6.61.2 (§ 6-4-204), upon conviction thereof, may be imprisoned in the state penitentiary for a period not exceeding ten (10) years and fined not more than ten thousand dollars ($10,000.00). (Laws 1977, ch. 92, § 1.)

Appendix C

October 1981 Congressional Hearings Regarding Failure of the Justice Department to Implement the Parental Kidnaping Prevention Act, Taken from the *Congressional Record*, October 21, 1981.

By Mr. WALLOP (for himself and Mr. Cranston):
S. 1759. A bill to clarify Congressional intent regarding the full application of section 1073 of title 18, United States Code, to State felony parental kidnaping cases: to the Committee on the Judiciary.

Parental Kidnaping

Mr. WALLOP. Mr. President, today I join with my colleague from California (Mr. Cranston) to introduce a bill which clarifies one section of the Parental Kidnaping Act. The act was passed last December, and was to be fully implemented by the 1st of July. However, after carefully monitoring the Justice Department's procedures to carry out their responsibilities under the act, I have concluded that the Department is not properly implementing the program.

The Parental Kidnaping Act has three sections. One section requires all States to adopt the uniform child custody code. Another authorizes the Federal Parent Locator Service to assist States in locating parents who have taken their children in contravention of a child custody decision. The third section authorizes the FBI to assist States and local authorities in locating a parent when a felony warrant has been issued. It is this last provision with which I am concerned today.

The Justice Department issued a memorandum at the beginning of the year which set very restrictive requirements for FBI assistance in parental kidnaping cases. The restrictions have prevented the effective management of this section of the act. The bill I am introducing today would clarify congressional intent regarding FBI assistance to State and local authorities.

Recently, I presented testimony to the House Judiciary Committee on this problem. The testimony is a thorough outline of the problem and I ask unanimous consent that my comments be printed in the RECORD at this point. I would also request that the text of the bill be printed in the RECORD following my statement.

There being no objection, the bill and statement were ordered to be printed in the RECORD as follows:

S. 1759

Be it enacted by the Senate and House of Representatives of the United States of America in Congress assembled, That (a) subsection 10 of the Parental Kidnaping Prevention Act of 1980 (Public Law 96-611) is amended by—

(1) inserting "(1)" before "In";

(2) striking out "section 302" and inserting in lieu thereof "section 7";

(3) adding at the end of paragraph (1) (as so redesignated) the following new sentence: "Congress further declares, notwithstanding any other provision of law, that such section 1073 apply to State felony parental kidnaping cases without restriction and in the same manner as to all other State felony cases"; and

(4) adding at the end the following new paragraph:

"(2) Not later than 30 days after the date of enactment of this section, the Attorney General of the United States shall eliminate all guidelines that require information that the child is in physical danger or is being abused or neglected, corroboration, prior approval, or otherwise limit the application of such section 1073 in State felony parental kidnaping cases in a manner which frustrates the intent of Congress that such cases be subject to only the requirements applicable in the case of all State felonies under such section. Not later than 45 days after the date of enactment of this section, the Attorney General shall report to the appropriate Committees of the Congress as to how and when the Department of Justice has complied with the provisions of this section and shall provide such Committees with copies of all memorandum, directives or other communications issued by the Department of Justice, including the Federal Bureau of Investigation, with respect to implementation of this section".

(b) subsection (b) of section 10 of such Act is amended by—

(1) inserting a comma and "by State and by type of agency or individual initiating such application," in paragraph (1) after "applications";

(2) inserting a comma and 'by State," in paragraph (2) after "complaints"; and

(3) inserting a comma and "including a description of disposition of each application and the reasons therefore," in paragraph (3) after "information".

Statement of Senator Malcolm Wallop

My sincere thanks to you, Mr. Chairman, and to your distinguished colleagues for convening this timely and important hearing on the implementation of the Parental Kidnaping Prevention Act of 1980, an act with which I have been associated from its inception. Since the law was passed last December, my staff has been monitoring its implementation by the Department of Health and Human Services and by the Department of Justice, and has been tracking to a more limited extent the private custody litigation pending in state courts involving the new law. As the original sponsor of S. 105, the bill from which sections 6-10 of Public Law 96-611 are substantially derived, I note at the outset my considerable disappointment with the failure of the Justice Department to conform its Fugitive Felon Act policies to the express language and legislative history of section 10 of the new law. If this hearing sparks a correction on the part of the Criminal Division and the F.B.I. with respect to the issuance of Unlawful Flight to Avoid Prosecution ("UFAP") warrants in state felony parental kidnaping cases involving interstate or international flight as the law requires, in my opinion it will prove to have been an extremely constructive proceeding, indeed.

The Parental Kidnaping Prevention Act ("PKPA") was enacted on December 28, 1980, to safeguard countless children from the harmful effects of child snatching, the wrongful removal or restraining of a child by a parent or parent's agent in violation of a custody decree or in violation of the other parent's rights as a joint custodian where a custody determination has not yet been made. The PKPA grew out of S. 105, a bill I introduced on January 23, 1979, which was modeled upon an amendment I had successfully offered to S. 1437, the criminal code reform legislation considered by the Senate in the 95th Congress. By the end of the 96th Congress, a bipartisan group of 25 senators had cosponsored S. 105, and over 60 House members had cosponsored H.R. 1290, a companion measure introduced by Representative Charles Bennett.

In January, 1980, the Senate Judiciary Subcommittee on Criminal Laws held a joint hearing on S. 105 with the Labor and Human Resources Subcommittee on Child and Human Development, which was followed in June by a hearing before the House Judiciary Subcommittee on Crime on related bills. The hearings were instructive in several respects.

First, the concealment of children who have been wrongfully removed or retained by a parent has stunning effects on the left-behind parent, who is typically emotionally and financially drained by the unrelenting search for the missing child, as well as for the victim child, who suffers anger, fear and sometimes irreparable psychological trauma.

Second, various agencies of state and federal government were unresponsive to the plight of the victim child and left-behind parent, either through neglect of their lawful responsibilities or for want of legal authority to provide meaningful assistance in parental kidnapping and restraint cases.

Third, the handful of jurisdictions that had not enacted the Uniform Child Custody Jurisdiction Act ("UCCJA") were serving, however, unintentionally, as havens for child-abducting parents, and even some states that had adopted the UCCJA were loosely interpreting that law, the effect of which was to provide abductor-parents with the means to circumvent the jurisdictional requirements and anti-parental kidnaping spirit of that statute.

The consensus from the hearings was that a federal solution was needed for a problem that was essentially interstate in nature. Shortly after the hearings, I offered S. 105 as an amendment to the domestic violence legislation which was agreed to in the Senate on September 4, 1980. In its consideration of the parental kidnaping amendment, a House-Senate Conference Committee accepted the two chief civil sections of the proposal without amendment, and accepted a modified criminal provision. The conference version of S. 105 was ultimately passed by both houses on December 13, 1980 as part of H.R. 8406, a bill providing for Medicare reimbursement for pneumococcal vaccines.

As enacted, the Parental Kidnaping Prevention Act: (1) requires the appropriate authorities of every state to enforce and refrain from modifying custody and visitation rights ordered by courts which have exercised jurisdiction in compliance with the jurisdictional criteria set forth in the law; (2) authorizes the Federal Parent Locator to act on requests from States to locate children who have been abducted or retained and the parents who have abducted or retained them; and (3) expressly declares, I would emphasize, the intent of Congress that the Fugitive Felon Act applies to state felony parental kidnaping cases involving interstate or international flight. The Conference Report on H.R. 2977, the Domestic Violence Prevention and Services Act, contains a concise description of each of these provisions. The relevant pages of that report are attached as an appendix to my statement.

Before tackling the most serious implementation problem, that is, the Justice Department's unacceptable response to section 10 of the law, I would comment briefly on the implementation of the other parts of the law.

When the PKPA was enacted, only 43 states had adopted the UCCJA. One of the desired effects of the Full Faith and Credit provision, section 8 of Public Law 96-611, was to induce the remaining non-UCCJA states to adopt that uniform state law since universal enactment of the UCCJA is consistent with the policy objective of the PKPA. I am pleased to report that three states—South Carolina, West Virginia and New Mexico—adopted the UCCJA subsequent to the enactment of the PKPA, and UCCJA legislation is pending in the City Council of the District of Columbia and in Massachusetts. With respect to case law, there have been thus far very few state court decisions involving section 8 of the PKPA. While at some future date we may wish to reconsider that provision, it would be prudent to postpone any such consideration until a body of cases have been decided, and the legal and academic communities have had an opportunity to thoroughly scrutinize the effect of the law on child custody legislation.

The Parent Locator Service is not yet available to the States wishing to utilize it to locate abducting-parents and missing children. That the Department of Health and Human Services has reacted slowly to the mandate of section 9 of Public Law 96-611 is disturbing to me since the law required only minor adjustments in existing child support enforcement regulations. The delay is of far more immediate concern to the many parents throughout the country who had expected the service to be available soon after the law was passed. Instead, nearly 10 months has elapsed, and these parents are still without recourse to the FPLS to help find their missing children.

I have written to Secretary Schweiker urging the Department to expedite the promulgation of the regulations and the federal-state agreement required by the law. The agreement must be submitted to the States for approval by the Governor or his or her delegate. It is imperative that this section of the PKPA be fully implemented as soon as possible. Every day of delay is potentially another day of separation between parents and their children.

Last, but certainly not least, I turn to the matter of the implementation of section 10 of Public Law 96-611. As mentioned earlier in this statement, the House-Senate Conference Committee substituted for the section of S. 105 that would have created a new federal misdemeanor offense for child snatching, a provision expressly declaring congressional intent that the Fugitive Felon Act applies to parental kidnapping cases. This modification struck a balance between federal and state law enforcement responsibilities in state felony parental kidnapping cases involving flight. The object was to bring the F.B.I. into investigations of abduction and restraint cases which the state prosecutor was intent on prosecuting upon the extradition of the perpetrator. Although the Fugitive Felon Act, 18 U.S.C. 1073, applies on its face to all state felonies, the Justice Department had carved out an exception for parental kidnappings, apparently based on the statutory exemption of parents from the federal kidnapping law, 18 U.S.C. 1201, from which they inferred that Congress similarly intended to limit the application of the Fugitive Felon Act in cases involving parents.

In enacting section 10 of the PKPA, Congress specifically rejected the Justice Department's restrictive standards for the issuance of fugitive complaints which essentially treated parental kidnapping cases differently than all other felony offenses. The pre-PKPA Justice Department guidelines required as conditions precedent to the issuance of Fugitive Felon warrants, and I quote, "convincing evidence that the child was in danger of serious bodily harm as a result of the mental condition or past behavior patterns of the abducting parents."

On December 31, 1980, three days after the law was passed, the Criminal Division of the Justice Department issued "revised" guidelines which purported to implement the Fugitive Felon section of the PKPA. Unfortunately, the new guidelines were little more than a reformulation of the pre-PKPA policy; under the new policy, the Criminal Division required, quote, "independent credible information establishing that the child is in physical danger or is being seriously abused or seriously neglected."

On March 9, 1981, I initiated a letter joined in by nine other senators and congressmen to Attorney General Smith requesting that he undertake a review and revision of the fugitive felon directive in accordance with the new law. The belated reply accompanied the report required to be filed by the Justice Department 120 days after enactment of the law, both of which were submitted to Congress on June 26, 1981. Copies of the letter and report are included as an appendix to my statement.

The contents of the letter and report hardly justified the long delay, for the "revised revised" policy set forth in these documents represents a barely perceptible improvement over the immediately preceding policy formulation. Of primary concern is the fact that these current guidelines continue to require as a condition precedent of the issuance of Fugitive Felon warrants, quote, "independent credible information that the child is in physical danger or is then in a condition of abuse or neglect." Additionally, prior approval must be obtained from the Justice Department in Washington before a U.S. attorney can issue a fugitive complaint.

Mr. Chairman, the current policy frustrates the express intent of the new law. Congress intended that state felony cases would be treated in the same manner as all other state felony charges, and that no special criteria would be applied to restrict the application of the Fugitive Felon Act in state felony parental kidnapping cases in which the state prosecutor intends to extradite and prosecute the fugitive once he or she is apprehended by the F.B.I. Yet, the Justice Department's requirements remain unique to child snatching cases; no similar criteria attach to the issuance of Fugitive Felon warrants in any other state felony cases.

Moreover, these requirements essentially change the character of the underlying offense for which the warrant is available from parental kidnapping, as the law specifically requires, to child abuse or neglect, a result which clearly contradicts the express language of the law. To add insult to injury, the requirements cannot possibly be satisfied by complainant-parents who do not know the whereabouts of their abducted children and therefore cannot provide the requisite (quote,) "credible information that the child is in physical danger or is then in a condition of abuse or neglect."

On account of the Justice Department policy, the federal-state cooperative relationship which the law was intended to forge has unfortunately not materialized. Instead, meaningful federal investigative assistance in state felony parental cases remains unavailable to prosecutors in all but a few cases. The June 26 report leaves no doubt but that very few warrants have been issued since the passage of the PKPA: of the 24 applications that met the "statutory requirements for assistance," a mere 6 UFAP warrants were issued. As an aside, I wonder whether the 24 applications met the Department's guidelines.

The application of the restrictive criteria is only one reason why the warrants are not being issued as intended by the law. The Department's requirement of prior Criminal Division approval of UFAP complaints has also proved to be a very substantial impediment to the issuance of fugitive warrants. Cases have been brought to my attention wherein the local United States Attorney has decided in favor of issuing a fugitive felon warrant in particular state felony cases, only to have that decision overturned by the Justice Department in Washington. In addition, the philosophy of the Justice Department that felony parental kidnapping cases are domestic, rather than criminal matters, has continued unabated despite the clear expression on the part of Congress to the contrary.

Mr. Chairman, for as long as the Justice Department maintains its present policy, one thing is certain. Very few cases of parental kidnapping will involve the F.B.I., and the F.B.I., Justice Department and Congress will be left with nothing more than sheer conjecture as to the actual number of cases which would fall to the federal government to investigate if the new law was applied without restriction. In the absence of such firm data, Congress has no basis to effectively evaluate its decision to involve the federal government in the investigation of parental kidnapping cases.

Nor I might add, can the Justice Department substantiate its claim that the investigation of parental cases require an undue amount of their time and effort. If we are to assess the effectiveness of the law as a response to the tide of parental kidnappings nationwide, it must be fully enforced to provide meaningful data for our evaluations. This would likewise prove instructive for the Department, itself.

Mr. Chairman, I offer the following recommendations to improve the effectiveness of section 10 of the new law. First, the Department should vigorously enforce the law so that data is available to Congress for an indepth assessment of the efficacy of applying the Fugitive Felon Act to state felony parental kidnapping cases, which in turn will serve as a clear warning to parents that abductions or retentions of children will not be tolerated. Second, the guidelines which treat child snatching cases differently than all other state felony charges should be eliminated, as should be the requirement of prior approval from Washington. Third, the reports required to be filed pursuant to section 10(a) of the law should indicate who the applicant is, and the state in which the application is made. This will facilitate future oversight of the Justice Department's implementation efforts.

Mr. Chairman, I thank you again for your obvious commitment to the full and effective implementation of the Parental Kidnapping Prevention Act.

Mr. CRANSTON. Mr. President, I am pleased to join with the distinguished Senator from Wyoming (Mr. WALLOP) in introducing this legislation to amend the Parental Kidnaping Prevention Act of 1980, Public Law 96-611 in order to insure its full implementation by the Department of Justice.

Mr. President, it has been my pleasure over the past few years to work with the Senator from Wyoming on the Parental Kidnaping Prevention Act. He has been a persistent and dedicated leader in efforts to deal with the devastating problem of parental kidnaping. The Senate has repeatedly and in a totally bipartisan fashion supported these efforts which culminated last year with the enactment of Public Law 96-611. It was my privilege to chair the conference committee which developed the final format which was the basis for the provisions of Public Law 96-611.

Unfortunately, Mr. President, a substantial amount of what we sought to accomplish by the Parental Kidnaping Prevention Act of 1980 has been undermined by the Department of Justice's persistent refusal to implement section 10 of the act. Section 10, as I will explain in more detail in a moment, expressly states that it is the intent of Congress that the Department of Justice apply the provisions of section 1073 of title 18 of the United States Code—the unlawful flight to avoid prosecution (UFAP) statute—to cases involving interstate or international flight to avoid prosecution under the State felony parental kidnaping statutes. Nevertheless, the Department of Justice has refused to comply with this express intent of the Congress; instead, the Department has imposed arbitrary and unjustifiable restrictions on the application of section 1073 to parental kidnaping cases.

Mr. President, the legislation we are introducing today simply and unequivocably states that section 1073 shall apply in State felony parental kidnaping cases in the same manner as it does in all other State felony cases and directs the Attorney General to eliminate all guidelines that impose additional restrictions in parental kidnaping cases or otherwise frustrate the intent of Congress in this matter.

LEGISLATIVE HISTORY

Mr. President, in order that my colleagues may understand the background of this legislation, I would like to describe briefly the development of the Parental Kidnaping Prevention Act of 1980.

Although various measures dealing with the problem of parental kidnaping have been introduced in both the Senate and the House over the past decade, the legislation that formed the basis for the Parental Kidnaping Prevention Act of 1980 grew out of provisions first approved by the Senate in January of 1978 as an amendment offered by Senator WALLOP to S. 1437, the proposed criminal code recodification. The House, however, failed to act upon S. 1437 during the 95th Congress. At the beginning of the 96th Congress, the parental kidnaping provisions were reintroduced by the Senator from Wyoming (Mr. WALLOP) as S. 15. This legislation, of which I was an original cosponsor, enjoyed broad bipartisan support with 24 cosponsors representing a broad range of political philosophies.

In April of 1979, as chairman of the former Subcommittee on Child and Human Development of the Labor and Human Resources Committee, I chaired a hearing in Los Angeles, Calif., on this legislation and the problem of parental kidnaping. Testimony at that hearing from both parents and law enforcement personnel indicated the tremendous problems created by the lack of Federal legislation.

The witnesses described the peculiar interstate nature of the problem of child stealing and how the conflicting State laws and jurisdictional barriers actually encouraged abducting parents to flee from State to State with these children, avoiding both the civil and criminal justice system.

In January of 1980, here in Washington, I chaired, with the distinguished Senator from Maryland (Mr. MATHIAS), a joint hearing of the Child and Human Development Subcommittee and the Criminal Justice Subcommittee of the Judiciary Committee on S. 105. Again, the testimony stressed the need for a Federal response to help stem interstate flight in child stealing cases. State law enforcement officers testified at both hearings on how the lack of Federal involvement undermined the effectiveness of their State statutes.

The Senate Judiciary Committee approved the provisions of S. 105 and incorporated them into S. 1722, the 1980 proposed criminal code recodification measure. However, S. 1722 was never brought to the Senate floor and in August of 1980, Senator WALLOP offered an amendment, which I cosponsored, to add the basic provisions of S. 105 as a separate title to the proposed Domestic Violence Prevention Services Act,

H.R. 2977. The Senate unanimously approved this amendment and H.R. 2977 was subsequently passed by the Senate.

The provisions of title IV of H.R. 2977 as passed by the Senate had three basic components.

First, it provided for the application of full faith and credit between the States to custody orders entered into in conformity with the provisions of the act. These provisions were based on the Uniform Child Custody Jurisdiction Act which has now been enacted by almost all of the States. They were intended to discourage interstate "forum-shopping" and to resolve the civil interstate jurisdictional problems that contribute to childstealing.

Second, the amendment authorized States to enter into agreements with the Secretary of HHS for use of the Federal Parent Locator Service (FPLS) to assist in location of missing children. The FPLS was established in 1976 to assist in locating parents who have avoided making child support payments; the amendment simply allowed the extension of the program to the location of parents who abduct children.

Third, and finally, the amendment provided for the establishment of a new Federal offense for interstate child stealing.

The first two provisions of title IV were approved in conference with minor modification. The third, the criminal provision, was modified in conference to provide for the application of section 1073 of title 18 of the United States Code to parental kidnaping, rather than to establish a new Federal crime as had originally been proposed and approved by the Senate.

Mr. President, I would like to describe for a moment the circumstances that led the conferees to modify the criminal provisions of the Senate-passed amendment. The House conferees expressed reservations about accepting the Senate provision establishing a new Federal offense without first attempting to utilize the existing UFAP statute. The conferees were aware of the policy of the Justice Department of refusing to apply the UFAP statute to parental kidnaping cases unless there was a showing of a "serious threat of physical injury to the child" from the abducting parent by reason of his or her medical condition or acute pattern of behavior, for example, alcoholism, interpersonal violence. The Justice Department, in its testimony before the Congress and in its internal guidelines, has consistently taken the position that the UFAP statute should not be applied to parental kidnaping cases except in extreme cases.

The Justice Department's rationalization for refusing to apply the UFAP statute to parental kidnaping cases was an alleged "congressional intent" arising from the fact that Congress, in enacting in 1932 the Federal kidnaping statute, section 1201 of title 18, had provided for an exception for parental kidnaping. Hence, the Justice Department argued, Congress must have intended to avoid Federal involvement in any way in parental kidnaping cases.

The conferees, in the joint explanatory statement of the conference report accompanying H.R. 2977 emphatically rejected that view and incorporated into section 10 of the Parental Kidnaping Prevention Act a clear and unequivocable statement that it is the intent of Congress that the UFAP statute apply to parental kidnaping cases in the same manner it applies to other interstate felony cases.

Mr. President, I ask unanimous consent that excerpts from that conference report joint statement be printed in the RECORD at this point.

There being no objection, the excerpts were ordered to be printed in the RECORD, as follows:

EXCERPTS FROM THE CONFERENCE REPORT TO
ACCOMPANY H.R. 2977
House Report 96-1401, pgs. 41-43

TITLE IV
Parental kidnaping
Findings and Purposes

The Senate amendment contains a statement of findings relating to the problem of interstate disputes and conflicts in matters relating to child custody and visitation matters and provides that the purpose of this title is to promote cooperation among the States in the enforcement of custody and visitation orders, discourage continuing interstate controversies and conflicts, and deter interstate abductions of children.

The House has no comparable provision.
The House recedes.

Full Faith and Credit Provisions

The Senate amendment provides that the appropriate authorities of every State shall enforce and not modify any child custody determination entered by a court of another State having jurisdiction consistent with the provisions of the title.

The House has no comparable provisions.
The House recedes.

Federal Parent Locator Service

The Senate amendment authorized the Secretary of Health and Human Services to enter into agreements with States for utilization of the Federal Parent Locator Service for the purpose of determining the whereabouts of any absent parent or child when such information is to be used to locate such parent or child for the purpose of enforcing any State or Federal law with respect to the unlawful taking or restraint of a child or making or enforcing a child custody determination.

The House has no comparable provision.
The House recedes with an amendment clarifying that the information provided under such agreement will be limited to information as to the most recent address and place of employment of any absent parent of the

child and making conforming changes in references to State and Federal law relating to child custody.

Criminal Provisions

The Senate amendment contains provisions which would establish a new federal criminal offense relating to parental kidnaping.

The House has no comparable provision.

The House recedes with an amendment deleting the provisions in the Senate amendment establishing a new federal criminal offense and substituting a provision setting forth Congressional intent that section 1073 of title 18, United States Code, is applicable to cases involving parental kidnaping and interstate or international flight to avoid prosecution under applicable State felony statutes and requiring the Attorney General of the United States to submit to the Congress reports with respect to the steps taken to comply with the intent of Congress.

It is the view of the Conferees that authority presently exists under 18 U.S.C. 1073 (the so-called "Fugitive Felon Act") for the exercise of federal jurisdiction in many cases involving parental kidnaping. However, that statute, which proscribes, inter alia, interstate or foreign flight to avoid prosecution under state felony statutes, is rarely used. This is the case because the Department of Justice policy as set forth in the U.S. Attorneys' Manual discourages the use of 18 U.S.C. 1073 as a basis for federal involvement in parental kidnaping cases.

Although section 9-69.410 of the Manual states that the primary purpose of the Act is "to assist in the location and apprehension of fugitives from State justice," section 9-69.421 of the Manual requires the express prior approval of the Criminal Division before a U.S. Attorney may issue a complaint under the Fugitive Felon Act in a parental kidnaping case. Section 9-69.421 states that such approval will occur only in "rare instances", and erroneously cites the "intent of Congress" supposedly implied in the parental exception to the federal kidnaping statute (18 U.S.C. 1201(a)) as a basis for this general policy against using the Fugitive Felon Act in cases involving flight to avoid state prosecution on felony charges growing out of parental kidnaping.

Although the Department of Justice should be permitted to reasonably exercise some prosecutorial discretion under the Fugitive Felon Act as under any other Federal criminal law, the Conferees find the reasoning cited in the U.S. Attorneys' Manual for the heretofore limited use of 18 U.S.C. 1073 in parental kidnaping cases to be illogical and largely irrelevant. The fact that Congress has not made parental kidnaping an offense under 18 U.S.C. 1201 does not in any way constitute "Congressional intent" as to whether or how often 18 U.S.C. 1073 should be employed as a jurisdictional basis for federal intervention in parental kidnaping cases. Section 1073 does not require that some other federal offense be found to form the basis of federal jurisdiction, nor does it anywhere suggest that the existence of an equivalent federal offense should be a factor influencing the Attorney General's use of discretion thereunder. The section itself is the jurisdictional basis.

The Conferees are of the opinion that the Attorney General should review and revise this section of the U.S. Attorneys' Manual to provide more specific guidance to the U.S. Attorneys in order to regularize the procedures to be followed by the Department of Justice and to correctly reflect Congressional intent with respect to the use of the Fugitive Felon Act in parental kidnaping cases as stated in section 405(a) of the bill and this Joint Explanatory Statement. Specifically, the Conferees expressly disapprove of the policy of the Department of Justice as set forth in section 9-69.421 of the United States Attorneys' Manual (August 16, 1979) to limit the application of 18 U.S.C. 1073 to those parental kidnaping cases where there is a showing that the "abducting parent, by reason of his or her medical condition or acute pattern of behavior (e.g., alcoholism, interpersonal violence), presents a serious threat of physical injury to the child." It is the Conferees view that section 1073 should be applied to State felony parental kidnaping cases in the same manner as in any other State felony case where the other jurisdictional requirements of section 1073 are satisfied.

Mr. CRANSTON. Mr. President, the compromise reached by the conferees in this matter presented, I believe, a fair and workable solution to the problem of interstate child abduction. First of all, it retained the primary responsibility for these cases within the State law enforcement system. Under the provisions of section 1073, a UFAP warrant is authorized where there is an application by a State law enforcement officer for the assistance in the apprehension of an individual who has fled to avoid State felony prosecution.

The State law enforcement officials determine whether to seek a UFAP warrant. The State law enforcement officers determine whether to file State felony charges and, once the individual is apprehended, prosecution is handled by State law enforcement officers.

Second, the role for the Federal law enforcement officers under the conferee's compromise was an entirely appropriate one within our Federal system. UFAP warrants are applicable only where there is interstate flight to avoid prosecution. This interstate nature makes the involvement of Federal law enforcement officers not only appropriate but necessary, given the limited ability of State law enforcement officers to carry out their duties effectively beyond State boundaries.

The compromise reached by the conferees in H.R. 2977 thus retained an appropriate balance between the respective responsibilities of State and Federal law enforcement officials and provided for Federal involvement as a means of assistance to State law enforcement activities when interstate flight was involved.

Mr. President, the compromise agreement sought simply to make clear Congress intent that section 1073 apply in parental kidnaping cases in the same manner it is applied to other State felony cases—nothing more or less.

The conference agreement on H.R. 2977 was approved by the House on October 1, 1980; unfortunately, the Senate was unable to complete final action on the conference report. The Senator from Wyoming subsequently, on December 9, 1980, offered the provisions of Title IV of the conference agreement as an amendment to S. 3259, relating to bankruptcy laws.

S. 3259 was unanimously passed by the Senate with the parental kidnaping provisions, but the House failed to act on this legislation, Senator WALLOP then, on December 13, offered the same provisions as an amendment to H.R. 8406, relating to medicare coverage of pneumococcal vaccine. Both the House and the Senate approved this legislation, and it was signed into law on December 28, 1980, as Public Law 96-611.

DEPARTMENT OF JUSTICE RESPONSE

Mr. President, on December 31, 3 days after Public Law 96-611 was signed into law, the Department of Justice prepared a message for transmission to U.S. attorneys purporting to provide for the implementation of the provisions of the new law relating to section 10. In fact, the new guidelines promulgated by the Department of Justice continued, with minor changes, the Department's pre-existing policy of refusing to apply section 1073 to parental kidnaping cases. The communication sent to U.S. attorneys stated, in part:

Congress now has expressly stated that 18 U.S.C. 1073 be applied in parental abduction situations. Certainly, in our view, this expression of congressional intent does not require routine Federal involvement in parental abduction situations and is consistent with the Department's general policy.

The guidelines further stated that the Department would authorize FBI involvement under section 1073 in parental kidnaping cases only where there is "independent credible information establishing that the child is in physical danger or is being seriously neglected or seriously abused." The Department has also required that UFAP warrants in parental kidnaping cases be approved by the Criminal Division in Washington, D.C., rather than allowing such warrants to be issued by the respective U.S. attorneys as in other UFAP cases.

Mr. President, I ask unanimous consent that the text of this transmittal be printed in the RECORD at the conclusion of my remarks.

Mr. President, on March 9, along with nine other House and Senate Members, I wrote to the Justice Department expressing strong opposition to the Department of Justice's new guidelines and its failure to comply with congressional intent. On June 26, the Department responded indicating that it was revising the guidelines to delete the requirement that the child abuse or neglect be serious but otherwise was continuing its policy of restricting the application of section 1073 in parental kidnaping cases.

Mr. President, I ask unanimous consent that the text of the March 9 and June 26 correspondence be printed in the RECORD at the conclusion of my remarks.

CONCLUSION

Mr. President, the Department of Justice has persistently refused to comply with congressional intent that parental kidnaping cases be treated just like any other State felony matter with respect to section 1073. The Department continues to characterize these cases "domestic matters" or "civil matters" irrespective of the fact that the vast majority of States have enacted State felony laws expressly covering parental kidnaping. As of this date, only 10 States do not have State felony statutes covering parental kidnaping. According to the Congressional Research Service, approximately 85 percent of the population of the United States reside in States which have enacted felony statutes.

Over the past several months, my office and many other congressional offices have been contacted by numerous local district attorneys and State law enforcement officers who have been frustrated in the enforcement of their State criminal statutes by the Justice Department's continuing refusal to implement the new law. Cases have come to my attention, where the criminal division has refused UFAP warrants despite the recommendation of the local U.S. attorney that a UFAP warrant be issued.

Mr. President, the Department of Justice actions in this matter have frustrated and totally undermined Congress' efforts to deal with interstate parental kidnaping cases. Efforts to persuade the Justice Department to comply with the new law have been essentially fruitless. Just last month in a hearing before the Subcommittee on Crime of the House Judiciary Committee, the Department reiterated its intent to continue to restrict issuance of UFAP warrants in parental kidnaping cases. Enactment of this measure appears to be the only realistic way to achieve implementation of this provision of the new law.

There being no objection, the material was ordered to be printed in the RECORD, as follows:

U.S. SENATE,
COMMITTEE ON FINANCE,
÷ashington, D.C., March 9, 1981.

HON. WILLIAM FRENCH SMITH,
U.S. Attorney General, U.S. Department of Justice, Washington, D.C.

DEAR MR. ATTORNEY GENERAL: We are writing to request your review of guidelines issued to United States attorneys by the Criminal Division on December 31, 1980 which purport to implement section 10 of the Parental Kidnapping Prevention Act of 1980, enacted as part of P.L. 96-611 on December 28, 1980. In our opinion, the new directive seriously misconstrues congressional intent with respect to the application of the Fugitive Felon Act to state felony child abduction cases involving interstate flight, and must promptly be amended in order for the new law to achieve its objectives of deterring childsnatching and fostering a cooperative relationship between state and federal law enforcement authorities in interstate childstealing cases.

By way of background, the Parental Kidnapping Prevention Act of 1980 grew out of legislation introduced in January 1979 by Senator Wallop to stem the wave of childsnatching in the United States. S. 105 and companion House measures contained three major provisions, one of which made it a federal misdemeanor to remove or retain a child in violation of an enforceable child custody determination. After hearings in both houses the Senate adopted S. 105 as an amendment to H.R. 2977, domestic violence legislation, which then went to conference.

House-Senate conferees deleted the misdemeanor provision and instead expressly declared that the Fugitive Felon Act, 18 U.S.C. 1073, is applicable to state felony parental kidnapping cases in the same manner as in any other state felony case where the other jurisdictional requirements of section 1073 were satisfied. In the Joint Explanatory Statement accompanying the Conference Report on H.R. 2977 at pages 41-43, the conferees expressly disapproved the policy of the Department of Justice as set forth in the United States Attorney's Manual which limited the application of the Fugitive Felon Act to those parental kidnapping cases where there is a showing that the "abducting parent, by reasons of his or her medical condition or acute pattern of behavior, (e.g. alcoholism, interpersonal violence) presents a serious threat of physical injury to the child." It was the H.R. 2977 conference version of the criminal provision which was enacted as part of P.L. 96-611.

The Criminal Division's directive ignores the language, spirit, and legislative history of the new law. In fact, it seems designed to frustrate totally what Congress was attempting to achieve—a change in policy. Instead, what has been done is essentially to issue the old policy in new words. The new guidelines continue to require independent credible evidence establishing physical danger or serious neglect or abuse of a child before a fugitive warrant will be issued. In addition, prior authorization by the Criminal Division is mandated. This completely disregards Congress' clear expression that fugitive felon warrants be issued in state felony childstealing cases on the basis of the same criteria and subject to the same procedures which govern the issuance of warrants for all other state offenses, none of which require such corroboration, prior approval, or other special tests. We are also disturbed by the Criminal Division's continued reference to felony childstealing as a "domestic matter." In clarifying the role for federal criminal authorities in parental kidnapping cases, Congress implicitly rejected the Department's long-standing characterization of these cases as simple domestic disputes.

Mr. Attorney General, the early feedback on the effect of the new guidelines is discouraging: at least one prosecutor has been denied a fugitive warrant notwithstanding a documented intent to extradite and prosecute the state law violation upon the apprehension of the fugitive, and other applications have not been acted upon at all.

We respectfully call upon you to undertake a review and revision of the fugitive felon directive in accordance with Section 10 of P.L. 96-611. We stand ready to assist this Administration in implementing the Parental Kidnapping Prevention Act of 1980 and invite you to consult freely with us toward that end.

Yours sincerely,

Malcolm Wallop, Henry J. Hyde, Dave Durenberger, Don Edwards, Charles E. Bennett, Harold S. Sawyer, Alan Cranston, F. James Sensenbrenner, Jr., William J. Hughes, Charles McC. Mathias, Jr.

U.S. DEPARTMENT OF JUSTICE,
OFFICE OF THE DEPUTY
ATTORNEY GENERAL
Washington, D.C., June 26, 1981.

HON. ALAN CRANSTON,
U.S. Senate,
Washington, D.C.

DEAR SENATOR CRANSTON: This is in further response to your letter of March 9, 1981, signed by nine other Senators and Members of Congress, objecting to the Department's policy guidelines limiting FBI involvement under the Fugitive Felon Act in "child snatching" cases, and requesting that these guidelines be revised to conform with the expression of Congressional intent set forth in section 10 of the Parental Kidnaping Prevention Act of 1980 (the Act) (Public Law 96-611).

Because of the concern expressed by you and your colleagues, the Attorney General requested a review of our policy guidelines be undertaken. Based on this review, the Department of Justice is convinced there is a demonstrated need for policy limitations on Federal involvement in "child snatching" cases under the Fugitive Felon Act. However, as a result of that review, the policy limitations have been modified as indicated below.

The Department's experience in these matters indicate that a "child snatcher" is a different kind of offender than the ordinary felon fleeing from state justice. We note that a significant number of states classify parental abduction or custodial interference as a misdemeanor not a felony. Moreover, it appears that state prosecutors often charge an abducting parent with a criminal violation as an accommodation to the victim parent, with no real intention of ultimately prosecuting the criminal charge against the abducting parent. Over the past several years, we have authorized FBI involvement in a significant number of these cases, consistent with existing policy guidelines. We have found that in repeated instances the state felony charges against the abducting parent have been dropped shortly after the complaining parent regained custody of the child. We suggest that the use of the Fugitive Felon Act in situations where state authorities have no actual intention of prosecuting the underlying criminal charges would amount to an abuse of legal process.

In the past four months, a variety of "child snatching" cases have been brought to our attention which, in our view, confirm the need for policy limitations. In two cases, the abducting parents were, in effect, given temporary custody in the asylum state despite outstanding felony "child snatching" warrants in other states. In two other cases, the parents were charged with felonies in spite of the fact they had custody decrees in other states. In at least three cases, the locations of the abducting parent were known, but law enforcement authorities in the asylum states refused to honor the out-of-state warrants, possibly because the asylum states classified child snatching as a misdemeanor. In two other cases, the asylum states refused extradition. In these latter cases, the request for FBI assistance apparently was an effort to avoid the extradition process. The Fugitive Felon Act, of course, is not an alternative to extradition, and individuals arrested on a Federal fugitive warrant should not be removed from the asylum state under Rule 40, Federal Rules of Criminal Procedure, when no Federal prosecution is intended. See *United States v. Love*, 425 F. Supp. 1248 (S.D.N.Y. 1977).

I wish to emphasize that the Department's policy is not intended to frustrate the spirit of section 10 of the Act. To the contrary, our policy is now less restrictive than in the past. Prior to the Act we required "convincing evidence that a child is in danger of serious bodily harm" before involving the FBI in a "child snatching" case. Under new guidelines established after enactment of the Act, we became involved in these matters if there was independent credible information that the child was being "seriously neglected or seriously abused".

As a result of that policy change, we authorized FBI involvement in six "child snatching" cases as of March 31, 1981, the cut-off date used for compiling data for the first report required by section 10(b) of the Act. Since March 31, 1981, we have authorized FBI involvement in at least seven additional cases. Recently, as a result of our policy review, the guidelines have been modified to permit FBI involvement under the Fugitive Felon Act in those instances where there is independent credible information establishing that the child is in physical danger or is then in a condition of abuse or neglect. We believe that this policy modification will result in a significant increase in Federal involvement, when compared with previous years.

Our present policy guidelines are an effort to comply with Congressional intent by extending Federal involvement to cases involving abuse and neglect. Consistent with our other criminal law enforcement responsibilities, we expect to furnish an increased level of assistance to the states in the legitimate enforcement of their criminal laws. At the same time, we hope to avoid the utilization of FBI investigative resources to enforce civil obligations.

I hope the foregoing information clarifies our position on this matter.
Sincerely,

EDWARD C. SCHMULTS,
Deputy Attorney General.

To: All United States attorneys.
RE: Parental Kidnaping Prevention Act of 1980.

On December 28, 1980, H.R. 8406, the Parental Kidnapping Prevention Act of 1980, was signed into law. Essentially the bill contains three provisions intended to ameliorate the problem of "child snatching."

The full faith and credit provision in the act (section 8), provides that appropriate authorities in every State shall enforce according to its terms, and shall not modify, except in limited circumstances, any child custody determination made consistent with the provisions of section 8 of the Act.

Section 9 of the act expands the use of the Parent Locator Service in the Department of Health and Human Services so that it can be used to locate a parent or child for the purpose of enforcing any State or Federal law with respect to the unlawful taking or restraint of a child, or making or enforcing a child custody determination.

Section 10 of the Act contains an expression of congressional intent that 18 U.S.C. 1073 (interstate flight to avoid prosecution) apply to cases involving parental kidnaping and interstate or international flight to avoid prosecution under applicable State felony statutes. Section 10 further requires that the Attorney General submit periodic reports setting forth steps taken to comply with this expression of congressional intent. Among other things, each report must contain data relating to the number of applications under 18 U.S.C. 1073 involving parental kidnaping and the number of complaints issued.

It has long been Department policy to avoid involvement in situations which are essentially domestic relations controversies. This policy has been based, in part, on the parental abduction exception in the federal kidnaping statute, from which we inferred a congressional intent that Federal law enforcement authorities stay out of such controversies. Consistent with that policy, the Department did not authorize FBI involvement under 18 U.S.C. 1073, for the purpose of apprehending a parent who is charged with a State felony in connection with the abduction of his own minor child, and who has traveled interstate to avoid prosecution. In some instances the Department has made exceptions to this policy where there was convincing evidence that the child was in danger of serious bodily harm as a result of the mental condition or past behavior patterns of the abducting parent. See U.S. Attorneys' Manual § 9-69.421.

Congress now has expressly stated that 18 U.S.C. 1073 be applied in parental abduction situations. Certainly, in our view, this expression of congressional intent does not require routine Federal involvement in parental abduction situations and is consistent with the Department's general policy militating against Federal involvement in domestic matters including abduction situations. Furthermore, the sound exercise of prosecutorial discretion and the need for careful utilization of Department manpower and resources, will require selectivity in seeking Federal fugitive warrants in these situations.

The primary purpose of the Fugitive Felon Act (18 U.S.C. 1073) is to permit the Federal Government to assist in the location and apprehension of fugitives from State justice. In evaluating any request from State or local authorities for assistance under the Fugitive Felon Act, there must be probable cause to believe that a fugitive charged with a State felony has fled interstate and that his flight was for the purpose of avoiding prosecution. Furthermore, it must be clear that State or local authorities are determined to take all necessary steps to secure the return of the fugitive and that it is their intention to bring him to trial on the State charge for which he is sought. It has been our experience that State prosecutors often will charge an abducting parent with a felony as an accommodation to the victim parent, with no real intention of ultimately prosecuting the abducting parent. Therefore, efforts should be made to identify those requests which seek to use the investigative resources of the FBI to compel the discharge of civil obligations, rather than serving a legitimate criminal law enforcement purpose.

In an effort to fulfill congressional intent consistent with its other responsibilities, the Department will authorize FBI involvement under 18 U.S.C. 1073 in parental kidnaping where there is independent credible information establishing that the child is in physical danger or is being seriously neglected or seriously abused. Examples of independent credible information include police investigations or prior domestic complaints to police or welfare agencies.

In view of the reporting requirements of section 10 of the act, it is imperative that the local office of the FBI be telephonically supplied with information regarding each parental kidnaping directly referred to the United States Attorney's Office so that the FBI may gather data for the legislatively required reports.

In order to maintain a uniform national policy, and in view of the Department's general policy against involvement in domestic relations controversies, criminal division authorization still must be obtained before seeking a fugitive felon warrant in parental abduction situations. Attorneys familiar with this policy are available on 724-7526 or 6971.

LAWRENCE LIPPE,
Chief, General Litigation and Legal Advice Section, Criminal Division.

Appendix D
Hague Convention on the Civil Aspects of International Child Abduction

Final Act of the Fourteenth Session

The undersigned, Delegates of the Governments of Argentina, Australia, Austria, Belgium, Canada, Czechoslovakia, Denmark, the Arab Republic of Egypt, Finland, France, the Federal Republic of Germany, Greece, Ireland, Israel, Italy, Japan, Jugloslavia, Luxemburg, the Netherlands, Norway, Portugal, Spain, Surinam, Sweden, Switzerland, Turkey, the United Kingdom of Great Britain and Northern Ireland, the United States of America and Venezuela, and the Representatives of the Governments of Brazil, the Holy See, Hungary, Monaco, Morocco, the Union of Soviet Socialist Republics and Uruguay participating by invitation or as Observer, convened at The Hague on the 6th October 1980, at the invitation of the Government of the Netherlands, in the Fourteenth Session of the Hague Conference on Private International Law.
Following the deliberations laid down in the records of the meetings, have decided to submit to their Governments—

A   The following draft Conventions—
I
CONVENTION ON THE CIVIL ASPECTS OF INTERNATIONAL CHILD ABDUCTION

The States signatory to the present Convention,
Firmly convinced that the interests of children are of paramount importance in matters relating to their custody,
Desiring to protect children internationally from the harmful effects of their wrongful removal or retention and to establish procedures to ensure their prompt return to the State of their habitual residence, as well as to secure protection for rights of access,
Have resolved to conclude a Convention to this effect, and have agreed upon the following provisions—

CHAPTER 1 – SCOPE OF THE CONVENTION

Article 1
The objects of the present Convention are:
a to secure the prompt return of children wrongfully removed to or retained in any Contracting State; and
b to ensure that rights of custody and of access under the law of one Contracting State are effectively respected in the other Contracting States.

Article 2
Contracting States shall take all appropriate measures to secure within their territories the implementation of the objects of the Convention. For this purpose they shall use the most expeditious procedures available.

Article 3
The removal or the retention of a child is to be considered wrongful where:
a it is in breach of rights of custody attributed to a person, an institution or any other body, either jointly or alone, under the law of the State in which the child was habitually resident immediately before the removal or retention; and
b at the time of removal or retention those rights were actually exercised, either jointly or alone, or would have been so exercised but for the removal or retention.
The rights of custody mentioned in sub-paragraph *a* above, may arise in particular by operation of law or by reason of a judicial or administrative decision, or by reason of an agreement having legal effect under the law of that State.

Article 4
The Convention shall apply to any child who was habitually resident in a Contracting State immediately before any breach of custody or access rights. The Convention shall cease to apply when the child attains the age of 16 years.

Article 5
For the purposes of this Convention:
a 'rights of custody' shall include rights relating to the care of the person of the child and, in particular, the right to determine the child's place of residence;
b 'rights of access' shall include the right to take a child for a limited period of time to a place other than the child's habitual residence.

CHAPTER II – CENTRAL AUTHORITIES

Article 6
A Contracting State shall designate a Central Authority to discharge the duties which are imposed by the Convention upon such authorities.
Federal States, States with more than one system of law or States having autonomous territorial organizations shall be free to appoint more than one Central Authority and to specify the territorial extent of their powers. Where a State has appointed more than one Central Authority, it shall

designate the Central Authority to which applications may be addressed for transmission to the appropriate Central Authority within that State.

Article 7
Central Authorities shall co-operate with each other and promote co-operation amongst the competent authorities in their respective States to secure the prompt return of children and to achieve the other objects of this Convention.
In particular, either directly or through any intermediary, they shall take all appropriate measures —

a to discover the whereabouts of a child who has been wrongfully removed or retained;
b to prevent further harm to the child or prejudice to interested parties by taking or causing to be taken provisional measures;
c to secure the voluntary return of the child or to bring about an amicable resolution of the issues;
d to exchange, where desirable, information relating to the social background of the child;
e to provide information of a general character as to the law of their State in connection with the application of the Convention;
f to initiate or facilitate the institution of judicial or administrative proceedings with a view to obtaining the return of the child and, in a proper case, to make arrangements for organizing or securing the effective exercise of rights of access;
g where the circumstances so require, to provide or facilitate the provision of legal aid and advice, including the participation of legal counsel and advisers;
h to provide such administrative arrangements as may be necessary and appropriate to secure the safe return of the child;
i to keep each other informed with respect to the operation of this Convention and, as far as possible, to eliminate any obstacles to its application.

CHAPTER III — RETURN OF CHILDREN

Article 8
Any person, institution or other body claiming that a child has been removed or retained in breach of custody rights may apply either to the Central Authority of the child's habitual residence or to the Central Authority of any other Contracting State for assistance in securing the return of the child.
The application shall contain —
a information concerning the identity of the applicant, of the child and of the person alleged to have removed or retained the child;
b where available, the date of birth of the child;
c the grounds on which the applicant's claim for return of the child is based;
d all available information relating to the whereabouts of the child and the identity of the person with whom the child is presumed to be.
The application may be accompanied or supplemented by —
e an authenticated copy of any relevant decision or agreement;
f a certificate or an affidavit emanating from a Central Authority or

other competent authority of the State of the child's habitual residence, or from a qualified person, concerning the relevant law of that State;
g any other relevant document.

Article 9
If the Central Authority which receives an application referred to in Article 8 has reason to believe that the child is in another Contracting State, it shall directly and without delay transmit the application to the Central Authority of that Contracting State and inform the requesting Central Authority, or the applicant, as the case may be.

Article 10
The Central Authority of the State where the child is shall take or cause to be taken all appropriate measures in order to obtain the voluntary return of the child.

Article 11
The judicial or administrative authorities of Contracting States shall act expeditiously in proceedings for the return of children.
If the judicial or administrative authority concerned has not reached a decision within six weeks from the date of commencement of the proceedings, the applicant or the Central Authority of the requested State, on its own initiative or if asked by the Central Authority of the requesting State, shall have the right to request a statement of the reasons for the delay. If a reply is received by the Central Authority of the requested State, that Authority shall transmit the reply to the Central Authority of the requesting State or to the applicant, as the case may be.

Article 12
Where a child has been wrongfully removed or retained in terms of Article 3 and, at the date of the commencement of the proceedings before the judicial or administrative authority of the Contracting State where the child is, a period of less than one year has elapsed from the date of the wrongful removal or retention, the authority concerned shall order the return of the child forthwith:
The judicial or administrative authority, even where the proceedings have been commenced after the expiration of the period of one year referred to in the preceding paragraph, shall also order the return of the child, unless it is demonstrated that the child is now settled in its new environment.
Where the judicial or administrative authority in the requested State has reason to believe that the child has been taken to another State, it may stay the proceedings or dismiss the application for the return of the child.

Article 13
Notwithstanding the provisions of the preceding Article, the judicial or administrative authority of the requested State is not bound to order the return of the child if the person, institution or other body which opposes its return establishes that:
a the person, institution or other body having the care of the person of the child was not actually exercising the custody rights at the time of removal or retention, or had consented to or subsequently acquiesced in the removal or retention; or
b there is a grave risk that his or her return would expose the child to

physical or psychological harm or otherwise place the child in an intolerable situation.

The judicial or administrative authority may also refuse to order the return of the child if it finds that the child objects to being returned and has attained an age and degree of maturity at which it is appropriate to take account of its views.

Article 14

In considering the circumstances referred to in this Article, the judicial and administrative authorities shall take into account the information relating to the social background of the child provided by the Central Authority or other competent authority of the child's habitual residence. In ascertaining whether there has been a wrongful removal or retention within the meaning of Article 3, the judicial or administrative authorities of the requested State may take notice directly of the law of, and of judicial or administrative decisions, formally recognized or not in the State of the habitual residence of the child without recourse to the specific procedures for the proof of that law or for the recognition of foreign decisions which would otherwise be applicable.

Article 15

The judicial or administrative authorities of a Contracting State may, prior to the making of an order for the return of the child, request that the applicant obtain from the authorities of the State of the habitual residence of the child a decision or other determination that the removal or retention was wrongful within the meaning of Article 3 of the Convention, where such a decision or determination may be obtained in that State. The Central Authorities of the Contracting States shall so far as practicable assist applicants to obtain such a decision or determination.

Article 16

After receiving notice of a wrongful removal or retention of a child in the sense of Article 3, the judicial or administrative authorities of the Contracting State to which the child has been removed or in which it has been retained shall not decide on the merits of rights of custody until it has been determined that the child is not to be returned under this Convention or unless an application under this Convention is not lodged within a reasonable time following receipt of the notice.

Article 17

The sole fact that a decision relating to custody has been given in or is entitled to recognition in the requested State shall not be a ground for refusing to return a child under this Convention, but the judicial or administrative authorities of the requested State may take account of the reasons for that decision in applying this Convention.

Article 18

The provisions of this Chapter do not limit the power of a judicial or administrative authority to order the return of the child at any time.

Article 19

A decision under this Convention concerning the return of the child shall not be taken to be a determination on the merits of any custody issue.

Article 20
The return of the child under the provisions of Article 12 may be refused if this would not be permitted by the fundamental principles of the requested State relating to the protection of human rights and fundamental freedoms.

Article 21
An application to make arrangements for organizing or securing the effective exercise of rights of access may be presented to the Central Authorities of the Contracting States in the same way as an application for the return of a child.

The Central Authorities are bound by the obligations of co-operation which are set forth in Article 7 to promote the peaceful enjoyment of access rights and the fulfillment of any conditions to which the exercise of those rights may be subject. The Central Authorities shall take steps to remove, as far as possible, all obstacles to the exercise of such rights.

The Central Authorities, either directly or through intermediaries, may initiate or assist in the institution of proceedings with a view to organizing or protecting these rights and securing respect for the conditions to which the exercise of these rights may be subject.

CHAPTER V – GENERAL PROVISIONS

Article 22
No security, bond or deposit, however described, shall be required to guarantee the payment of costs and expenses in the judicial or administrative proceedings falling within the scope of this convention.

Article 23
No legalization or similar formality may be required in the context of this Convention.

Article 24
Any application, communication or other document sent to the Central Authority of the requested State shall be in the original language, and shall be accompanied by a translation into the official language or one of the official languages of the requested State or, where that is not feasible, a translation into French or English.

However, a Contracting State may, by making a reservation in accordance with Article 42, object to the use of either French or English, but not both, in any application, communication or other document sent to its Central Authority.

Article 25
Nationals of the Contracting States and persons who are habitually resident within those States shall be entitled in matters concerned with the application of this Convention to legal aid and advice in any other Contracting State on the same conditions as if they themselves were nationals of and habitually resident in that State.

Article 26
Each Central Authority shall bear its own costs in applying this Convention.

Central Authorities and other public services of Contracting States shall not impose any charges in relation to applications submitted under this Convention. In particular, they may not require any payment from the applicant towards the costs and expenses of the proceedings or, where applicable, those arising from the participation of legal counsel or advisers. However, they may require the payment of the expenses incurred or to be incurred in implementing the return of the child.
However, a Contracting State may, by making a reservation in accordance with Article 42, declare that it shall not be bound to assume any costs referred to in the preceding paragraph resulting from the participation of legal counsel or advisers or from court proceedings, except insofar as those costs may be covered by its system of legal aid and advice.
Upon ordering the return of a child or issuing an order concerning rights of access under this Convention, the judicial or administrative authorities may, where appropriate, direct the person who removed or retained the child, or who prevented the exercise of rights of access, to pay necessary expenses incurred by or on behalf of the applicant, including travel expenses, any costs incurred or payments made for locating the child, the costs of legal representation of the applicant, and those of returning the child.

Article 27
When it is manifest that the requirements of this Convention are not fulfilled or that the application is otherwise not well founded, a Central Authority is not bound to accept the application. In that case, the Central Authority shall forthwith inform the applicant or the Central Authority through which the application was submitted, as the case may be, of its reasons.

Article 28
A Central Authority may require that the application be accompanied by a written authorization empowering it to act on behalf of the applicant, or to designate a representative so to act.

Article 29
This Convention shall not preclude any person, institution or body who claims that there has been a breach of custody or access rights within the meaning of Article 3 or 21 from applying directly to the judicial or administrative authorities of a Contracting State, whether or not under the provisions of this Convention.

Article 30
Any application submitted to the Central Authorities or directly to the judicial or administrative authorities of a Contracting State in accordance with the terms of this Convention, together with documents and any other information appended thereto or provided by a Central Authority, shall be admissible in the courts or adminstrative authorities of the Contracting States.

Article 31
In relation to a State which in matters of custody of children has two or more systems of law applicable in different territorial units —
a any reference to habitual residence in that State shall be construed as referring to habitual residence in a territorial unit of that State;

b any reference to the law of the State of habitual residence shall be construed as referring to the law of the territorial unit in that State where the child habitually resides.

Article 32
In relation to a State which in matters of custody of children has two or more systems of law applicable to different categories of persons, any reference to the law of that State shall be construed as referring to the legal system specified by the law of that State.

Article 33
A State within which different territorial units have their own rules of law in respect of custody of children shall not be bound to apply this Convention where a State with a unified system of law would not be bound to do so.

Article 34
This Convention shall take priority in matters within its scope over the *Convention of 5 October 1961 concerning the powers of authorities and the law applicable in respect of the protection of minors*, as between Parties to both Conventions, Otherwise the present Convention shall not restrict the application of an international instrument in force between the State of origin and the State addressed or other law of the State addressed for the purposes of obtaining the return of a child who has been wrongfully removed or retained or of organizing access rights.

Article 35
This Convention shall apply as between Contracting States only to wrongful removals or retentions occurring after its entry into force in those States.
Where a declaration has been made under Article 39 or 40 the reference in the preceding paragraph to a Contracting State shall be taken to refer to the territorial unit or units in relation to which this Convention applies.

Article 36
Nothing in this Convention shall prevent two or more Contracting States, in order to limit the restrictions to which the return of the child may be subject, from agreeing among themselves to derogate from any provisions of this Convention which may imply such a restriction.

CHAPTER VI – FINAL CLAUSES

Article 37
The Convention shall be open for signature by the States which were Members of the Hague Conference on Private International Law at the time of its Fourteenth Session.
It shall be ratified, accepted or approved and the instruments of ratification, acceptance or approval shall be deposited with the Ministry of Foreign Affairs of the Kingdom of the Netherlands.

Article 38
Any other State may accede to the Convention.
The instrument of accession shall be deposited with the Ministry of Foreign Affairs of the Kingdom of the Netherlands.

The Convention shall enter into force for a State acceding to it on the first day of the third calendar month after the deposit of its instrument of accession.
The accession will have effect only as regards the relations between the acceding State and such Contracting States as will have declared their acceptance of the accession. Such a declaration will also have to be made by any Member State ratifying, accepting or approving the Convention after an accession. Such declaration shall be deposited at the Ministry of Foreign Affairs of the Kingdom of the Netherlands; this Ministry shall forward, through diplomatic channels, a certified copy to each of the Contracting States.
The Convention will enter into force between the acceding State and the State that has declared its acceptance of the accession on the first day of the third calendar month after the deposit of the declaration of acceptance.

Article 39
Any State may, at the time of signature, ratification, acceptance, approval or accession, declare that the Convention shall extend to all the territories for the international relations of which it is responsible, or to one or more of them. Such a declaration shall take effect at the time the Convention enters into force for that State.
Such declaration, as well as any subsequent extension, shall be notified to the Ministry of Foreign Affairs of the Kingdom of the Netherlands.

Article 40
If a Contracting State has two or more territorial units in which different systems of law are applicable in relation to matters dealt with in this Convention, it may at the time of signature, ratification, acceptance, approval or accession declare that this Convention shall extend to all its territorial units or only to one or more of them and may modify this declaration by submitting another declaration at any time. Any such declaration shall be notified to the Ministry of Foreign Affairs of the Kingdom of the Netherlands and shall state expressly the territorial units to which the Convention applies.

Article 41
Where a Contracting State has a system of government under which executive, judicial and legislative powers are distributed between central and other authorities within that State, its signature or ratification, acceptance or approval of, or accession to this Convention, or its making of any declaration in terms of Article 40 shall carry no implication as to the internal distribution of powers within that State.

Article 42
Any State may, not later than the time of ratification, acceptance, approval or accession, or at the time of making a declaration in terms of Article 39 or 40, make one or both of the reservations provided for in Article 24 and Article 26, third paragraph. No other reservation shall be permitted.
Any State may at any time withdraw a reservation it has made. The withdrawal shall be notified to the Ministry of Foreign Affairs of the Kingdom of the Netherlands.
The reservation shall cease to have effect on the first day of the third

calendar month after the notification referred to in the preceding paragraph.

Article 43
The Convention shall enter into force on the first day of the third calendar month after the deposit of the third instrument of ratification, acceptance, approval or accession referred to in Articles 37 and 38.
Thereafter the Convention shall enter into force—
1   for each state ratifying, accepting, approving or acceding to it subsequently, on the first day of the third calendar month after the deposit of its instrument of ratification, acceptance, approval or accession;
2   for any territory or territorial unit to which the Convention has been extended in conformity with Article 39 or 40, on the first day of the third calendar month after the notification referred to in that Article.

Article 44
The Convention shall remain in force for five years from the date of its entry into force in accordance with the first paragraph of Article 43 even for States which subsequently have ratified, accepted, approved it or acceded to it.
If there has been no denunciation, it shall be renewed tacitly every five years.
Any denunciation shall be notified to the Ministry of Foreign Affairs of the Kingdom of the Netherlands at least six months before the expiry of the five year period. It may be limited to certain of the territories or territorial units to which the Convention applies.
The denunciation shall have effect only as regards the State which has notified it. The Convention shall remain in force for the other Contracting States.

Article 45
The Ministry of Foreign Affairs of the Kingdom of the Netherlands shall notify the States Members of the Conference, and the States which have acceded in accordance with Article 38, of the following—
1   the signatures and ratifications, acceptances and approvals referred to in Article 37;
2   the accessions referred to in Article 38;
3   the date on which the Convention enters into force in accordance with Article 43;
4   the extensions referred to in Article 39;
5   the declarations referred to in Articles 38 and 40;
6   the reservations referred to in Article 24 and Article 26, third paragraph, and the withdrawals referred to in Article 42;
7   the denunciations referred to in Article 44.
In witness whereof the undersigned, being duly authorized thereto, have signed this Convention.
Done at The Hague, on the _____ day of _____ 19___ in the English and French languages, both texts being equally authentic, in a single copy which shall be deposited in the archives of the Government of the Kingdom of the Netherlands, and of which a certified copy shall be sent, through diplomatic channels, to each of the States Members of the Hague Conference on Private International Law at the date of its Fourteenth Session.

NOTES*

1. U.S. Congress. House Committee on the Judiciary. Subcommittee on Crime. Hearings, 93rd Congress, 2nd Session, on H.R. 4191 and H.R. 8722, Amendments to the Federal Kidnapping Statute. *Congressional Record.* Washington: U.S. Government Printing Office, 1974. Hearings held February 27 and April 10, 1974, p. 77

2. Anne Dolcini, "Child Stealing," *Novato Advance*, March 11, 1981.

3. Lew Koch, "New Group Leads War on Child Snatchers," *Coping*, July 21, 1975.

4. Dave Smith, "After All the Anguish, They Still Fight," *Los Angeles Times*, April 11, 1977.

5. U.S. Congress, 1974 Hearings. Op Cit., p. 85.

6. Merideth McCoy, Parental Kidnaping Issue Brief No. IB77177. Washington D.C.: Library of Congress, Congressional Research Service, Major Issues System, October 30, 1980, p.1.

7. Elin McCoy, "Childhood Through the Ages," *Parents*, New Jersey: Parents Magazine Enterprises, January 1981, p. 62.

8. Virginia Coigney, *Children Are People Too: How We Fail Our Children and How We Can Love Them* (New York: William Morrow and Company, Inc. 1975), p. 25.

9. Susan Brownmiller, *Against Our Will* (New York: Bantom Books in Association with Simon & Schuster), p. 312.

10. Lois G. Forer, *Criminals and Victims* (New York: W.W. Norton & Company), p. 177.

11. Anne Dolcini, Op Cit.

12. U.S. Congress. House Committee on the Judiciary. Subcommittee on Crime. The Parental Kidnapping Prevention Act of 1979. H.R. 1290. *Congressional Record*. Washington, D.C.: U.S. Government Printing Office, 1980. Hearings held on June 24, 1980.

13. List included in Arnold Miller's "Testimony of Children's Rights, Inc.," June 24, 1980 Congressional Hearings., Op. Cit.

14. Mary Duckworth, "Child-snatchers break hearts, not laws," Augusta, Georgia *Chronicle-Herald*, February 20, 1977.

15. Del Martin, *Battered Wives* (San Francisco: Glide Publications, 1976), p. 106.

16. Geraldine Strozier, "When a Child is Snatched by a Parent," *Detroit Free Press*, March 18, 1976.

17. Leslie Albin, "Children's Rights Inc. Seeks Law to Curb Parental Child Abduction," Orlando, Florida *Sentinel Star*, May 23, 1977.

*(Full titles of all Congressional Hearings on last page of "Suggested readings")

18. John C. Keeney, 1974 Congressional Hearings, Op. Cit.

19. Mark M. Richards, 1980 Congressional Hearings, Op. Cit.

20. Daniel D. Molinoff, "Divorced Parents Who Kidnap Their Own Children," *Parade Magazine*, October 16, 1977.

21. Scott Winokur, "The Child Stealers," *The San Francisco Examiner*, October 5, 1980.

22. Eileen Baris Luboff & Constance L. Posner, *How To Collect Your Child Support & Alimony* (Berkeley: Nolo Press, 1977), pp. 11-13. Out of Print.

23. Arnold Miller and Rae Gummel, "History", Children's Rights Inc. Chapter Guide, Children's Rights, Inc., 3443 17th St., N.W., Washington, D.C. 20019, 1977.

24. Children's Rights, Inc., 1980 Congressional Hearings, Op. Cit.

25. Ivan Sharpe, "The Epidemic of Kidnapping by Parents," *The San Francisco Examiner*, May 2, 1978.

26. Department of Health, Education and Welfare, *The First Annual Report to the Congress on the Child Support Enforcement Program*, Washington, D.C.: Government Printing Office, 1977, pps. 24, 26.

27. Sheila Kast, " 'Child Snatching' Reads Like Scenario for Detective Movie," *The Washington Star*, August 3, 1975.

28. Ibid.

29. John Huey, "To Man Whose Job Is Child Snatching, End Justifies Means," *The Wall Street Journal*, March 24, 1976.

30. John Gill, *Stolen Children*, (New York: Seaview Books, 1981), p. 53-54.

31. Bruce Most, "The Child-Stealing Epidemic," *The Nation*, May 7, 1977.

32. Ibid.

33. John Gill, "Putting A Stop To Child-Snatching," *Newsday*, July 6, 1978.

34. Dave Smith, Op Cit.

35. U.S. Department of Health Education and Welfare, *Child Abuse and Neglect*, Vol. 1, Washington, D.C.: Government Printing Office, 1975, p. 13.

36. California Dept. of Justice Information Pamphlet #3, *Child Abuse: The Problem of the Abused and Neglected Child*, August 1976, p. 1.

37. Testimony of Children's Rights, Inc. 1980 Congressional Hearings, Op. Cit.

38. Ibid.

39. Debby Brian, "System Doubles Grief for Victimized Parents," *The News-Sentinel*, Fort Wayne, Indiana, February 5, 1977.

40. Deborah Shwartz, "Child Snatching: The Ultimate Custody Battle," *The Children's Advocate of Berkeley*, 1981.

41. Scott Winokur, Op. Cit.

42. Linda Field, "Custody Kidnapping: A Common Concern," *Newsday*, April 12, 1977.

43. Patricia Quinn, 1974 Congressional Record, Op. Cit.

44. Paul Liberatore, "Marin Dad Grieves for Kidnapped Children," *Independent Journal*, September 14, 1978.

45. United Press International, "Kidnaping Father Freed by Judge," *San Franscisco Chronicle*, March 16, 1982.

Suggested Reading

CHILD-STEALING

Abrahms, Sally and Bell, Joseph N. "Have you seen these Children?" *Ladies Home Journal*. New York: Charter Media Publishing Group. April 1981

Black, Bonnie Lee, *Somewhere Child*. New York: Viking Press, 1981.

Fielding, Joy. *Kiss Mommy Goodbye (a novel)*. New York: Doubleday & Co., 1981.

Gill, John. *Stolen Children*. New York: Seaview Books, 1981.

Katz, Stanley N. Child Snatching: *The Legal Response to the Abduction of Children*. Washington, D.C.: American Bar Association Press, 1981.

U.S. Congress. House Committee on the Judiciary. Subcommittee on Crime. Hearings, 93rd Congress, 2nd Session, on H.R. 4191 and H.R. 8722, Amendments to the Federal Kidnapping Statute. *Congressional Record*. Washington: U.S. Government Printing Office, 1974. Hearings held February 27 and April 10, 1974.

U.S. Congress. Senate Committee on the Judiciary. Subcommittee on Criminal Justice. Committee on Labor and Human Resources. Subcommittee on Child and Human Development. Joint hearings, 96th Congress, 2nd Session, on The Parental Kidnapping Prevention Act of 1979, S. 105. *Congressional Record*. Washington: U.S. Government Printing Office, 1980. Hearings held January 30, 1979.

U.S. Congress. Senate Committee on Labor and Human Resources. Subcommittee on Child and Human Development. Hearings, 96th Congress, 1st Session, on examination of the problem of "Child Snatching." *Congressional Record.* Washington: U.S. Government Printing Office, 1979. Hearings held April 1979.

U.S. Congress. House Committee on the Judiciary. Subcommittee on Crime. The Parental Kidnapping Prevention Act of 1979. H.R. 1290. *Congressional Record.* Washington: U.S. Government Printing Office, 1980. Hearings held June 24, 1980.

RELATED CRIMES

These books provide a legal and historical perspective on why crimes like child-stealing are treated as they are.

Brownmiller, Susan. *Against Our Will.* (Rape). New York: Simon & Schuster, 1975

Butler, Sandra. *Conspiracy of Silence.* (Incest). San Francisco: New Glide Publications, 1978.

Fontana, Vincent J. *Somewhere a Child is Crying: The Battered Child.* New York: The MacMillan Company, 1973.

Hoff, Patricia, ed. *Interstate & International Custody Disputes: A Collection of Materials.* Washington: American Bar Association. 1982.

Langley, Roger and Richard C. Levy. *Wife Beating, The Silent Crisis.* New York: Pocket Books. 1977.

Martin, Del. *Battered Wives.* San Francisco: New Glide Publications, 1976.

SELF-HELP

deKiefer, Donald. *How to Lobby Congress.* New York: Dodd, Mead & Company. 1981.

Elias, Stephen. *Legal Research: How to Find and Understand the Law.* Nolo Press, 950 Parker Street, Berkeley, California. 94710.

Humm, Andy. *How to Organize a Self-Help Group.* Publication of the National Self-Help Clearing-house, Graduate School & University Center of the City University of New York, 33 W. 42nd St, New York, N.Y. 10036.

Kersch, Mary Ellen. *How to Fight City Hall: A Guide for Citizen and Environmental Action.* Gabriel Books, P.O. Box 224, Mankato, Minnesota 56001

Loeb, David. *How to Change Your Name.* Nolo Press, 950 Parker St., Berkeley, California. 94710.

Zagone, Frank. *How to Adopt Your Stepchild.* Nolo Press, 950 Parker St., Berkeley, California 94710. (Includes information on "abandonment" proceedings)

GENERAL

Adams, Paul et al. *Children's Rights: Toward the Liberation of the Child.* New York: Praeger, 1971.

Coigney, Virginia. *Children Are People Too: How We Fail Our Children and How We Can Love Them.* New York: William Morrow and Company, Inc. 1975.

Forer, Lois G. *Criminals and Victims* (Chapter 12). New York: W.W. Norton & Company, 1980.

Hearst, Patricia C. *Every Secret Thing.* New York: Doubleday & Company, 1982.

McCoy, Elin. "Childhood Through the Ages". *Parents* Magazine. January 1981.

Rapoport, Rona, Robert Rapoport and Ziona Strelitz with Steven Kew. *Fathers, Mothers and Society: Perspectives on Parenting.* New York: Vintage Books. 1980.